# AN INTRODUCTION TO
# LIFE-COURSE CRIMINOLOGY

# PRAISE FOR THE BOOK

'This is an excellent introduction to a topic of central importance for criminologists. It has the merit of being very clearly written, and the authors cover a wide range of materials – theories and data; European and American research; quantitative and qualitative studies. Throughout, they provide helpful examples from their work on the Stockholm Life Course Project. Highly recommended.'
**Sir Anthony Bottoms, Emeritus Wolfson Professor of Criminology, University of Cambridge**

'Carlsson and Sarnecki's An Introduction to Life-Course Criminology captures the excitement of the life course perspective within criminology, a lens and set of preoccupations that have become increasingly central to the field. This lively and engaging volume will not only give other scholars and students alike a full appreciation of key concepts and historical roots, but open a window on what is at stake theoretically, and how recent research informs contemporary debates. Illustrations from the authors' own important longitudinal study are especially useful, as they make tangible sometimes slippery notions (e.g., agency) and complicated pathways (the desistance process). This would be an ideal text for a class on life course criminology and an excellent supplement for more general courses, and will be an outstanding resource for researchers with interests in this area.'
**Peggy Giordano, Distinguished Professor of Sociology, Bowling Green State University**

'Written by an emerging scholar in Carlsson and an internationally acclaimed criminologist in Sarnecki, the book is historically rich, theoretically provoking, methodologically sound, and policy relevant. Weaving in their own work with the Stockholm Life Course Project, this book casts a bright light into the futures of life course criminology and deserves to be read.'
**Alex R. Piquero PhD, Ashbel Smith Professor of Criminology, University of Texas at Dallas**

'The field of life-course criminology has clearly come of age. Carlsson and Sarnecki's important new text is a wise and generative gift for the next generation of life course scholars. The authors clarify and synthesize decades of research on crime and the life course across multiple disciplines, and lay out the challenges still to come. It is a perfect introduction to a fascinating body of work.'
**Shadd Maruna Dean, Rutgers School of Criminal Justice**

# AN INTRODUCTION TO
# LIFE-COURSE CRIMINOLOGY

## CHRISTOFFER CARLSSON
## & JERZY SARNECKI

Los Angeles | London | New Delhi
Singapore | Washington DC

Los Angeles | London | New Delhi
Singapore | Washington DC

SAGE Publications Ltd
1 Oliver's Yard
55 City Road
London EC1Y 1SP

SAGE Publications Inc.
2455 Teller Road
Thousand Oaks, California 91320

SAGE Publications India Pvt Ltd
B 1/I 1 Mohan Cooperative Industrial Area
Mathura Road
New Delhi 110 044

SAGE Publications Asia-Pacific Pte Ltd
3 Church Street
#10-04 Samsung Hub
Singapore 049483

Editor: Amy Jarrold
Editorial assistant: George Knowles
Production editor: Sarah Cooke
Copyeditor: Lynda Watson
Proofreader: Katie Forsythe
Indexer: Judith Lavender
Marketing manager: Sally Ransom
Cover design: Francis Kenney
Typeset by: C&M Digitals (P) Ltd, Chennai, India
Printed and bound by CPI Group (UK) Ltd,
Croydon, CR0 4YY

**Library of Congress Control Number: 2015940124**

**British Library Cataloguing in Publication data**

A catalogue record for this book is available from
the British Library

ISBN 978-1-44627-590-0
ISBN 978-1-44627-591-7 (pbk)

MIX
Paper from
responsible sources
FSC
www.fsc.org   FSC® C013604

# CONTENTS

# CONTENTS

# CONTENTS

# LIST OF TABLES AND FIGURES

## Figures

# Tables

# ABOUT THE AUTHORS

**Christoffer Carlsson** (b. 1986) has a PhD in Criminology from The Department of Criminology at Stockholm University. His main field of work is life-course criminology, where he has published extensively. In 2012, he received the European Society of Criminology's Young Criminologist Award for his work on turning points and desistance processes.

**Jerzy Sarnecki** (b. 1947) came to Sweden from Warsaw, Poland as a refugee in 1969. He has a PhD in Sociology from Stockholm University (1978) and is Professor of Criminology at Stockholm University and University of Gävle. He has done extensive research on youth crime, criminal networks, and criminal policy, and is the author of several textbooks in criminology. Having worked on The Stockholm Life-Course Project since the late 1970s, Sarnecki has been the project director for the 2nd and 3rd waves of the study. He is also co-chair of the jury for the prestigious Stockholm Prize in Criminology.

# ACKNOWLEDGEMENTS

The authors wish to thank the Swedish National Bank's Jubilee Fund, the Swedish Prison and Probation Service, the Swedish National Board of Institutional Care, and the Department of Criminology at Stockholm University, for financing of The Stockholm Life-Course Project, which forms much of the basis of this book. We are also very grateful for the great encouragement and assistance we have received from Natalie Aguilera, Amy Jarrold, Sarah Cooke and George Knowles at SAGE Publications during our work.

We also want to pay our respect to the first generation of scholars who launched and worked on The Stockholm Life-Course Project, and without whose enormous efforts this work would not have been possible. These include Gösta Carlsson, Birgitta Olofsson, Gustav Jonson, Anna-Lisa Kälvesten, Sven Ahnsjö, Kerstin Elmhorn, Kristine Humble, and Gitte Settergren Carlsson.

Finally, to our colleagues at the Department of Criminology at Stockholm University, and to our respective friends and families: thank you.

# 1

# LIFE-COURSE CRIMINOLOGY: AN INTRODUCTION

In November 2010 Francis T. Cullen, a well-known criminologist and the then recipient of the prestigious Edwin Sutherland Award, delivered his Sutherland Address during the annual American Society of Criminology (ASC) meeting in San Francisco. In this address, he noted that 'life-course criminology is now criminology' (Cullen, 2011: 310). Cullen's intention was not, we think, to argue that all criminological inquiries are or should be informed by a life-course perspective (although an increasing number are). Rather, it was to suggest that life-course criminology is now an integral part of criminology as a whole. Indeed, although the main ideas of the field are as old as criminology itself (probably older), it did rise to fame very quickly.

The main task of this book is to unpack life-course criminology for the reader. In this first chapter, we briefly introduce the topic and questions of life-course criminology, provide a history of the research field, and outline the structure of the book. Our initial tasks are to present the field of life-course criminology and then to map the distance from the 1970s when research on crime and the life course began, to the 2010 ASC meeting when Cullen made the above remark.

## Crime and the Life Course as a Field of Study

Norwegian criminologist Torbjörn Skardhamar (2010: 1) distinguishes life-course criminology from classical theories of crime in a very simple way:

While classical theories of crime mostly discussed differences in offending *between* people (or strata of the population), DLCC [Developmental- and Life-Course Criminology] is primarily concerned with differences in offending *within* individuals over time.

For Skardhamar, what separates life-course criminology from other criminological enterprises is simply a change in perspective, from a focus on differences in criminal offending *between* people, to a focus on differences of offending *within* people. That is, life-course criminology is concerned with individuals as they move through time and place, and how criminal offending changes or continues with these movements. While the relationship between crime and age is as old as criminology itself (Quetelet, 1831), its modern relevance was mainly established in the 1970s with a study by Wolfgang et al. (1972) on the Philadelphia Birth Cohort. The central finding of this well-known publication was that a small number of offenders – between 5 and 10 percent of a given population – were responsible for the majority of crimes committed by that same population. Wolfgang et al. termed these 'chronic offenders', and it raised serious questions: who were these individuals? Could they be identified in advance? What could make them cease their offending?

The main task of life-course criminology has since been to understand an empirically identified paradox. In the words of Moffitt (1993: 674), antisocial behavior 'shows impressive continuity over age, but … its prevalence changes dramatically with age'. In other words, the best 'predictor' for future criminal activity, is past criminal activity (continuity). However, in any given population, the number of active offenders (prevalence) decreases with age.

The task, then, became to untangle mainly two questions: what makes some people persist in crime longer, and have more frequent and serious criminal careers than others? And, what makes people desist from crime? Today, an enormous literature has attempted to answer these questions, and related sub-questions, and we will revisit them later.

Let us linger on terminology for a bit. As the reader will soon find out, life-course criminology introduces quite a number of new terms and concepts to account for crime and deviance across the life course. Some of these are theoretical (such as life course, trajectory, and transition) while others are of a more technical nature (such as frequency, escalation, de-escalation, and duration). We will get to these in due time. For now, it is important to point out that 'life-course criminology' is often considered synonymous to 'developmental criminology' and 'criminal career research'. Depending on the writer or speaker using the term, however, the distinction between *life-course* and *developmental* criminology can be quite significant, because some argue that there are important, underlying perspectives at work here: using *developmental*, you tend to see human life as mainly unfolding in a normative, almost given series of steps. If you use life-course, on the other hand, you subscribe to the life-course perspective of seeing human life as much more fluid, dynamic and unpredictable. We return to these quite complicated arguments later in this book.

Modern criminology was mainly sociological in its origin. The well-known theorists discussed in most textbooks include people such as Clifford Shaw and Henry McKay, Edwin Sutherland, David Matza, Travis Hirschi, and many others. These researchers form part of the history and theoretical core of criminology, and they all approached crime and delinquency as a sociological phenomenon. In contrast, life-course criminology is often considered *interdisciplinary*, where insights from biology, psychology, sociology, economics, and political science converge. In this introductory book we mainly consider the intersections of psychology and sociology, as these approaches have been the most influential so far, but we also include biology (see Chapters 3 and 5). Here we alert the reader to our own background, since no introduction to such a broad research field can be completely unbiased and non-selective. We are trained in the socio-logical strand of criminology. That being said, we attempt to give the reader an introduction to the field as an interdisciplinary enterprise, and reflect the strengths of the psychological and biological approaches, as well as highlighting the limitations of the sociological branch of the field.

## An Imagination for Studying the Life Course

The development of life-course criminology is contingent on life-course studies in a more general sense. The idea that human development occurs in stages, with the latter stages of development based on the previous ones, first appeared in psychology. Developmental psychology had undergone a rapid development in the early 1900s by such scholars as Sigmund Freud, who focused on human psychosexual development, and Jean Piaget, who outlined the different stages of human cognitive development.

In sociology, this approach began in the 1970s, with the work of Glen H. Elder, Jr. In *Children of the Great Depression* (1974) Elder traced the lives of a group of children who grew up in Oakland, California under the Great Depression. Beginning in 1931, fifth graders from five schools, and their parents, were measured on a number of topics. Follow-up studies were conducted in the 1940s, 1950s, and 1960s. This mode of inquiry made it possible for Elder to study the contingency of having grown up during the Great Depression, and how that impacted on the future lives of those children. It also led the way toward a more sophisticated, conceptually clear notion of the life course than had previously been the case.

When we speak of the *life course*, we do so in a quite specific way. By life course, we mean the 'age-graded sequence of roles, opportunities, constraints, and events that shape the biography from birth to death' (Shanahan and Macmillan,

2008: 40). 'Age-graded' is important here. It means, plainly, that the roles we enter and the events that happen to us in life tend to occur in quite predictable ways. This does not mean that there is not any room for variation, only that what happens to us tends to happen to other people too, and at roughly the same age.

Two central concepts are embedded within the notion of the life course: *trajectories* and *transitions*. A *trajectory* is 'a pathway or line of development over the life span', such as education, work, or criminal behavior (Sampson and Laub, 1993: 8). *Transitions*, in turn, are life events, such as one's high school or college graduation, first job, or first marriage. They are embedded within trajectories and tend to mark the exit from one social role (e.g. 'student') and the entry to another (such as 'worker'). Trajectories and transitions tend to unfold in a normative pattern, as we noted above. They are, moreover, embedded in the social institutions of education, work, family life, and so on. One's biography is thus tied to the social structure of society. There are certain features of life that are natural – i.e. we are born, we age for some time, and we die – but how our lives are constructed along that path is historically specific. That is, they are dependent on time and place and the result of specific forms of social organization.

Within sociology, one of the great, famous research programs was outlined by C. Wright Mills in his seminal work *The Sociological Imagination* (1959). In this work, Mills argues that the social sciences need to be relevant and sensitive to the lives of the people those same sciences claim to study. The study of human behavior should begin with humans, their behavior and the social situation in which this behavior occurs – not with highly abstract concepts that have little or nothing to do with the people and their situations. The intersection of human biographies and social structures form the starting point, 'the capacity to range from the most impersonal and remote transformations to the most intimate features of the human self – and to see the relations between the two' (Mills, 1959: 7). The person who has trained him- or herself to develop a sociological imagination, Mills continues on the same page, will 'understand what is happening in themselves as minute points of intersections of biography and history within society'.

In connecting the ideas of person, time, and place, Mills' program is a powerful and important predecessor to the life-course perspective, which in greater detail may be said to try and answer some of the questions Mills never did, such as: *how* do we do that? What is the importance of *age* at the intersection of biography and structure? What makes most people have unique, biographical elements in some ways, and what makes most of them still follow very similar trajectories and go through the same transitions?

When we focus on the life course, we thus focus on the way people's behavior, feelings, and thoughts continue and change with age, as they go through various transitions and experiences, and move along trajectories. As might be suspected, at this general level it's not really a theory of anything, but rather a way of thinking and seeing human lives and how they develop, unfold, and take expected and unexpected turns over time.

To take just one example, as researchers, in our occupational trajectory we typically go through a transition from being graduate students to PhDs, and from there on to associate professors and (hopefully!) full professors. We also have other trajectories, however, for example, a residential trajectory: we have grown up in our childhood families and homes, then move out, get our own apartments, and so on. In Stockholm, where we are living and working, getting the apartment you want can be quite expensive and it is more likely that you will get a loan from a bank if you are an associate or full professor, than if you are a graduate student, because as a professor you have a higher salary and a more stable form of employment. Residential transitions, in turn, are likely to be somewhat dependent on what happens in still other spheres of life, such as family life. Thus, trajectories and transitions interlock, connect, and become partly contingent on one another; social arrangements tend to mesh together and what happens in one sphere of life can impel or obstruct processes of continuity and change in other spheres. These processes are all, of course, intersected by different forms of social stratification, such as class (in Sweden, researchers tend to belong to the middle-class segment of society, and this fact impacts on all the trajectories and transitions we briefly outlined above).

As the life-course perspective emerged, so did a number of 'core principles' (Elder, 1998) of the perspective. While life-course criminology tends to subscribe to these principles, they may be more usefully thought of as guidelines. Principles suggest firm and static rules for how research should be done and what features should be considered. In practice, they are more often used as guidelines, or, in a sense, tricks – they are useful ways of thinking about the unfolding of human lives, and also suggest what we as researchers should be sensitive and attentive to as we go about our research:

1. The historical nature of time and place.
2. The timing of human lives.
3. The linking of human lives.
4. Human agency.

These four guidelines are interconnected, but for the purpose of clarity we go through them separately below.

## 1. The Historical Nature of Time and Place

Everything has to occur somewhere, and sometime, and where and when something happens is important for understanding that very 'something'. Human development is dependent on social and historical conditions and processes: where and when we live impacts on *how* we live and *how* our life course unfolds (Elder, 1998). Some social conditions change very rapidly, such as the Great Depression of the 1930s, the outbreak of World War II in Europe in 1939, or the fall of Communism in the late 1980s. Those changes rapidly and severely rearrange social life. Consider, as an example, education and work during and after the Great Depression. During the Depression, many people went through the transition from being a student to a worker, only to find that there was little meaningful employment to be found. As a result, many experienced negative employment patterns through adulthood (Elder, 1974). For those who were slightly younger and graduated only some 10 or 15 years later, however, things looked very different: World War II was over and the economy was expanding in an extremely rapid, drastic way and opportunities to find work were everywhere to be found. Compared to the older group of graduates, this younger group had drastically different trajectories.

Now, these are very drastic and dramatic social changes (for a Swedish example, see Nilsson et al., 2013). Economic recessions and world-altering wars are extremely rare events. These days, in our part of the world, most of the time social life changes much more slowly and gradually, but the general guideline of being sensitive to time and place is still as valid. For example, take the early 21st century's capacity to heavily reduce the amount of manual labor that is needed for a society's economy to function. Today, most occupations require advanced education and vast technical skills. This means that today's young people need to delay their entry into employment to a greater extent than those who were young 40 years ago, because they need to pursue higher education. This has consequences for the everyday life of people, but also for their long-term trajectories when it comes to education, employment, and – perhaps – family formation. It is also likely that the situation might differ between, say, metropolitan and rural areas. If we compare the trajectories of those born in the countryside in the 1960s to those born in big cities during the 1990s, the important transitions are likely to differ, which supports the overall guideline: where and when you live matters. To give an additional example, think about the phenomenon criminologists often term opportunity structure. Both the extent and nature of criminal activity such as theft is affected by the amount of possible objects to steal, and in Western societies during the 20th century, the opportunity structure for crimes of theft increased dramatically (von Hofer, 2008). Today, as far as we know, theft decreases in many parts of the Western world, while crimes related to the Internet are increasing rapidly (perhaps a consequence of what Cohen and Felson [1979] called a change in routine activities).

Similarly, consider the impact of changes in social control, especially social control of the young. Here we have moved from a society characterized by vertical (i.e. superior adults control the young) to horizontal control, where social control is primarily exercised among equal peers, which influence the character of crime and people's criminal trajectories (Sarnecki, 2005).

## 2. The Timing of Human Lives

As life-course researchers, we are not only interested in the events that happen to an individual as he or she moves along the life course, but we are also very much interested in *when* they happen. The timing of events is crucial, because the same event may give rise to very different results, depending on how old the individual is when it occurs. The individual is changing throughout life, depending partly on the natural aging process, and partly on the constant ongoing interactions with the social environment.

The timing of events in human lives is partly dependent on the social organization of a society. Think about it. When somebody says that 'he is too young for this' or 'she is too old for that', the person is referring to an often invisible (but sometimes visible, such as written laws) set of norms governing what stages people should go through, and when: education in adolescence; moving out of the family home at the end of adolescence; starting higher education and/or entering the labor market in early adulthood; finding more stable employment and (heterosexual, monogamous) relationship and family formation in adulthood; retirement in late adulthood, and so on.

Of course, far from all individuals actually engage in every role at precisely the expected age, but the majority tends to engage in most of them and at roughly the expected time. These normative expectations, we must remember, are grounded in a specific segment of contemporary Western society – the male, white, heterosexual middle class – but individuals outside of that segment are also embedded in this structure. They can also be expected to struggle more, since how individuals experience social structures and social institutions, as well as their ability to make transitions into and between them, are very much dependent on their past and present 'location in social structures of inequality, based on class, race, gender and other social statuses' (Berger and Quinney, 2005: 176).

So, when things happen and in what order they happen are crucial to a life-course-informed understanding of human behavior in general, and criminal behavior in particular. Let us be frank about it. It is often one thing to be arrested for a small crime for the first time at age 30, when you presumably have had the chance to build up a conventional life, a relatively firm self-image, and a good reputation among your friends, relatives, and colleagues. To be sure, it is not very pleasant, but it is unlikely to be a life-altering experience. It is a very different experience, however, to be arrested for the same crime at age 10, 12, or 15. These are formative years, not only socially but also psychologically, and the various actors in your immediate environment – your family, school, and so on – are likely to view the arrest as an indicator of problems to come, and take measures. These measures, early studies showed, tend to powerfully affect the vulnerable youth's mind, sense of self and future behavior (Lemert, 1951). The label 'deviant' or 'criminal' is more likely to stick to the 10-year old than to the 30-year old.

But, we must not assume that the principle of timing is that easy or general; already at this early stage, we need to complicate the picture somewhat. In other circumstances, the effect of timing can be the *opposite*. Being arrested for certain crimes can have far more devastating effects on the future life trajectory for the adult, well-established individual than for a minor. Take for example, having sex with somebody who is below the legal age (in Sweden this age is 15). When committed by a minor, such behavior can be perceived as a lack of maturity. For an adult, however, it is a serious sexual deviance and a serious crime. In this case, we can understand the timing effect using Hirschi's (1969) social control theory. According to this theory, an individual with strong ties to society has much more to lose if he or she gets caught for a violation of social norms than a person without such a strong attachment, commitment and involvement in society, and adult individuals are more likely than minors to have developed such ties.

## 3. The Linking of Human Lives

What we do impacts on what those in our surroundings do. Similarly, when those around us act it may affect our feelings, thoughts, and actions. What kind of family we grow up in, whether we have siblings or not, and whether they are younger or older than us, whether we have many or few friends as we grow up, and how their lives are different from ours (or not) – all these lives powerfully inform and characterize our own personal histories (Benson, 2013).

Human lives are linked together, affecting one another and the resulting trajectories and transitions of their lives. Taking the example of juvenile delinquency, consider the importance that peers seem to have. There is no reason to assume that peer influence is limited to adolescence only, but it seems to be the case that peer influence reaches its highest importance between the middle teens and early adulthood (Warr, 2002). Incidentally, this is also the phase where criminal offending peaks for the majority of all offenders. As we grow older, the majority of us leave crime behind, and this is also the same phase where the importance of peers begins to decrease. Our lives instead begin to be linked to intimate partners, colleagues, and others. We ourselves, in turn, may affect others as we move along the life course.

## 4. Human Agency

Given the normative structuring of the life course, how is variation possible? Here we need to introduce another, final guideline to the study of life courses: *human agency*. Its general meaning is very broad, but the basic notion is that people are purposive. They act based on past experiences and their striving toward the future. This does not mean that every act is based on reflection and rational decision-making; on the contrary, many things we do is the result of habit and routine (Weber, 1978: 21f).

Human agency has been conceptualized in many ways. For Elder, the guideline of human agency holds that people 'construct their own life course through the choices and actions they take within the opportunities and constraints of history and social circumstances' (Elder, 1998: 4). To stress the importance of human agency for understanding the life course does thus not imply that the individual's will is 'free'. As Matza explains, will is 'a sense of option that must be rendered *in context* … Will need not be untrammeled, abstracted or 'free', nor need behavior be determined, preordained or predictable' (Matza, 1969: 116, emphases added).

As people age and move along the life course, their motivations change and this is reflected in the content of their human agency. But conversely, people's human agency can influence their movement between social institutions and places in social structure. So, for example, conventional motivation can produce conventional behavior, but the reverse is also possible, as conventional behavior can produce conventional motivation (see Becker, 1960). Recognizing the dynamics of human agency is an important factor in the realization that human behavior can never be totally predictable.

The notion of human agency, conceived of in one way or another, has been deeply influential to life-course criminology and studies on desistance from crime (Bottoms, 2006). Having made this very brief sketch of the field's basic characteristics, however, we can now turn to the criminological history of it. As we do so, we can also outline additional central concepts.

## A Brief History of Life-Course Criminology

The first longitudinal studies in criminology had already started in the 1930s, when Sheldon and Eleanor Glueck published *Five Hundred Criminal Careers* (Glueck and Glueck, 1930).[1] In the beginning, however, these researchers had in mind a short follow-up time. This was the case in many studies. That one of the Gluecks' studies, *Unraveling Juvenile Delinquency*, eventually became the (so far) longest follow-up study in the history of criminological research, is due to the fact that the study was resumed by Sampson and Laub in the 1980s and 1990s (Laub and Sampson, 2003; Sampson and Laub, 1993). We return to the theory development based on this study in Chapter 3.

---

[1] They were eventually supplemented by additional studies: *Five Hundred Delinquent Women* (1934), *One Thousand Juvenile Delinquents* (1934), and *Unraveling Juvenile Delinquency* (1950).

Another early longitudinal study is the so-called Cambridge Somerville Youth Study, which was launched in 1939, to investigate the effects of preventive measures against juvenile delinquency. The study included around 500 boys who were followed up on several occasions by Joan McCord (2007). This research was of great importance for future treatment research because it showed that, in some cases, well-intentioned treatment measures can be directly harmful to the individual who receives them. It also showed that a long follow-up time is sometimes necessary, before any actual treatment effects can be observed.

While continuity and change in behavior over time had been part of developmental psychology for quite some time (see Brim and Kagan, 1980), it was not until the 1970s and 1980s that sociological criminology began to explore the topic in depth. This was also the time when criminal career research and life-course criminology bloomed and rose to fame. Initiated in the 1960s and published in 1972, Wolfgang et al. undertook a seminal study of around 10,000 boys born in 1945 in Philadelphia, who lived there from the age of 10 until they were at least 18. Due to the study design, the researchers were able to track the longitudinal sequencing of offenses committed by the cohort boys. Perhaps even more importantly, their study was one of the first to find that a small portion of the sample (6 percent) accounted for roughly 50 percent of the offenses committed by the whole group of boys. As we suggested above, this finding sparked debate and controversy that continues to this day: who were these boys? What made them commit so many offenses, and what could be done to make them stop?

The Philadelphia Birth Cohort Study was thoroughly quantitative in its methodology. Around the same time, however, qualitative studies that specifically addressed life-course criminological questions, and focused more on the processual nature of social life, began to emerge. In an interview study published in the influential journal *Criminology*, Thomas Meisenhelder (1977) conducted an exploratory study of 20 non-professional property offenders exiting from criminal careers (today, the phase Meisenhelder explored would probably be termed the phase of *desistance*). Meisenhelder's basic findings can be summarized in two points: first, he found that exiting was motivated by the offender's desire to avoid (further) imprisonment and his wish to 'settle down'. Second, in order for the offender to succeed in his project of exiting, he must be able to establish social bonds to conventional society. 'In general', Meisenhelder noted, 'these findings support social control as a theory of criminal behavior' (1977: 319).

A few years later, Meisenhelder (1982) returned to the question of exiting criminal careers, but now added a new dimension to it: the phase of certification. This phase, Meisenhelder noted, is the last phase in leaving crime. In the phase of certification, the offender goes through an identity transition, both in the eyes of himself and in the eyes of others; from that of being a 'criminal' to that of being a conventional person and recognized as such by members of the conventional community. Today, the study of such processes of social interaction in order to further explain and understand criminal careers, occupies a central place in life-course criminology (e.g. Carlsson, 2012; Maruna, 2001).

## Key Dimensions and Concepts

The year of 1986 is important for criminal career research. This year, The National Academy of Sciences published the two-volume study *Criminal Careers and Career Criminals*, edited by Blumstein, Cohen, Roth and Visher (1986). The volumes outline the basic features of criminal career research, including some central concepts and their definitions. Within sociology, the term 'career' was originally used in studies of occupations but then broadened 'to refer to any social strand of any person's course through life' (Goffman, 1961: 127). In the 1986 study, Blumstein and his colleagues took the concept and redefined it: the *criminal career* is defined as the 'longitudinal sequence of crimes committed by an individual offender' (Blumstein et al., 1986: 12). Everyone who at least once commits a crime thus has a criminal career; the majority of us have a rather short one, consisting of one or a few offenses, whereas a small minority have a considerably longer career, consisting of more and (often) serious offenses.

One can, of course, discuss the appropriateness of using the term career (which is usually used to describe an individual's progress in employment) to describe crime, as it in most cases can hardly be regarded as a profession. We thus use the concept as an analytical tool, and not in the perhaps everyday sense of the word (which might suggest an upward movement through positions in a hierarchical structure, such as a company or organization). They also outline the key dimensions and concepts of the criminal career, which we go through step by step here but also return to in subsequent chapters.

First of all, *participation* distinguishes those who engage in crime at least once, from those who never do so. Second, *onset* refers to the initiation of the criminal career, that is, the individual's first infraction of a criminal law. Thus, *age of onset* refers to the individual's age when he or she first engages in a crime. As we will see later, age of onset is important, for the earlier onset occurs for an individual offender, the greater is the risk for frequent and serious criminal offending by that same individual. By *frequency*, Blumstein and his colleagues refer to the rate of an individual's criminal activity, that is, how many offenses he or she commits during a certain period of time. This rate they term Lambda, or $\lambda$. Some offenders have a very high rate of offending, while others have a very low. Blumstein et al. (1986) argue that differences in $\lambda$ between offenders is largely dependent on demographic features, such as ethnicity, gender, and class, and other factors such as drug use and age of onset. Importantly, the rate of offending also changes *within* offenders as they move along the life course. The seemingly simple and innocent measure (and meaning) of $\lambda$ was to become an important issue of debate in criminology.

By *seriousness*, they simply refer to the seriousness of the individual's criminal activity, and how the degree of seriousness escalates or de-escalates over time. *Career length*, or *duration*, is the amount of time the individual is an active offender, that is, the amount of time between onset and the end of the criminal career, which is termed *desistance*.

The research program outlined by Blumstein et al. (1986), combined with the previous study by Wolfgang et al. (1972) and the rise of life-course studies in the social sciences in a more general sense (e.g. Elder, 1974) contributed to the rise of life-course criminology. The theoretical as well as methodological advances within this field have greatly influenced criminology as a whole. We hope to illustrate this for the reader as we go along, but to give just one example, take The Stockholm Prize in Criminology, arguably one of the more prestigious awards within the discipline. Since 2006, the recipients have included Alfred Blumstein and Terrie Moffitt (2007), Robert Sampson and John Laub (2011), David P. Farrington (2013), and Daniel S. Nagin (2014) – all of whom occupy central positions of influence within the field of life-course criminology.

However, as the attentive reader might have noted in this brief history of the field, the early phases of life-course criminology seemed to be very non-theoretical, and instead heavily driven by empirical data. This, we believe, is an adequate assessment of the early years of criminal career research. This was followed, however, by a wave of researchers who formulated theoretical outlines in order to understand and explain the empirical findings laid out by these early and subsequent studies of crime and the life course. We go through these theories in detail in Chapter 3.

## Life-Course Studies in Europe and Scandinavia

The research that we refer to above has with few exceptions been conducted in the USA. You could actually argue that the main achievements of this research have taken place there. However, even early on in the history of life-course criminology, a substantial number of criminological studies of longitudinal character were conducted in Europe. Killias et al. (2012) review nearly 100 such studies in different European countries. The studies come from such countries as England, Germany, Netherlands, and Sweden, but also Estonia and Finland.

The oldest and possibly most well-known of the European life-course studies of crime is The Cambridge Study in Delinquent Development. It was founded in 1961 by Donald J. West, but has for many years been directed by David P. Farrington. The study includes 411 boys who were born in 1953 and studied for the first time when they were eight years old, and lived in a working-class neighborhood in South London. It included variables on socioeconomic conditions, schooling, friendship, parent–child relationships, extracurricular activities, and criminal records. Researchers also carried out psychological tests to study the causes of crime and delinquency. Information in the survey includes reports from peers, family size, child-rearing behavior, job histories, leisure habits, truancy, popularity, physical attributes, tendencies toward violence, sexual activity, and self-reported delinquency. Nowadays, the Cambridge Study in Delinquent Development is a multi-generational study.

In Scandinavian countries, with centralized systems of national identification numbers and many official registers covering the entire population, prerequisites for quantitative life-course research were considered to be very good. Scandinavian researchers were also very early to engage with the question of age and crime. Using Swedish and Norwegian criminal records, Sveri (1960) found an empirical pattern similar to the common age/crime curve, and suggested that 'most children under the influence of their "gang" indulge in criminal activities, but cease when they emerge from the "gang" age' (Sveri, 1960: 218). Sveri was thus aware of the transient nature of offending among those who engage in crime in adolescence: it is 'improper to stamp every "gang" formation as harmful, as do certain criminologists', he noted on the same page. 'Group activities are a normal part of the process of development of the individual.' Some of those who engage in crime, however, also persist (although Sveri does not use that terminology) and become 'professional criminals' in adulthood (Sveri, 1960: 218).

Arguably the most well-known Scandinavian life-course study is Project Metropolitan.[2] Envisioned by the Norwegian historian and sociologist Kaare Svalastoga in 1960, the project was originally supposed to include all Nordic countries. It was eventually only launched in Denmark and Sweden, and we focus on the latter here. The research program had an explicitly longitudinal approach, the main question being why some fare better in life than others, with a specific focus on criminal and deviant behavior (Janson, 1975). Launched in 1964, Project Metropolitan includes everybody born in Stockholm in 1953 who was living in Stockholm during 1963 (around 15,000 people).

The original data collection included a range of surveys, interviews, and tests, including surveys of every cohort member's family situation, socioeconomic status, his or her behavior in several domains (but not juvenile delinquency[3]), attitudes, interests, and plans for the future, including work. For the subsequent analyses of crime, official criminal records were collected and pieced together from a variety of official sources and records, up until 1984. The results show that between 1966 and 1984 around 20 percent of the cohort (predominantly men)

---

[2] In the 2000s, the project was renamed The Stockholm Birth Cohort Study (Stenberg, 2013). In our description of Project Metropolitan we rely on Stenberg's recent historical review, except where explicitly noted.

[3] The reason behind this is found in Janson (1982: 14): 'To get the cooperation of school authorities and the PTA in the School Study [where the self-report study was carried out] we agreed not to ask about sex life and delinquency.'

was recorded for at least one crime. In general, those who engaged in crime came from households with weak socioeconomic resources, broken families and parents who used or had used drugs. Mirroring the common finding in contemporary life-course criminology, that of both continuity and change in behavior, the vast majority of offenders nevertheless desisted after adolescence. However, those who initiated their criminal offending early (prior to age 19) and then continued made up around 75 percent of the men's total criminal offending. Those who persisted in crime also ran a clear, increased risk of having worse living conditions and being socially excluded in adulthood, compared to those who desisted.

By the mid-1980s, a major mass-media debate on this project started. The criticism concerned legal and ethical aspects, but also methodological dimensions of the project and life-course research in general. Criticism of the project resulted in it being temporarily stopped and part of the data was destroyed. It was eventually resumed under a new name, the Stockholm Birth Cohort Study. As a result of these turbulences, researchers active in the study may add data from official records but are not allowed to complement the material with interviews, or other data collected directly from the participants.

Project Metropolitan was sociologically driven. In contrast, the IDA-program (Individual Development and Adjustment) was psychological in its orientation. Initiated in 1965 by psychologist David Magnusson, IDA follows a cohort of around 1,300 children born in the Swedish city of Örebro during the 1950s. Using an array of tests and assessments to capture the children's childhood, they have been followed up through official records for 30 years since the initial study (Bergman and Andershed, 2009; Stattin and Magnusson, 1991).[4] Perhaps mirroring the psychological basis of IDA, it was and is more concerned with the study of risk and protective factors than Project Metropolitan was (e.g. Stattin et al., 1997).

Outside of Sweden, Norwegian life-course criminological studies have made not only important empirical contributions to the field, but also highlighted important methodological limitations in the influential statistical technique known as group-based modeling. Mainly through the works of Skardhamar (2009, 2010), Skardhamar and Lyngstad (2011), and Monsbakken et al. (2013) the predominant explanations of continuity and change in crime (such as Moffitt's developmental taxonomy, which we go through in Chapter 3, and the relationship between partnership and/or employment and desistance) have been questioned and developed further, utilizing the strengths of Norwegian register data.

---

[4] The methodological person-centered approach – as opposed to a variable-centered one – IDA outlined and used in their analysis (see Bergman and Magnusson, 1990), was later taken up by Sampson and Laub and formed the basis of their analysis of the Glueck data (see Sampson and Laub, 1993: 204; see also Chapters 3 and 4 in this book).

Similarly, in Denmark, Kyvsgaard (1998) used official register data to study a Danish cohort longitudinally and explored a variety of features of the criminal career. Utilizing the strength of the Danish register data, Kyvsgaard was able to give 'a more varied picture of the criminal career than do most other studies' (Kyvsgaard, 1998: 239) and found that it is more common for offenders to desist from crime than to continue it. Kyvsgaard also highlighted the importance of aging. Although it is very common for young offenders to desist from crime (we know this from age/crime curves of prevalence), the desistance-rate 'among middle-aged and older offenders ... passes the rate of the young ones' (Kyvsgaard, 1998: 237). In line with Savolainen (2009), who studied the connection between employment and desistance longitudinally in Finland, Kyvsgaard found a clear relationship between employment and desistance: fewer offenders without jobs desist, compared to those who are working, and those offenders who do not belong to the work force at all have the lowest desistance rate.

Equally important contributions have recently come from the Netherlands, with such studies as the Criminal Career and Life-Course Study (CCLS). The CCLS follows over 5,000 offenders – a national representative sample of 4 percent of all criminal cases in the Netherlands in 1977 – and their family members during large parts of their life course. Incorporating data on life events such as death, marriage, divorce, having children, the CCLS allows the researchers to study the important interdependencies between criminal development and such life-course transitions. The results have been published in leading criminological journals (Block et al., 2010; Blokland and Nieuwbeerta, 2005).

As this brief review of European life-course criminology suggests, it has already, since the birth of the research field, been actively engaged in designing influential studies and contributing to the knowledge of criminal careers, most notably through such studies as the Cambridge Study of Delinquent Development, the Stockholm Birth Cohort, and CCLS. As the later examples by such researchers as Skardhamar, Kyvsgaard, and Savolainen show, they have also continued to be so.

## 'The Big Debate'

Before we continue, we must pay attention to what has been called 'The Big Debate' in criminology. It occurred during the 1980s and the formative phase of criminal career research and is an important part of the history of life-course criminology. It was the relationship between age and crime that stood in the center of the debate. It had long been known that crime rates rise considerably throughout adolescence to a peak in the late adolescent years, and then decline.

Now, the traditional interpretation of the decline was that it primarily was a matter of frequency: people continued to offend, but with lower intensity. The number of active offenders was thus thought to remain the same over time. However, criminal career researchers claimed that this interpretation was inadequate; the vast majority of those who initiate criminal offending actually *stop*. It was not a matter of frequency or intensity, but a matter of *participation*. This alternative interpretation of the age–crime relationship led to another con-tested implication: it followed that it might be necessary to develop different explanatory models for such phenomena as frequency and participation. That is, one set of factors or processes may cause one's participation in crime, whereas another set might influence one's offending frequency and duration in crime.

Here is where the argument began in the 1980s. It took place predominantly in a number of journal articles published in The American Society of Criminology's influential flagship journal *Criminology*. On the one side stood the early criminal career researchers, such as Alfred Blumstein, David Farrington, and Jacqueline Cohen. On the other side stood, perhaps most notably, Michael Gottfredson and Travis Hirschi (although they were not the only ones).

Let us begin with Gottfredson and Hirschi. Their main contention was that, independent of any sociological explanation, age matures people out of crime. This is not the case for some offenders, they argued, but for all offenders. The decline of crime with age is thus not due to a decline in participation, but a decline in offending frequency among all offenders. Underlying this stance was their criminal propensity position. Simply put, according to Gottfredson and Hirschi, some people are more prone than others to carry out crime, and this propensity is relatively stable across the life course (we revisit this position in Chapter 3). From about age 8 and on, an individual has developed his or her criminal propensity; a propensity which may manifest itself in various ways depending on circumstances and chance, so people with the same propensity might actually commit rather various forms of crimes. It follows from this argument that factors such as onset of crime, frequency, duration, and desistance are unnecessary for our under-standing of criminal careers. Variations in criminal offending depend on where the individual currently is on the age–crime curve, because age is the one funda-mental factor that affects criminal offending over time. The age-effect is invariant, meaning that it is found in all societies at all times and therefore does not require explanation. The only criminological task is to disclose why some individuals have a higher criminal propensity than others. This line of reasoning is entirely consistent with their self-control theory (Gottfredson and Hirschi, 1990; see Chapter 3), according to which, low self-control is the cause of criminal propensity and developed in early childhood.

The criminal career advocates, on the other hand, had, as we noted above, a different take on the relationship between age and crime. They contended that different factors, events, and processes may influence different stages of the criminal career. It might therefore be necessary to construct different explanations for the different steps of a criminal career. The debate was thus partly grounded in theory, but it was also a methodological issue: a debate about research design.

Gottfredson and Hirschi argued that cross-sectional research, which compares different individuals at the same time, was enough. Cross-sectional research compares individuals on personality traits, socioeconomic status, gender, ethnicity, residential area, number of delinquent friends, etc., and then studies these variables' relationship to crime. It follows logically from their theoretical position, where the basic cause of criminal offending is established early in life. It is a relatively cheap methodology to use, since it can all be done in one time.

The criminal career researchers, on the other hand, argued that criminologists should rely on longitudinal research in order to fully understand the continuities and changes in criminal careers. Longitudinal research is a research methodology that we revisit later in the book, but in essence it follows the same individuals over time, through repeated measurements. It is both time- and resource-consuming. The rationale for doing this, however, is that cross-sectional studies can only establish correlates of criminal behavior. They cannot untangle the causal unfolding of events and sequences, because they cannot establish the time-order of events. For example, we know that low school performance is a 'risk factor' for criminal offending. The correlation between these two variables can be established with the help of cross-sectional methodology. But what comes first? It is possible that criminal offending precedes low school performance, but it is equally possible that low school performance precedes criminal offending. Or, does one start to associate with delinquent peers because one has already initiated criminal offending, or does one engage in criminal offending because one has started to hang out with criminally active friends?

In this book we are primarily concerned with life-course studies of crime, but we also consider the criminal propensity approach, particularly in Chapter 3. More than 25 years later, criminologists are still testing and developing the criminal propensity vs. criminal career positions. However, as Nagin and Land (1993) among others have found, the two positions might be less oppositional than they first seemed to be, as both have gained empirical support. This has been one of the main contributions of the debate, seeing as it helped spawn a large bulk of influential studies that contributed to the development of both criminological theory and policy.

At the word 'policy' we must pause and add another dimension to the debate. When the debate is re-told and reviewed in textbooks it is often done in the way we have here. However, as Hagan (2010) importantly reminds us, the issue was not, and is not, limited to theoretical positions, empirical findings, and research designs. It also has a political dimension. An illustrative example here is the concern with Lambda, or $\lambda$. We sneaked in a comment above about how this measurement – of the frequency of offending among active offenders – was to become an important issue of the debate. The contentious question was, might some offenders persist in offending at a near constant rate regardless of age? In a wonderfully provocative paper title, Gottfredson and Hirschi (1986) made their position clear: 'The true value of lambda would appear to be zero'. They considered the idea that some offenders commit crimes at a constant rate was 'an academic myth' (Hagan, 2010: 110). In line with Gottfredson and Hirschi's (1990) theoretical position and empirical illustrations of the age–crime curve, all offenders de-escalate and eventually cease their offending with age. On the other hand, the criminal career researchers argued that the non-zero rate of λ might be real and profound.

The political dimension enters powerfully here: the possible constancy of λ suggested a possibility to accurately identify the offenders whom Wolfgang et al. (1972) had termed 'chronic offenders'. The criminal career approach held, in other words, the potential promise of and justification for selective incapacitation (i.e. the strategy to, through imprisonment, prevent particularly dangerous individuals from committing new crimes). In Gottfredson and Hirschi's (1986, cited in Hagan, 2010: 113) words: 'To the policy-oriented, the idea of a career criminal suggests the possibility of doing something to or for a small segment of the population with notable reductions in crime rates.' Such policies, they noted, 'inevitably incarcerate people after they have moved beyond the teen years, the age of maximum participation in crime' (Gottfredson and Hirschi, 1995: 34). It is thus both an expensive and unnecessary intervention, with low prospects for any considerable reduction in crime rates.

The criminal career researchers 'formally maintained an agnostic position' on this issue (Hagan, 2010: 113). They were aware of the policy implications inherent in the two approaches, where Gottfredson and Hirschi's position suggested that interventions be focused on reducing overall participation in crime (that is, policies directed at the general population). The criminal career advocates were also open to the possibility of a more restrictive, concentrated focus on the 'chronic' offenders. 'So far', Blumstein et al. (1988: 7) noted, 'the evidence on both approaches is sufficiently inconclusive that neither is clearly preferable, and pursuit of either should not preclude interest in the other.'

The debate moved on, and it is still alive and kicking as we write this. We encourage the reader to go back and revisit this debate later, as the questions and problems at stake might emerge more clearly and seem more relevant after having read, particularly, Chapters 3 and 4.

# The Structure of this Book

As you may have noticed, already in this first chapter we have covered a lot of ground. Having introduced the field of life-course criminology and the study of criminal careers here, we continue with a brief chapter on criminological theories and criminal careers. Chapter 2 thus shows how the central features of life-course criminology were present in much of what we today think of as 'classical' criminology (the works and theories of Edwin Sutherland, Howard S. Becker, David Matza, etc.), but how those features also tended to be on the margins of the field.

In Chapter 3, we move on to review and discuss today's dominant life-course criminological theories. This is a long chapter, but it does cover a lot of ground. Rather than making a brief overview of a large chunk of theories, we choose to focus on a rather small number of theories and go through them in some depth and detail. We believe this is a more fruitful approach for the student.

Next is Chapter 4, where we go through the various methodologies of the life-course criminological enterprise. Here we also briefly present the research project The Stockholm Life-Course Project (SLCP), which serves as our main empirical, illustrative example in the subsequent chapters (see below). Life-course criminology, we believe, is most easy to grasp and understand when made concrete, and using The SLCP is a way to do that, as it is a project we have been actively involved in as researchers. Most importantly, however, The SLCP includes many of the central features that most life-course criminological research projects have.

Following the chapter on methodology, the next chapters engage in a more step-by-step review of the different stages of the criminal career, beginning with risk, risk factors and prediction in Chapter 5. In Chapter 6, we turn to the onset of crime. Next, we cover continuity in criminal activity, or persistence, paying attention to the 'minor' lulls, drifts, and phases of intermittency that characterizes many criminal careers. Chapter 8 deals with desistance from crime.

As we go through the field of life-course criminology, we also mention and discuss its limits, and the way those limits are always changing due to the ever-increasing amount of life-course criminological research, development, and exploration of new ideas and phenomena. The ninth and final chapter both summarizes and looks forward.

## Suggestions for Further Reading

Blumstein, Alfred, Cohen, Jacqueline, Roth, Jeffrey A. and Visher, Christy A. (eds) (1986) *Criminal Careers and Career Criminals*. Washington, DC: National Academy Press.
In this 1986 publication, Blumstein and colleagues introduce much of the central conceptual apparatus of criminal career research.

Cullen, Francis T. (2011) 'Beyond adolescence-limited criminology – choosing our future: the American Society of Criminology 2010 Sutherland Address', *Criminology*, 49(2): 287–330.

In his 2010 Sutherland Address, with which we began this chapter, Cullen spells out the influence life-course criminology has had on criminology as a whole, and also suggests a possible future for the field.

Elder, Glen H. (1998) 'The life course as developmental theory', *Child Development*, 69(1): 1–12.
Whereas the 1986 publication by Blumstein et al. introduced much of the central concepts for studying criminal careers, this is one of Elder's (many) outlines of the life-course perspective.

Blumstein, Alfred, Cohen, Jacqueline and Farrington, David (1988) 'Criminal career research: its value for criminology', *Criminology*, 26(1): 1–35.
Gottfredson, Michael and Hirschi, Travis (1988) 'Science, public policy, and the career paradigm', *Criminology*, 26(1): 37–55.
Blumstein, Alfred, Cohen, Jacqueline and Farrington, David (1988) 'Longitudinal and criminal career research: further clarifications', *Criminology*, 26(1): 57–74.
These three articles, all in the same issue of *Criminology* (no. 26, issue 1) constitute parts of criminology's 'Big Debate' and are essential reading (in fact, the whole issue is devoted to the debate with many insightful papers and comments).

# 2
# CRIMINOLOGICAL THEORIES
# AND CRIMINAL CAREERS

In this chapter, we begin our attempt at unpacking the field of crime and the life course in greater detail. As was suggested in the previous chapter, life-course criminology rose to fame and controversy in questions surrounding the heart of the criminological enterprise: why do people engage in rule-breaking behavior? How can we explain the empirical finding that most do so only a few times and then quit, while a few continue much longer? Proponents of the criminal career approach gave one answer, while those of the propensity approach gave another, with subsequent policy implications to follow. Life-course criminology insists that if we want to find answers to these questions, we must follow individuals through time and place. As it turns out, this insight – the fundamental importance of individual pathways through time – is found at the very heart of criminology.

Life-course criminology should be understood not as a separate field but rather as a development and extension of criminology's traditional, theoretical locus. This extension mainly consists of systematically paying attention to the importance and meaning of the process of aging, the different stages individuals go through, and the contingencies of these stages with regards to crime and deviance.

## Criminological Theories and Criminal Careers

Sociology was founded in Europe at the turn of the century, through the classical works of such historical figures as Karl Marx, Émile Durkheim, Alexis Toqueville, Ferdinand Tönnies, Max Weber, and Georg Simmel. What these thinkers shared was a simple but powerful insight. As two modern, prominent criminologists put it, they realized that 'all social practices of any consequences have to be studied in the context of the society in which they are situated' (Rosenfeld and Messner, 2011: 130). If we want to understand peoples' lives, it follows that we must understand them in their social and historical context.

Modern, sociological criminology was born at the University of Chicago at the beginning of the 20th century. Founded by Albion Small in 1895, the Department of Sociology became one of the centers of sociological research in the USA, and educated a breadth of students who would go on to become prominent criminologists, including Clifford Shaw, Henry McKay, Edwin Sutherland, James F. Short Jr., Howard S. Becker, and David Matza. At the University of Chicago, the early sociologists applied what was in practice a life-course perspective to understand social phenomena. So, for example, Thomas and Znaniecki (1974) used huge amounts of research on life histories of Polish peasants to study experiences among immigrants across generations, firmly situating them in time and place to understand how their lives unfolded. Similarly, Nels Anderson (1923) explored the lives of 'hobos' in their distinct social and historical organization. Under the leadership of Robert E. Park – who was one of Georg Simmel's students – in the 1920s, the Department of Sociology turned its attention to the city as a 'natural laboratory'. It is here, in the city, we must begin.

# The Chicago School

In their study of juvenile delinquency and urban areas, Shaw and McKay (1942) find that delinquency depends on factors inherent in a community itself. They famously call this social disorganization. These communities tend to be characterized by a variety of features, including low economic status, ethnic heterogeneity, weak social control of its inhabitants, values that favor delinquency, a structure of intergenerational transmission of crime where older people influence the young, and, importantly, residential instability.

Shaw and McKay's study is a study of communities and crime rates in Chicago, not individual offenders, but for our discussion there is a relevant element in it. What they find is that people who have not committed any crime prior to living in such communities, start doing so once they move there. When they leave the community, they tend to stop. Individual case studies of these ideas outline them in much greater detail (Shaw, 1930), but implicit in this notion is a transition from one place to another, from one life-course stage to the next: typically, people grow up in these areas and when they start higher education, get employment or meet a partner, they move out.

Of course, having grown up in such an area might also affect one's future in an important fashion, i.e. impel persistence in crime in several ways. For example, people living in 'socially disorganized' neighborhoods tend – to a lesser extent than those living elsewhere – engage in higher education and enter the labor market. The point is that very early in the history of modern criminology, Shaw and McKay sensitize us to the contingency of time and place, the people who live there, their activities and the values they share, and their possible influence on the young person to develop and continue a criminal career.

Similarly, for Sutherland, communities can be distinguished based on their differential social organization (Sutherland, 1947). In some social environments, definitions favorable to the violation of criminal law prevail over definitions unfavorable to the violation of those laws, and such areas are likely to have higher crime rates. People transmit these definitions through interacting with each other. As he notes, when 'persons become criminal they do so because of contacts with criminal patterns' (Sutherland, 1947: 7). Through interacting with others, people acquire the skills, beliefs, attitudes, and rationalizations that facilitate criminal offending.

This is often understood as related to onset, but Sutherland also insists that the same analytical scheme can be used to understand the next steps in the development of a criminal career: the theory is a 'statement of lifetime processes, running through the entire career of the person' (Goff and Geis, 2011: 45). The theory consists of elements that vary over time: people interact with some peers in childhood, others in adolescence, and still others in adulthood. A few peers might be there through all stages, but many change. It follows from this that people learn different things at different stages in life and what we learn affects how we act, including criminal offending. Delinquent behavior developed in childhood can persist through life but change is also possible, a theme Sutherland develops in his work with Chic Conwell, the professional thief (Sutherland, 1937), and in later editions of differential association theory. Consider the following extract from a classic edition of Sutherland's *Principles of Criminology*:

> Something like a process of maturation appears [among habitual criminals]. Delinquencies begin at an early age and increase in frequency and seriousness. Delinquencies start as a recreational incident and become an integrated pattern of life. Criminal maturity is reached in early middle age, about thirty or thirty-five. Some criminals then abandon their crimes abruptly, others adopt less strenuous types of crimes, others engage in quasi-criminal activities in connection with politics, gambling, prostitution, and the liquor business, while others become vagrants. This process, however, is only roughly characteristic of the careers, and exceptions may be found regarding the age of beginning criminality and the age of leaving the profession. (Sutherland, 1947: 97)

The notion of a criminal career, and the insight that people's criminal offending change with age, does thus not belong to life-course criminology. We revisit Sutherland's theory of differential association and the importance of peers later, as we discuss the theoretical developments that have resulted from life-course criminological studies such as those conducted by Moffitt (1993).

# Matza and the Question of Maturational Reform

Crucial insights about criminal careers can also be found in the work of Matza (1964). Matza begins by attacking the then prevailing theories of crime on a number of points, but there is mainly only one that interests us here:

> Anywhere from 60 to 85 per cent of delinquents do not apparently become adult violators. Moreover, this reform seems to occur irrespective of intervention of correctional agencies and irrespective of the quality of correctional service ... Most theories of delinquency take no account of maturational reform ... Why and by what process is the continuity from juvenile delinquency to adult crime implicit in almost all theories of delinquency not apparent in the world of real events? (Matza, 1964: 22)

Although the finding – that most juvenile delinquents do not become adult offenders – had been noted previously, often implicitly but sometimes explicitly (see Dunham and Knauer, 1954), it is perhaps Matza who most powerfully brings it to the center of the criminological enterprise. Matza's answer to the problem of delinquency theories is maturational reform: 'Among the manifold and complex reasons for the drift out of delinquency is one that is immediately pertinent', Matza writes (1964: 54). This reason is the transition to adulthood. As the juvenile delinquent approaches this transition, he[1] is faced with alternatives:

> with the passing of time they may effortlessly exhibit the conventional signposts of manhood–physical appearance, the completion of school, job, marriage, and perhaps even children ... The approach of adulthood is [thus] marked by the addition of new affiliations. (Matza, 1964: 55)

This process – that of maturation – makes the individual gradually realize that he should leave delinquency behind.

'Maturational reform' is a way to express change in behavior with increasing age. This is picked up by Hirschi (1969), who, in an interview with Laub (2002: xxxi), claims that his now well-known formulation of social control theory 'was meant to explain maturational reform'. In the vein of life-course studies, such a retrospective account needs to be read with some caution. If Hirschi's task was to explain maturational reform, it seems a bit odd to only include (male) adolescents in the study.

At any rate, Hirschi's explanation, of course, was the four elements of social control theory: attachment, commitment, involvement, and belief. As the delinquent ages, the institutions of adulthood (employment, family life, etc.) exercise their control on him or her, a control that eventually leads to desistance. For Hirschi, the maturational reform identified by Matza is, essentially, the process through which people in various ways become bound to society in the transition

---

[1] Matza writes with the male pronoun.

to adulthood, and thus desist from crime (Hirschi, 1969; Hirschi and Rudisill, 1976). We find Hirschi (1969: 163) expressing this in his original formulation of control theory:

> In the ideal case, the adolescent simultaneously completes his education, begins his occupational career, and acquires adult status. He is thus continuously bound to conformity by participation in a conventional game.

Unfortunately, Hirschi continues on the same page, 'many adolescents in effect complete their education without at the same time being able to begin their occupational careers'. The result is a situation where the individual is free to pursue 'adult privileges' without having to take on 'adult responsibilities', making delinquent behavior (e.g. smoking, drinking, minor offenses, etc.) a likely outcome. This notion of a 'maturation gap' will, albeit in a somewhat different shape, occur in life-course criminology some 35 years later and occupy a fundamental place in one of the most influential criminological life-course theories in the field, namely, Terrie Moffitt's dual developmental taxonomy (see Chapter 3).

Having made this brief review and tried to point out some of their life-course criminological elements, it is also important to note the critique directed at them from a life-course criminological perspective:

> the dominant criminological theories of the last three decades ... have also been treated as largely static in their predictions. This is not to say that they are devoid of developmental *implications* ... only that the leading theoretical trio is rooted in 'between-individual' rather than temporal thinking. (Sampson and Laub, 1997: 138, emphasis in original)

In other words, their focus was still on understanding differences between individuals: the theories attempt to explain criminal behavior by exploring why some people are exposed to more pro-criminal definitions than others (Sutherland), why some people rather than others have weaker ties to conventional society (Hirschi), and so on. Beyond that point the theories are mostly silent.

Whereas many criminological perspectives are static when it comes to the dimension of time, there is one that is explicitly dynamic, and developmental: the labeling perspective.

## Labeling and Sequential Models of Deviance

Becker (1963: 22) distinguishes between 'simultaneous' and 'sequential' models of deviance, and the latter is of particular interest here. With very few exceptions, life-course criminological explanations are implicitly or explicitly based on the latter of these two models.

The first, a simultaneous model, is one that 'assumes ... that all the factors which operate to produce the phenomenon under study operate simultaneously' (Becker, 1963: 22). The main task is to discover which variable or process best 'predicts' the behavior we study. 'But', Becker continues,

> all causes do not operate at the same time, and we need a model which takes into account the fact that patterns of behavior *develop* in orderly sequence ... Each step requires explanation, and what may operate as a cause at one step in the sequence may be of negligible importance at another step. (Becker, 1963: 23, emphasis in original)

Thus, taking the example of becoming a marihuana user, Becker argues that one set of factors or processes are necessary for learning the technique of marihuana smoking, another set emerges as necessary when it comes to learning to perceive the effects of smoking, and yet another set of factors and processes are necessary for the smoker to learn to enjoy the effects. The three steps unfold sequentially and each step is dependent on the one that precedes it. This, a sequential model, is a basic tenet of life-course criminology. It does not suggest that there *must* be different explanations for different steps of the criminal career, but only that we allow for the possibility that that *might* be the case.

Within criminology, Becker (1963) is perhaps most famous for his contribution to the development of the labeling perspective. The labeling perspective is, in fact, strikingly life-course criminological in its dynamic view of people and social life. It is 'the only [classical] criminological theory that is truly developmental in nature because of its explicit emphasis on processes over time', Sampson and Laub (1997: 138) note. Whereas the labeling perspective was considered part of – or at least an important precursor to – the 'radical' or 'critical' turn in criminology that took place during the 1960s and 1970s, it is today part of the classical criminological canon. An important factor that gave this perspective wide acceptance was the empirical support it received from longitudinal research (Farrington, 1977; Farrington and Murray, 2014).

The labeling theorists' main thesis is that when society, mainly through powerful authorities (parents, school teachers, social workers, police officers, etc.), designate and treat people as 'deviant' or 'criminal', this often results in what Lemert (1967) called secondary deviance, or the development of what Becker (1963) termed a deviant career. Becker's thesis adopts the 'career' concept from the sociology of occupations and argues that the concept can formally refer to 'several varieties of career outcomes, ignoring the question of success' (Becker, 1963: 24). One dimension of careers is particularly important, namely, the sequencing of movement from one stage or position to another through place and time. These movements, Becker argues, are informed by career contingencies. These contingencies affect and inform when and how such movements (we could say transitions) take place and one of the most crucial steps in this process of building a stable pattern of deviant behavior (i.e. persistence) is the experience of being caught and publicly labeled as a deviant (Becker, 1963: 31).

Similar career contingencies are those we outlined above, in discussing the process of becoming a marihuana user. We will have reason to return to Becker's deviant career conception later, especially when we explore the importance of informal social control for continuity and change in criminal careers.

## On the Criminological Margin

As the attentive reader notes, we have only included a handful of examples taken from a criminological history in which many more exist. In this brief review, we have noted that the central life-course criminological questions – age and place – had already been formulated before the rise of the research field. What might have been missing was the idea of the 'chronic offender', but that idea too is possible to infer from, for example, Matza's extract above. If the vast majority commit crime in youth and then cease, it reasonably follows that a small group of offenders should be persisting in crime (the empirical observation, however, was missing until 1972, when Wolfgang, Figlio, and Sellin published their findings from the Philadelphia Birth Cohort Study).

The questions that were to become the focal points of life-course criminological inquiry had thus been suggested long before the rise of the field, but prior to the 1970s these remarks were made briefly and in passing, limited to the criminological margin and periphery in pursuit of other projects and in the search for answers to other questions. This is not an unusual phenomenon in academic, scientific fields, least of all in criminology.

Consider, as an example of this, yet again the approach to deviance called the labeling approach. It has its origins in one of the classic Chicago School perspectives, symbolic interactionism (Blumer, 1969) and became influential in the 1960s through the writings of Becker (1963), Goffman (1963), and Lemert (1967), among others. More than 20 years earlier, Franklin Tannenbaum published his *Crime and The Community* (1938) in which he presented his 'dramatization of evil' thesis. Tannenbaum began with an observation of the staggering normalcy of delinquency. A range of delinquent behaviors are part of an adolescent's 'normal life' and, with the transition from adolescence, s/he ceases to engage in such behavior. However, the response delinquency often triggers in other actors (e.g. parents, teachers, social workers, the police) tends to be one of intervention. A powerful police intervention can initiate a process of change in the way the delinquent is viewed and perceived by others and, eventually, a change in the way the delinquent perceives of him- or herself. The delinquent's 'evil' actions become dramatized and made part of the delinquent's self-identity; s/he may begin to consider him- or herself as somebody who does 'evil' things, with subsequent persistent delinquency and criminal offending as a result.

Tannenbaum's account is one that is remarkably similar to the ones later outlined by the labeling perspective in the 1960s, where researchers such as Becker, Goffman, Lemert, and others picked up his thesis and developed it both theoretically and empirically. Until then, however, Tannenbaum's thesis remained in the periphery of criminology. Our point here is to show that precursors to emerging fields and branches of research nearly always exist, and life-course criminology is no exception. This historical dimension is important, for the field of life-course criminology explicitly or implicitly is contingent on these previous observations.

## Suggestions for Further Reading

Becker, Howard (1963) *Outsiders: Studies in the Sociology of Deviance*. New York: The Free Press.
Becker's famous outline of the labeling perspective, and sequencing of the deviance process in particular, is the only 'classic' perspective that is inherently developmental. Some 30 years later, it will become an integral part of life-course criminology.

Hirschi, Travis (1969) *Causes of Delinquency*. New Brunswick, NJ: Transaction Publishers.
Hirschi's first control theory is – somewhat ironically – one of the most influential theories in life-course criminology, in the guise of Sampson and Laub's (1993) theory.

Matza, David (1964) *Delinquency and Drift*. New Brunswick, NJ: Transaction Publishers.
Matza's take on the criminological enterprise places the aging out process in the center, demanding it to be explained by criminologists. At the time, nobody could do it. It's a stellar read.

# 3
# LIFE-COURSE THEORIES OF CRIME AND DEVIANCE

In the early stages of criminal career research, the field was dominated by a focus on empirical findings and their policy implications. Theoretical developments of crime and the life course lagged behind. From the early 1990s and onward, however, this changed considerably as a breadth of life-course theories of crime and deviance emerged in the field, incorporating various elements from the traditions of developmental psychology, life-course sociology, and criminological theory. Today, these criminological theories are among the most influential theories within the discipline as a whole. In this chapter we go through a number of these theories and we do so in some detail. Instead of giving a schematic, brief description of each theory (as is often done) we aim to go through each theory step by step, to give the reader a closer account of how each theory attempts to explain criminal careers, crime, and the life course. We then revisit the different steps of each theory in the subsequent chapters as we specifically deal with elements of the criminal career (persistence, intermittency, desistance, etc.). Theories can be difficult to learn and understand, and the repetition is useful.

A theory is a proposed explanation of a given phenomenon (Merton, 1945; Swedberg, 2012). If we are to understand and be able to use a given theory, we first have to understand what that theory is attempting to explain. Some criminological theories – such as Sutherland's theory of differential association, or Gottfredson and Hirschi's self-control theory – are 'general', basically meaning that they claim to be able to explain all crimes committed by all people in all places, at all times. Other theories are much more modest in their claims. Farrington's Integrated Cognitive Antisocial Potential (ICAP) Theory, for example, only claims to be able to explain 'everyday crimes' such as interpersonal violence, theft, vandalism, robbery, and illegal drug-use and drug-dealing committed by working-class men in big cities, such as Philadelphia, Boston, London, Copenhagen, and Stockholm (Farrington, 2005). Here and there in our below discussion, we point out these issues to the reader.

Before we get going, however, it is important to remind ourselves of the specific, over-arching research problem that life-course theories of crime try to address and explain. We have already introduced this problem in Chapter 1. The basic issue seemingly takes the form of an empirical paradox. Crime and (other) anti-social behavior show impressive *continuity* over age, but, at the same time, their prevalence *changes* dramatically with age. In other words, the best 'predictor' for future criminal activity is past criminal activity (continuity). However, in any given population, the number of active offenders (prevalence) decreases with age. The two empirical findings seem to be contradictory. How can these two findings be reconciled and integrated in the same, theoretical framework? In other words, what makes some people persist in crime, and what is it that makes most offenders quit? This question has given rise to a number of related, more specific questions, which we also address below.

We distinguish the life-course criminological explanations of continuity and change in criminal careers according to two very broad themes: *static* and *dynamic* theories. The distinction is to be taken not literally but more as a guide-line, suggesting that theories differ and imply different implications. As Piquero et al. (2007) note, the content, shapes and pathways the criminal career takes in any given case is likely a result of *both* static and dynamic processes.

Because the field of life-course criminology is so large – and still growing, possibly more than ever – we have limited this chapter's review to five theories: two 'static' (Gottfredson and Hirschi's, and Moffitt's theories), and three 'dynamic' (Sampson and Laub's, Giordano et al.'s, and Farrington's theories). We have chosen them for several reasons: partly, because they are among the most influential and most tested; and partly, because they give a quite good overview of the field, including the more sociologically oriented approaches (Gottfredson and Hirschi, Sampson and Laub, and Giordano et al.) as well as the more discipline-integrated ones (Moffitt and Farrington).

## Static Theories of Criminal Careers

Static theories of crime and the life course are sometimes referred to as ontogenetic theories, or theories of population heterogeneity (Nagin and Paternoster, 2000). This concept aims to capture an allegedly empirical phenomena; that people's propensity to engage in crime differ within a given population. Simply put, some individuals more than others are prone to do crime. Human development, moreover, is seen as a normative process of 'maturational unfolding' so that behavior tends to emerge in the same sequence and at the same age for the vast majority of individuals. Such theories of crime tend to share at least three features.

First, the basic causes of criminal behavior (including changes in criminal offending over time) are found at the individual level of features, traits, and endowments, all established early in life. These features differ between individuals so, for example, for Gottfredson and Hirschi (1990) some people have low self-control, while others have high. Those with low self-control are then more prone to offending and this propensity will be stable over time. Second, these features result in inter-individual stability in behavior, so that people who have a higher level of offending in adolescence are also expected to have a higher level of offending in adulthood. Third, changes in within-individual offending over time are products of normative changes that occur as people age.

As we noted above, considering the breadth of life-course criminology, a complete review of all static theories is impossible for us to present here. Instead of briefly sketching the outlines of a bulk of theories, we choose to limit ourselves to two theories and go through them in greater detail, step by step, to give the reader a more comprehensive view of how these theories – and their creators – see crime and the life course, and attempt to explain their relationship. Those two are the theories of Gottfredson and Hirschi (1990), and Moffitt (1993).[1]

## *A General Theory of Crime*: The Importance of Self-Control

Considering Gottfredson and Hirschi's firm rejection of the life-course criminological enterprise, as we saw in Chapter 1, it may seem strange to include them here. However, somewhat ironically, their theory of self-control is one of the most discussed, empirically tested (more or less validly, we should add) theories in the field. It is therefore an important piece of the story we tell in this book.

Note the word 'general' in the title of their book, *A General Theory of Crime*. The word implies considerable boldness: a general theory of crime can explain all crimes, at all times, by all persons. It might be fruitful for the reader to keep in mind that, using this theory, we should be able to explain 'everyday crimes' such as violence and theft, as well as complicated finance crimes, committed by young or old, women or men, today or 50 or a 100 years ago.

Gottfredson and Hirschi begin at the beginning: with a conception of crime and human nature. The genesis of their approach is found in the Classical School of Beccaria, Bentham, and Hobbes: 'all human conduct can be understood

---

[1] Other theories include those of Glueck and Glueck (1950), Mednick (1977), and Wilson and Herrnstein (1985).

as the self-interested pursuit of pleasure or the avoidance of pain. By definition, therefore, crimes too are merely acts designed to satisfy some combination of these basic tendencies' (Gottfredson and Hirschi, 1990: 5). Crimes, as they define them, are 'acts of force or fraud undertaken in self-interest' (p. 15). Where classical theory – and social control theory – fail, they argue, is in their inability to account for the empirical finding that 'people also differ in the extent to which they are vulnerable to the temptations of the moment' (p. 87).

To unpack this vulnerability, they go to the characteristics of criminal acts. The basic cause of crime, they argue, can 'be derived directly from the nature of criminal acts' (p. 88). Criminal acts, then, provide immediate, easy, and/or simple gratification of desires, are exciting, risky, or thrilling, require little or no skill or planning, and provide meager long-term benefits. Other things being equal, some individuals are more prone to choose to commit crime than are others and the reason behind that is a latent trait they term self-control. Gottfredson and Hirschi (p. 90) explain this term as people who are impulsive, insensitive, physical, risk-taking, short-sighted and nonverbal and will therefore tend to engage in criminal acts such as smoking, drinking, drug use, etc.

Now, Gottfredson and Hirschi caution that crime is not a necessary consequence of having low self-control. Crime can be counteracted by 'situational conditions or other properties of the individual' (p. 89) but, that being said, those who possess a high degree of self-control 'will be substantially less likely at all periods of life to engage in criminal acts'. In other words, when combined with appropriate opportunities and attractive targets, low self-control leads to crime.

Self-control is spread on a continuous scale. What, then, makes somebody develop a higher or lower degree of self-control? Because the road toward or away from crime starts early in an individual's life, Gottfredson and Hirschi know that the origins of an individual's level of self-control must be laid even earlier (otherwise, it would not be a cause of crime). The origin of our self-control is quite complex:

> The first [source] is the variation among children in the degree to which they manifest such traits to begin with. The second is the variation among caretakers in the degree to which they recognize low self-control and its consequences and the degree to which they are willing and able to correct it. (p. 96)

They do *not* argue that criminal behavior is inherited, or that some people are 'born criminals'; in fact, they explicitly reject that notion. However, individual differences can impact on the prospects for effective socialization. Effective socialization is, moreover, always possible, whatever the individual's original disposition. In other words, when an individual is born there is always an indeterminate quality to his or her future level of self-control (and thus the probability that he or she will engage in crime).

In short, a very large portion of our self-control comes from early family experiences and the way we are brought up. That is, the situation in the family and the quality of parenting during a child's early years is crucial. Many characteristics associated with low self-control, Gottfredson and Hirschi argue, 'show themselves in the absence of nurturance, discipline, or training' (p. 95). Child-rearing is thus a basic tenet of an individual's future self-control: the child's behavior must be monitored, deviant acts (when they occur) must be recognized, and punished.

If the family, for one reason or another, is unwilling or incapable of exercising this power over the child, it does not mean that the individual by definition develops a low self-control. On the contrary, there is one other powerful institution that affects the child during his or her early years:

> Those not socialized sufficiently by the family may eventually learn self-control through the operation of other sanctioning systems or institutions. The institution given principal responsibility for this task in modern society is the school. (p. 105)

In the school, the child learns 'to better appreciate the advantages and opportunities associated with self-control' and becomes more socialized, regardless of family experiences and upbringing (p. 106). Around age 8, an individual's level of self-control is set and then stable throughout life: in the subsequent individual's development, there is 'little or no movement from high self-control to low self-control' (p. 107).

Here is where Gottfredson and Hirschi present a famous and debated argument. We know the shape of the age/crime curve: a steep rise in adolescence with a peak at around age 17, followed by an almost as steep decline during the following years. In other words, say we have a group of 100 boys. At age 10, 20 of those boys are engaged in crime. At age 17, the number of boys actively engaged in crime has increased to 90. At age 20, it has decreased to 50. At age 29, the number has decreased even more to, say, 10. That is to say, the prevalence of offenders within the group changes dramatically. However, since low self-control is stable after age 8, it cannot be changes in individuals' self-control that cause the shape of the curve; it must be something else. It is, simply, age. Offenders basically 'age out' of crime. Studying various age–crime curves, Gottfredson and Hirschi find the same shape of the curve everywhere they look, regardless of historical period, gender, or ethnicity. Thus, their famous argument that the 'age–crime relation is invariant' (p. 126). Turning to the notion of desistance, Gottfredson and Hirschi return to Matza (see Chapter 2), and state that desistance is nothing but maturational reform, and 'maturational reform is just that, change in behavior that comes with maturation' (p. 136).

Since socialization does not end in adolescence but continues through life, Gottfredson and Hirschi reach the conclusion that 'the proportion of the population in the potential offender pool should tend to decline as cohorts age' (p. 107). 'Developmental' variables, such as relationship formation, employment, and association with delinquent peers, exert no *causal* influences on criminal behavior and the timing of desistance; instead, age is the fundamental factor and all others merely 'spurious' (Thornberry et al., 2012: 53).

> Since this decline [of crime with age] cannot be explained by change in the person or by his exposure to anticriminal institutions, we are left with the conclusion that it is due to the inexorable aging of the organism. (Gottfredson and Hirschi, 1990: 141)

Now, in this extract there is an important, somewhat hidden dimension: that of the stability postulate. Although crime declines with age for everybody, regardless of their level of self-control, individual differences remain stable: those with low self-control will always offend, the theory predicts, at a higher rate than those with high self-control. In other words, as we follow two groups, one with low and one with high self-control, through time, the offending rates should (1) follow the age/crime curve, but (2) the low self-control group should always offend at a higher level than the high self-control group.

As a result of this, Gottfredson and Hirschi argue that cross-sectional research, which compares different individuals at the same time, is enough to study crime and criminal careers. It follows logically from their theoretical position as self-control, the cause of criminal offending, is established early in life. Gottfredson and Hirschi's position is one of considerable boldness and attractiveness. We now move on to a brief evaluative discussion on the theory.

### The Merits and Problems of A General Theory of Crime

Gottfredson and Hirschi's theory has the scientific beauty of simplicity: an individual's self-control and his or her movement along the age continuum explains his or her criminal offending. This is a great merit of the theory. However, being a general theory of crime, there are some important issues inherent in it.

For example, the fact that low self-control is positively correlated with crime is hard to dispute: a breadth of possible indicators of self-control (what some term risk factors, such as impulsivity) have been closely correlated with crime in various studies (Farrington, 2003), and the notion that there are between-individual differences when these indicators are measured is well-known: some people simply tend to be more impulsive or risk-taking than are others. However, it is one thing to argue that there is a correlation between low self-control and crime, that is, people who score low on self-control indicators tend to score high on criminal offending. It is a very different thing to claim that there is a *causal relationship* at work, where it is the low level of self-control that causes the individual to engage in crime. In their work, Gottfredson and Hirschi have trouble proving this claim, since it is an empirical question but the main inference they use to support it is theoretical. To actually test the claim would, in effect, entail using a methodology Gottfredson and Hirschi are against; longitudinal research, where the sequencing of events can be controlled for. There is a related issue in the proposition that self-control is stable after age 8; to actually test the stability of self-control would require longitudinal data.

Another issue concerns the word 'general'. Can the theory account for white-collar crime? Despite a specific focus on this (see Gottfredson and Hirschi, 1990, Ch. 9) their argument is problematic on logical grounds.[2] People who engage in white-collar crime and do so from a relatively high position in a business hierarchy have, in the majority of cases, demonstrated that they are capable of delaying gratification and rewards, and focusing on long-term goals, since they have gone through years of higher education. Being able to delay gratification and rewards is an indicator of *high* self-control, not low.

Additionally, there is the problem of the so-called stability postulate. On the one hand, as demonstrated by Paternoster et al. (2001) among many others, individual differences do seem to matter. However, there is 'little empirical support' for the core notion of relative stability over time (Thornberry et al., 2012: 57): those with a lower level of self-control do not constantly offend at a rate above those with a higher level of self-control.

Finally, there is the problematic claim that the age/crime curve is universal. There are multiple issues with this claim, here we only highlight the perhaps most central of them. It is a question of methodology. Remember, the age/crime curve is an aggregate. As such, it may 'hide' individual, alternative age/crime curves that disappear when hundreds, sometimes thousands of individuals' criminal offending (as construed by some measure or other) are lumped together in one curve. There may, for example, be individuals who consistently commit crimes throughout their lives, and do so at a non-decreasing, or even increasing rate. In that case, Gottfredson and Hirschi's age/crime argument stands on very shaky ground. This possibility, that the age/crime curve may hide several distinct types of offending patterns, is in fact a central thesis of the theory we turn to now.

## Moffitt's Dual Developmental Taxonomy

Terrie E. Moffitt's (1993) explanation of crime and the life course is one of the earliest and most famous theories in the field. According to Farrington (2010: 254) 'there has been more empirical research on this theory than on any others'. Her theory is partly based on previous research but, most importantly, also leans heavily on results from one of the famous longitudinal studies, the Dunedin Multidisciplinary Health and Development Study. It is a prospective, longitudinal cohort study, consisting of all children born at the only maternity hospital in Dunedin, New Zealand, between April 1, 1972, and March 31, 1973 who were still residing in Dunedin when the study began three years later, in 1975; a total of 1,037 participants. New data – consisting of psychological, medical, and sociological measures, as well as official record data – has been collected every two years.

---

[2] The following remark is adopted from Soothill et al. (2009: 26).

In her attempt at unpacking the riddles of crime and the life course, she begins in a way very similar to how we began this book in Chapter 1. The task she sets herself is to 'reconcile two incongruous facts about antisocial behavior: (a) It shows impressive continuity over age, but (b) its prevalence changes dramatically over age, increasing almost ten-fold temporarily during adolescence' (Moffitt, 1993: 674). Moffitt's solution to this problem is similar to self-control theory in several respects but differs in one crucial way. While self-control is distributed on a continuous scale, Moffitt presents an offender dichotomy, or dual taxonomy: life-course persistent offenders (LCP), and adolescence-limited offenders (AL).

The age/crime curve thus 'conceals two qualitatively distinct categories of individuals, each in need of its own distinct theoretical explanation' (p. 674). The typical search for 'general' theories of crime, Moffitt argues, is an analytical mistake. Instead, crime can be explained by two distinct causal mechanisms.

## The Life-Course Persistent Offenders

Let us begin with the LCP offenders, who are very small in number. Here, continuity in behavior is the hallmark:

> Across the life course, these individuals exhibit changing manifestations of antisocial behavior: biting and hitting at age 4, shoplifting and truancy at age 10, selling drugs and stealing cars at age 16, robbery and rape at age 22, and fraud and child abuse at age 30; the underlying disposition remains the same, but its expression changes form as new social opportunities arise at different points in development. (p. 679)

This continuity in behavior, moreover, is not only consistent over time but also across situations. So, LCP offenders may lie at home, cheat in school or steal from work, fight in bars in their spare time, and so on.

The origins of the LCP offender's criminal actions are to be found in the neuro-psychological makeup of the individual. By neuropsychological factors, Moffitt refers to 'the extent to which anatomical structures and physiological processes within the nervous system influence psychological characteristics such as temperament, behavior development, cognitive abilities, or all three' (p. 681). These deficits, as Moffitt calls them, lead to low IQ, impaired verbal and cognitive skills, clumsiness, awkwardness, inattentiveness, irritability, impulsiveness, and a low level of self-control. Early signs of acting out, such as in the form of aggression, are thus also a sign of this deficit.

This is the beginning of the story. Up until now, Moffitt has argued as if environment was held constant. Unfortunately,

> children with cognitive and temperamental disadvantages are not generally born into supportive environments, nor do they even get a fair chance of being randomly assigned to good or bad environments ... Vulnerable infants are disproportionately found in environments that will not be ameliorative because many sources of neural maldevelopment co-occur with family disadvantage or deviance. (p. 681)

What is going on here, are two things: first, the child's disadvantages are often not countered by a stable, safe family environment. On the contrary, those disadvantages tend to be amplified because such children are often born into families with members who themselves have a history of disadvantages and deviance. Second, what takes place is an interaction between the child and the family, as 'personality and behavior are shaped in large measure by interactions between the person and the environment' (p. 682). So there is a form of transactional dialectic at work, where the child acts, the family reacts, the child reacts, the family reacts again, and so on:

> the juxtaposition of a vulnerable and difficult infant with an adverse rearing context initiates risk for the life-course-persistent pattern of antisocial behavior. The ensuing process is a *transactional one* in which the challenge of coping with a difficult child evokes a chain of failed parent-child encounters. (p. 682, emphasis added)

This combination – of neurological deficits and an 'adverse rearing context' for the child – forms a process of development characterized by an early onset of various problem behaviors both in the home and the school:

> If the child who 'steps off on the wrong foot' remains on an ill-starred path, subsequent stepping-stone experiences may culminate in life-course-persistent antisocial behavior. For lifecourse-persistent antisocial individuals, deviant behavior patterns later in life may thus reflect early individual differences that are perpetuated or exacerbated by interactions with the social environment: first at home, and later at school. (p. 682)

So far, Moffitt claims to have presented an explanation for the development and onset of antisocial behavior, including onset of crime. Now she has as her next task to explain the important life-course criminological topic of why these individuals continue, or persist, in crime beyond childhood, into adolescence and adulthood.

In doing so, she essentially uses two distinct, but related forms of continuity: those of *cumulative continuity*, and *contemporary continuity*. By contemporary continuity, Moffitt aims to capture the direct link between the original childhood problems, and adult problems. So, for example, children who are ill-tempered in childhood tend to be hot-tempered as adults as well, causing problems for them at work. In other words, the 'traits' that originally got the child into trouble in childhood, such as impulsivity, irritability, and poor self-control, persist into adulthood and cause problems in adulthood as well.

By cumulative continuity, however, Moffitt aims to capture the *in*direct link between the original problems and the adult outcome: 'early individual differences may set in motion a downhill snowball of cumulative continuities' (p. 683). So, for example, early tantrums are predictive of lower educational attainment. Educational attainment, in turn, is predictive of lower occupational status. To continue our example of tantrums – or being ill-tempered in childhood – having tantrums in childhood is predictive of lower stability when it comes to social relations in adolescence, which, in turn, are predictive of having lower stability in social relations in adulthood. Now, being able to acquire work and develop stable, conventional social relations are two important reasons as to why individuals are able to desist from crime (we return and explore this issue in more detail later). 'Life-course persistent persons', however, 'miss out on opportunities to acquire prosocial alternatives at each stage of development' (p. 683).

At this stage, Moffitt has come halfway through solving the riddle of continuity and change in crime; she has explained the first by arguing that the LCP offenders from a very young age are consistently engaged in various problem behaviors over time, unable to leave this path even if they eventually want to do so. Now, she has to account for the latter; change. She does this by introducing the other category in her taxonomy; the adolescence-limited offender (AL).

## The Adolescence-Limited Offender

This offender category is by far the most common one. That is, most people who engage in crime belong to this category: 'adolescent-limited delinquency', Moffitt notes, 'is ubiquitous' (p. 685). It is so common for young people to engage in crime, in fact, that it is statistically unusual to *not* have committed a crime during adolescence. There are mainly two features of the AL offender that are different from the LCPs'.

First, whereas the LCP offenders consistently engage in antisocial behavior across different contexts – i.e. they are rule-breakers in school, on the street, in their homes – the AL offender's behavior is characterized by discontinuity. That is, he or she may engage in crime on his or her spare time, but in school the same person is a good student and at home he or she is a good, well-behaved adolescent.

Second, and crucially for Moffitt's argument, the AL offender has no history of antisocial behavior. Whereas the LCP offender has been engaged in all kinds of problematic behaviors since he or she was a small child, the AL offender has not. When the AL offender enters adolescence, criminal behavior simply tends to pop up. The AL offender often persists for a short while, and then ceases.

It is against this background that Moffitt formulates the questions her theory of adolescent-limited delinquency must be able to answer:

> A theory of adolescence-limited delinquency must account for several empirical observations: modal onset in early adolescence, recovery by young adulthood, widespread prevalence, and lack of continuity. Why do youngsters with no history of behavior problems in childhood suddenly become antisocial in adolescence? Why do they develop antisocial problems rather than other difficulties? Why is delinquency so common among teens? How are they able to spontaneously recover from an antisocial life-style within a few short years? (p. 686)

Whereas the origins of the LCP offender had to be sought in the early, even pre-natal development of the child, Moffitt now goes to the stage of development where delinquency peaks: the adolescent years, when puberty tends to kick in.

Why do so many adolescents engage in delinquency? Here, Moffitt introduces the notion of *social mimicry*; something she borrows from the canon of social learning theory in psychology. A similar argument, however, can be found in the criminological classics of Akers (1985) and Sutherland (1947). Mimicry is a term taken from studies of ethology. Mimicry occurs when two (or more) species want access to the same, desired resource. Seeing that one form of behavior is rewarding and gives access to the desired resource (such as food or water), the other species 'picks up' this behavior to also access that resource.

Moffitt thus suggests that the AL offender begins to mimic the behavior of the LCP offender. However, if social mimicry is to explain the onset of delinquency for so many adolescents, it must mean that engaging in crime gives access to a resource considered desirable by them. Indeed, Moffitt says, 'I suggest that the resource is mature status, with its consequent power and privilege' (Moffitt, 1993: 686).

At this stage, Moffitt makes a brief excursion that is fundamental to her explanation. It also touches upon a crucial life-course theme: the transition to adulthood, and the way it has changed with the modernization of the world. In modern society, she notes, the phase of adolescence has been stretched out, in the social sense: young people leave their parental home later than they used to, their entry into the labor market has been delayed, they form their own families later than people did in the past, and so on. The social, adult status has thus been postponed, but people's biological maturity has not. In fact, the development of improved health and nutrition has decreased the age of biological maturity. This tension causes problems:

> The ensuing gap leaves modern teenagers in a 5- to 10-year role vacuum … They are biologically capable and compelled to be sexual beings, yet they are asked to delay most of the positive aspects of adult life … They remain financially and socially dependent on their families of origin and are allowed few decisions of any real import. Yet they want desperately to establish intimate bonds with the opposite sex, to accrue material belongings, to make their own decisions, and to be regarded as consequential by adults … Contemporary adolescents are thus trapped in a *maturity gap*, chronological hostages of a time warp between biological age and social age. (p. 686f)

This phenomenon begins to color life for most teenagers as they enter high school, and it affects their self-images, confidence, and self-perceptions of autonomy. Now, these 'healthy adolescents' (p. 687) notice something: their life-course persistent peers (of which Moffitt says there are about one to two in every classroom) seems to suffer less from this maturity gap. At this stage in their lives, the LCP offenders are able to obtain desirable objects such as cars, clothes, and drugs through the practices of theft or vice, they tend to be more sexually experienced, appear to be relatively free from their parents' grip, and seem to go their own way, making their own rules as they go along. Their actions, moreover, are consequential and reverberate into the adult world, as evidenced by the presence of social workers, probation officers, and so on, in their lives. As a result, 'antisocial behavior becomes a valuable technique that is demonstrated by life-course-persistents and imitated carefully by adolescence-limiteds' (p. 687).

So, now Moffitt has explained the onset of delinquency for that vast portion of young people who live law-abiding lives and then sporadically engage in crime during adolescence. Next, her task is to explain their desistance from crime. Following the same logic she has applied before, she argues that as the adolescent eventually approaches and makes the transition into adulthood, criminal behavior ceases to be rewarding and instead becomes incompatible with the conventional, adult role. Further, they manage to cease their offending because they do not have the history of persistent problematic behavior that the LCP offender has: 'without a lifelong history of antisocial behavior, the forces of cumulative continuity have had fewer years in which to gather the momentum of a downhill snowball' (p. 690). Thus, when criminal behavior is no longer a needed or even possible source of status (on the contrary, it becomes a form of stigma), the AL offender desists from crime.

## Later Developments of the Taxonomy

Moffitt's theory of crime and the life course has resulted in a lot of debate, and critique has been raised against it, aimed at both the empirical adequacy of it, as well as against its conceptual blurriness (e.g. Sampson and Laub, 1993; Skardhamar, 2009). As a result, Moffitt has revisited her original outline of the theory several times, continuously revising it. Here, we briefly highlight the important critical aspects of her theory, as well as her subsequent adjustments.

First of all, there is the conceptual question of what Moffitt means by 'offender types'. Although Moffitt uses the term, Skardhamar (2009) notes in his critical review of the taxonomy, it is not clear how literal the types and how distinct their patterns of behavior are. In the social sciences, 'types' can mean anything from a kind of 'ideal type' – that is, constructs we use to make sense of social life without assuming that the types are as distinct in reality as they are in theory – to a form of Lombrosian, ontologically distinct subtype of human. Most likely, Moffitt considers her offender types as being, conceptually, somewhere in between these two. That is, although she does refer to them as 'hypothetical prototypes' (Moffitt, 2006: 700) she also tends to treat them quite literally.

Second, there is the question of how many offender groups there are. Moffitt, as we know, originally suggested only two: the LCP and the AL offenders. However, using a statistical method called semi-parametric group-based mode-ling, researchers subsequently have found the need to add additional offender groups to the theory, since the inclusion of additional groups better explains the variation in many data sets. In particular, Moffitt has addressed the proposition of incorporating both a third and fourth group of offenders. The third group would be one called 'childhood-limited', or 'low-level chronics', because they exhibit 'extreme, pervasive, and persistent antisocial behavior during childhood' but 'surprisingly engaged in only low to moderate delinquency … from the age of 15 to 18' (Moffitt, 2007: 53f). Additionally, the fourth group would entail those offenders called 'adult-onset offenders', that is, those who do not engage in crime until after the normative peak of onset (i.e. after the teenage years). This one is a bit more uncertain, however, because although many studies have shown that a significant number of offenders seem to have an adult onset, this may be an 'artifact of official measurement' (Moffitt, 2007: 55). If we rely on official measurements of onset, she notes, we are likely to approximate it to three or five years after actual onset has occurred. 'These so-called adult onset offenders', she concludes, 'can probably be accommodated by the adolescence-limited theory because … the alleged adult-onset group has not differed from ordinary adolescent offenders' (Moffitt, 2007: 56).

Whether the number of offender groups is two, three, or four, studies show a great diversity in the number of offender groups they find. Some find four or five (D'Unger et al., 1998; Piquero et al., 2007), others find three (Nagin and Land, 1993), six (Ezell and Cohen, 2005), or seven (Bushway et al., 2003). This debate on offender types is still very much alive more than 20 years after Moffitt originally formulated her theory. It is an important one, because it has clear implications for policy. For example, it is common to combine the idea of offender types (especially the LCP, or 'chronic' offender) to specific forms of selective incapacitation strategies (Blumstein, et al., 1986; Skardhamar, 2009).

## Dynamic Theories of Criminal Careers

In contrast to static theories, dynamic theories of crime and the life course assume that human behavior is never set or established. Our present can never be reduced to early traits or endowments, although they may be important facets of it. The self is not static 'but rather changes as those we interact with change, either by being replaced by others or by themselves acting differently, presumably in response to still other changes in those they interact with' (Becker, 1970: 292). The self is thus processual and always in a stage of becoming (which is not to say that there is no continuity). While early experiences may be important, the primary explanation for continuity and change in criminal offending is to be found in the changing social situations and circumstances people encounter as they move along the life course. Dynamic theories tend to devote a substantial amount of attention to the importance of aging, just like Gottfredson and Hirschi do. Here, however, age is not seen as invariant, but rather as a kind of *proxy*:

most experts who study age-related change believe that age is essentially a proxy for some unmeasured developmental process. That is, developmental theory posits that various aspects of human functioning (like antisocial behavior) change with age, but that there must be an underlying, if not always easily identified, mechanism that accounts for the change. (Sweeten et al., 2013: 934)

We limit our discussion to three influential theories: first, we explore Sampson and Laub's age-graded theory of informal social control. Within our description of Sampson and Laub's theory we also discuss Giordano, Cernkovich, and Rudolph's theory of cognitive transformations. The reason behind this is that they criticize and develop their theory on important points. Finally, we turn to Farrington's integrated cognitive antisocial potential (ICAP) theory.[3] As we go along, we should point out that several of these theories incorporate elements from the static theories, and our review of each theory is therefore not as lengthy as of the static ones. The dynamic theories also have many similarities among each other.

## Sampson, Laub and Social Control, Revisited

In the 1980s, Sampson and Laub found the famous *Unraveling Juvenile Delinquency* data, stored away in boxes at the Harvard Law School Library. The original data was collected in the 1940s and 1950s by Sheldon and Eleanor Glueck. It consists of 1,000 males, 500 delinquent and 500 non-delinquent boys who were similar on other important variables, such as age and class. In their 1993 book, *Crime In The Making: Pathways And Turning Points Through Life*, where Sampson and Laub present their theory, they have re-analyzed all the original data, following the males up to 32 years of age.

Interestingly, Sampson and Laub published their seminal work the same year as Moffitt originally formulated her developmental taxonomy (1993). They too attempt to solve the same riddle Moffitt takes on, but they do so in a very different way. Consider their basic thesis (Sampson and Laub, 1993: 7, our emphasis):

The basic thesis we develop is threefold in nature: (1) structural context mediated by informal family and school social controls explains delinquency in childhood and adolescence; (2) in turn, there is continuity in antisocial behavior from childhood to adulthood in a variety of life domains; and (3) informal social controls in adulthood to family and employment explain changes in criminality over the life span *despite* early childhood propensities.

Note the final part of the thesis, and the word 'despite'. Already at the outset, Sampson and Laub make clear that while they do not consider an individual's

---

[3] Other well-known theories include those of Catalano et al. (2005), LeBlanc (1997), Thornberry (1987), and Wikström (2005).

early crime propensity unimportant, to understand why criminal behavior changes over the life span we must study the changes that occur in informal social control as the individual moves along the life course.

What, then, is social control? Its sociological history is long and was perhaps made most famous by Hirschi, in his first attempt to explain crime in *Causes of Delinquency* (1969). For Sampson and Laub, social control means 'the capacity of a social group to regulate itself according to desired principles and values, and hence to make norms and rules effective' (Sampson and Laub, 1993: 18). The central idea of social control theory, therefore, is that 'crime and deviance result when an individual's bond to society is weak or broken' (p. 18). Now, social control can be formal, as when it is exercised by various government or state agencies, such as the law and its various enforcers through apprehension and punishment, or it can be *informal*, such as when it is exercised through the interpersonal, social bonds that link a society's members to the social institutions of family, school, and work. In line with Hirschi's 1969 formulation, informal social controls, Sampson and Laub argue, hold the key to understanding why individuals engage in crime, why they persist, and why they stop.

However, whereas Hirschi's outline was temporally static – in the sense that he basically only studied the effects of social control on crime in childhood and adolescence – Sampson and Laub explore 'the extent to which social bonds inhibit crime and deviance early in the life course, and the consequences this has for later development' (p. 18). They also study the within-individual changes in informal social controls that occur as people age. To give just one example, the family tends to be a powerful source of informal social control in the early childhood of an individual. As adolescence approaches, however, the family is joined by the school and the individual's peers as important sources of control. In the transition to adulthood, as we move on, the school's social control naturally tends to diminish and give way for another, much more important source: employment. As the individual moves along the life course, he or she is then continuously tied to society through various sources of informal social control.

For Sampson and Laub, the basic cause of crime and deviance early in life is *low*, informal social control within the family and school, and one's attachment to delinquent peers. Now, what about such structural factors as socioeconomic status, parents' employment, or family size? And what about individual difference constructs, such as the onset of early conduct disorders and having persistent tantrums as a child – do these have no influence on the child's engagement in crime at all? Yes, they do. But they do not have an immediate, direct influence on delinquency – instead, these structural and individual factors are mediated by the interpersonal levels of family, school, and peers. So, for example, growing up with low socioeconomic status or having persistent tantrums as a child, have no *direct* effect on whether or not you will commit a crime, but if you come from a home with low socio-economic status or have persistent tantrums you are more likely to perform more poorly in school and have a weaker attachment to that institution. This – poor school performance and weak attachment – has a *direct* effect on whether or not you will commit a crime. The same goes for the family, and your association to delinquent peers: the effect of having a structural- or individual-level 'risk' is mediated through the institutions of family, school, and peers.

This argument is quite simple but also has a certain explanatory elegance: first, it explains why people who engage in crime tend to do so during adolescence. It is during this life-course stage that people 'liberate' themselves from their family homes and parents, i.e. their social bonds are weakened in many ways. They become free to gravitate toward delinquent peers and thus deviate and experiment with crime. It also explains, however, why some young people engage in crime earlier than do others, do more serious crimes, and offend more frequently. The argument also explains why there are significant between-individual differences among people who engage in crime: they are *mediated* through the institutions of informal social control.

Having explained onset of crime, Sampson and Laub now have to account for the same phenomena we saw Moffitt deal with earlier: why the vast majority ceases to commit crime after only a short period of criminal activity, and why a small subset of offenders persist in crime beyond the transition to adulthood. Let us begin with the first part of the task, and see how Sampson and Laub explain why so many people desist in the transition to adulthood. Here is where they introduce the famous notion of turning points, a concept they continue to refine in subsequent elaborations and developments of their theory (e.g. Laub and Sampson, 2003; Sampson and Laub, 2005).

'Changes that strengthen social bonds to society in adulthood', they note, 'will lead to less crime and deviance' (Sampson and Laub, 1993: 21). This process is facilitated by the presence of potential 'turning points' in the offenders' lives. These turning points – military service, employment, marriage, and others – have the potential to make the offender (a) 'knife off' the past from the present, (b) invest in new relationships that foster social support and growth, (c) be under direct and/or indirect supervision and control, (d) engage in routine activities more centered on conventional life, and/or (e) perform an identity transformation. The strengthening of social bonds through such turning points 'increase social capital and investment in social relations and institutions' (Sampson and Laub, 1993: 21). Moreover, the quality, duration, and strength of the social bond are especially important features of those ties. In other words, for Sampson and Laub, it is not the marriage in itself that is important, but rather the strong social control, combined with the emotional bond that develops between the spouses, that a 'good marriage' entails. This goes for the institution of work as well.

> Adult social ties are important insofar as they create interdependent systems of obligation and restraint that impose significant costs for translating criminal propensities into action. (p. 141)

Variations in adult criminal offending can thus not be explained by childhood behavior alone. What really matters when it comes to an individual's behavior in adulthood – whether he or she persists or desists from crime – are the more short-term, immediate situational aspects of that individual's life. When informal social control strengthens around an individual, he or she is likely to leave crime behind and, thus, Sampson and Laub have explained why the vast majority desists around the time they leave adolescence behind.

These more immediate, situational aspects can of course be influenced by the individual's past life. That brings us to persistence, or why a small subset of all offenders continues to engage in crime and develop lengthy, serious criminal careers. Here you will see a clear connection to Moffitt's theory. Moffitt accounts for persistence in offending, remember, by using the notions of *cumulative* and *contemporary continuity*. Cumulative continuity is something Sampson and Laub consider pivotal for understanding why people persist in crime. They call it *cumulative disadvantage*:

> we emphasize a developmental model where delinquent behavior has a systematic attenuating effect on the social and institutional bonds linking adults to society ... For example, delinquency may spark failure in school, incarceration, and weak bonds to the labor market, in turn increasing later adult crime ... Serious sanctions in particular lead to the 'knifing off' ... of future opportunities such that labeled offenders have fewer options for a conventional life. (Sampson and Laub, 1997: 144f)

This process of cumulative disadvantage is strongly linked to important social institutions of social control: the family, the school, peers, and state sanctions. As the offender continues to engage in crime, he or she becomes more marginalized from the conventional, institutional fabric of society, which in turn increases the likelihood for still further criminal offending.

Here, you may have noted, is where Sampson and Laub adopt an argument from the labeling perspective (see Chapter 2). The criminal justice system has a considerable role to play in the process of 'knifing off' an individual's life chances. Being an 'ex-prisoner', for example, is likely to decrease one's chances of getting a job, and work, we must remember, is one of the central turning points in the process of desisting from crime.

What about individual differences, then? In contrast to Moffitt, Sampson and Laub disregard the notion of contemporary continuity (that the original problem behavior in childhood persists and causes contemporary problems, leading to persistent offending). This is logical for them, given their position that what matters in explaining adult behavior, is the individual's life situation in adulthood. Nevertheless, early individual differences still do matter, but only in a cumulative fashion:

> To assume that individual differences influence the choices one makes in life (which they certainly do), does not mean that the social mechanisms emerging from those choices can then have no causal significance. Choices generate constraints and opportunities that themselves have effects not solely attributable to individuals. As situational theorists have long pointed out, the same person – with the same attributes and traits – acts very different in different situations. (Sampson and Laub, 1997: 155)

Thus, we are back at the fundamentally dynamic position and perspective on how a human life unfolds, including a person's engagement, persistence in, and desistance from crime.

## Making Change Understandable: Giordano et al.'s Critique

Sampson and Laub's theory is well-known and tends to generate empirical support in most studies (see Thornberry et al., 2012). However, in the original formulation there are still at least two problematic features when it comes to the process of desistance. Giordano et al. (2002) focus on those features, and attempt to develop them more satisfactorily.

First of all, their theory is based on a sample of only males. It is an impressive sample, consisting of 500 male juvenile delinquents, and 500 male non-delinquents – but no females.

A more conceptual problem with the theory, they argue, is that the initial move toward a conventional life is not accounted for, but rather attributed to chance or luck due to the scaffolding of the environment, as the individual 'happens' to engage in employment or a 'good marriage' (see, for example, Laub et al., 1998). 'Nonetheless', Giordano et al. argue,

> individuals themselves must *attend* to these new possibilities, discard old habits, and begin the process of crafting a different way of life. At the point of change, this new lifestyle will necessarily be 'at a distance' or a 'faint' possibility. Therefore, *the individual's subjective stance* is especially important during the early stages of the change process. (2002: 1000, emphases added)

Giordano and her colleagues thus engage in a study of desistance, based on a sample including both males and females. In their analysis they direct attention to the cognitive shifts they see as preceding, accompanying, and following desistance from crime. Their main point is that offenders tend to vary in their 'openness' to change and their receptivity to certain catalysts, or 'hooks for change', such as higher education, employment, or relationship formation. These 'hooks' are important not only as sources of social control but also because they provide blueprints for how to maintain one's change and be able to replace one's former self with a new one (Maruna, 2001). Although social control is a gendered phenomenon, Giordano et al. do find that the main mechanism seems to be valid for both males and females, albeit with some smaller differences (in Chapters 5–8 of this book, we include a section where we highlight the possible, gender-specific dimensions of the criminal career).

In their later work, Laub and Sampson (2003) revise their theory on several points, but the core of the theory is mainly the same. In particular, they answer Giordano et al. (2002) and stress the importance of human agency. They term it the 'missing link' in persistence and desistance (Laub and Sampson, 2003: 141). Offenders, they note, are 'active participants in constructing their lives' within the constraints of structure and context (Laub and Sampson, 2003: 281). A subjective reconstruction of the self is likely at times of life-course transitions. When it comes to desistance, especially, human agency is an important theoretical concept (Bottoms, 2006), and we revisit it in more detail in Chapter 8.

## Farrington's ICAP Theory

Taking over after Donald West, David P. Farrington – a psychologist by trade – has been the director of the well-known Cambridge Study in Delinquent Development (CSDD) since 1982. Having published extensively in life-course criminology, it is only relatively recently that he has begun to formulate his own theory of crime and the life course, the Integrated Cognitive Antisocial Potential (ICAP) Theory (he first attempted to formulate it in 1992, but has developed it in writings from 2005 and onward).

In his attempt at explaining continuity and change in crime across the life course, Farrington integrates ideas from several perspectives and theories, including strain, control, learning, and rational choice approaches (Farrington, 2005). Its key construct, however, is *antisocial potential* (AP), which refers to the potential of an individual to commit antisocial acts, such as crime and delinquency, and – thereby – becoming an offender. Because it is so central to his theory we need to devote a considerable amount of attention to it:

> The distribution of AP in the population at any age is highly skewed; relatively few people have relatively high levels of AP. People with high AP are more likely to commit many different types of antisocial acts, including different types of offending. (Farrington, 2010: 261)

Now, what makes an individual's antisocial potential high? Here, Farrington introduces a range of important childhood risk factors, including hyperactivity-impulsivity-attention deficit, low intelligence or low school attainment, family criminality, family poverty, large family size, poor child-rearing, and disrupted families. Farrington also includes a central, strain-theoretical theme:

> Following strain theory, the main energizing factors that potentially lead to high … AP are desires for material goods, status among intimates, excitement and sexual satisfaction. However, these motivations only lead to high AP if antisocial methods of satisfying them are habitually chosen. (Farrington, 2005: 79)

Now, similar to all the theories we have discussed so far, Farrington also places a large importance on the family, and the process of socialization and attachment:

> AP will be high if children are not attached to (prosocial) parents, for example if parents are cold and rejecting. Disrupted families (broken homes) may impair both attachment and socialization processes ... AP will also be high if people are exposed to and influenced by antisocial models, such as criminal parents, delinquent siblings, and delinquent peers, for example in high crime schools and neighborhoods. (Farrington, 2005: 79)

As you can see, what Farrington is doing is an integration of central elements from various theories. In Farrington's account of an individual's development of his or her antisocial potential (whether high or low), we see traces from Gottfredson and Hirschi, Moffitt, and Sampson and Laub.

The translation from antisocial potential to antisocial *behavior* depends on 'cognitive ... processes that take account of opportunities and victims' (Farrington, 2010: 260). In other words, the commission of a criminal act depends on the interaction between the individual, with his or her level of antisocial potential, and the social environment:

> In general, people tend to make decisions that seem rational to them, but those with low levels of AP will not commit offenses even when (on the basis of subjective expected utilities) it appears rational to do so. Equally, high ... levels of AP ... may induce people to commit offenses when it is not rational for them to do so. (Farrington, 2010: 263)

Now, so far it seems that Farrington is merely putting new words on an argument we already know from Gottfredson and Hirschi, turning *self-control* into *antisocial potential*. Farrington, however, recognizes the more fluid, dynamic nature of life and now introduces a crucial element of antisocial potential:

> levels of AP *vary with age*, peaking in the teenage years, because of changes within individuals in the factors that influence ... AP (e.g. from childhood to adolescence, the increasing importance of peers and the decreasing importance of parents) ... Also, *life events affect AP*; it decreases (at least for males) after people get married or move out of high crime areas, and it increases after the separation from a partner. (Farrington, 2010: 261f, emphases added)

In other words, an individual's antisocial potential is never static or fixed; on the contrary, it changes as the individual moves along the life course and responds to changes in his or her environment. It may decrease, as in the case of getting a job, getting married or perhaps making a residential change to a neighborhood with fewer criminal opportunities. It can also increase, as in the case of losing a job, separating from a partner, or moving to a neighborhood where levels of crime are high and criminal opportunities come aplenty.

Another source of changes in an individual's antisocial potential is the consequences of criminal offending for the individual's future. Here we see the learning dimension in Farrington's theory: if the consequences are reinforcing (e.g. the offender gains peer approval or material goods) antisocial potential is likely to rise, if they are punishing (e.g. the offender receives a legal sanction or disapproval from an important authority figure, such as a parent) antisocial is likely to decrease. However, if the punishing consequences involve labeling or stigmatization for the offender, this may – in line with classical labeling theory – make it more difficult for him or her to achieve his or her aspired aims legally, contributing to an increase in antisocial potential and continuity (perhaps even escalation) in criminal offending.

This way – through the use of antisocial potential, a feature which is highly skewed in any given population and subject to change as the individual encounters changes in his or her environment – Farrington attempts to address the question of continuity and change in criminal behavior across the life course. As noted above, a central feature of Farrington's approach is the notion of risk and risk factors; a feature we revisit and discuss in detail in Chapter 5.

## Some Final Remarks

As we mentioned at the outset, a full review of all existing life-course theories is impossible. Farrington's anthology (2005) gives a pretty good overview of the field as it looked about 10 years ago, but life-course criminology is – like all science – in constant movement. The theories and topics we have covered so far, however, are still among the most fundamental in the field and they are continuously cited, tested, and developed. As we proceed in this book, we also mention and discuss additional theories and research projects to give the reader a more comprehensive overview of the field.

In this chapter, we have gone through a number of the basic building blocks of life-course criminological theorizing, and how they attempt to explain the closely connected phenomena of continuity and change in criminal careers. We have seen that they all subscribe to some basic, fundamental premises of the life-course perspective, but we have also seen that they differ in important respects. Some – Gottfredson and Hirschi, and Sampson and Laub – have adopted a more sociologically oriented approach, whereas Farrington and Moffitt attempt to understand criminal careers from a more psychological one.

Gottfredson and Hirschi, and Sampson and Laub tend to stress the phenomenon of *change* in criminal offending, whereas Moffitt argues that *continuity* is the hallmark for a specific segment of those who engage in crime (the life-course persisters). However, when it comes to the underlying construct that is causing the individual to engage and persist in crime, we see that there are other similarities: Gottfredson and Hirschi, and Moffitt (in the case of the life-course persisters) stress the static, fixed trait of self-control and antisocial behavior. Further, both theories locate this basic cause within the individual (although it might be influenced by external forces, such as the family). Farrington, too, locates the crucial construct – antisocial potential – within the individual but, in contrast, sees this construct as dynamic, subject to change as the individual changes and moves along the life course.

Sampson and Laub also see the causal, underlying construct – age-graded informal social control – as dynamic and ever-changing, but they locate the source of this construct in the interpersonal relationships the individual has to his or her surroundings.

What are we to make of these partly similar and partly very different takes on continuity and change in criminal careers? Rather than trying to synthesize the approaches, it seems fruitful to consider the plurality and theoretical versatility of the field. Yes, individual differences – whether it is differences in self-control, antisocial potential, or informal social control – matter, when it comes to the individual's future criminal career. However, it is equally important to remember that an individual's pathway across the life course is never fully set. Life events – such as engaging in higher education, getting a job, forming a family, and so on – may transform one's life and self in important, crime-inhibiting ways. Individual differences may influence the likelihood of those life events occurring in a given person's life, but whether they do occur or not can never be *reduced* to those individual differences. Human and social life is much too complex for that, full as it is with its coincidences, contingencies, and unexpected events.

The theories' differences also imply different implications for criminal policy and intervention. For Moffitt, the most effective intervention would be directed at the would-be life-course persisters and, predominantly, environmental factors. We know that many of the neuropsychological 'deficits' are influenced by factors such as prenatal substance abuse, severe child maltreatment and witnessing family violence. These can all be countered with various forms of early intervention programs. We are also increasingly coming to understand the plasticity of the brain and how interventions can address these issues. In fact, Moffitt argues that one reason why so many interventions fail is that they start too late.

The argument has been made that selective incapacitation is a likely outcome of Moffitt's argument, given that we are already 'too late' in many cases. Life-course persisters are likely to engage in long and serious criminal careers. They will hurt a lot of people (including themselves), and cost society a considerable amount of money. For Gottfredson and Hirschi, lengthy and selective incapacitation is meaningless. Such policies, inevitably, keep people locked up long after their teenage years and thus the peak-age of criminal offending. In other words, even the most serious criminal offenders will desist from crime after having made the transition to adulthood. That does *not* mean that they will not engage in self-destructive or antisocial behavior. Low self-control is static and its expression can take many forms across the life course, including alcohol problems and gambling. Gottfredson and Hirschi's position simply means that they will cease to engage in crime in the transition to adulthood, and thus cease to commit acts which are defined as law-breaking.

Sampson and Laub's position is similar here. In fact, they argue that selective incapacitation and lengthy prison/treatment sentences may actually be counter-productive. Why? Because they tend to isolate the individual from the institutional fabric of society and it is the bond between the individual and his or her society that is crucial: if the bond is strong – through such institutions as work and family life – it is likely that the individual will desist from crime. Without these turning points, persistence in crime is a likely outcome, and the implementation of harsh criminal justice policies may thus actually impel continuity in crime due to the process of cumulative disadvantage.

We revisit these and other implications later on, especially in Chapter 5 when we talk about risk factors and prediction, where we also elaborate on Farrington's position in these questions. First, however, we must consider the methodologies of the field (Chapter 4).

## Suggestions for Further Reading

Gottfredson, Michael and Hirschi, Travis (1990) *A General Theory of Crime.* Stanford, CA: Stanford University Press.
Despite their aim – to show that life-course- and longitudinal studies of crime are meaningless – Gottfredson and Hirschi's outline of a theory of self-control remains one of the most influential, contested, and tested theories within the field.

Moffitt, Terrie E. (1993) 'Adolescence-limited and life-course persistent antisocial behavior: a developmental taxonomy', *Psychological Review*, 100(4): 674–701.
In her 1993 paper, Moffitt presents the dual developmental taxonomy. When discussed in textbooks and by critics, Moffitt's theory is usually described in simplistic terms. Reading her original piece shows the nuance, elegance, and power of her argument.

Sampson, Robert J. and Laub, John H. (1993) *Crime in The Making: Pathways and Turning Points Through Life.* Boston, MA: Harvard University Press.
This is the original, highly influential statement of an age-graded theory of informal social control. Sampson and Laub re-build and re-analyze the famous Glueck data, following the Boston Boys to age 32.

Loeber, Rolf and Farrington, David P. (eds) (2012) *From Juvenile Delinquency to Adult Crime.* Oxford: Oxford University Press.
In this relatively new work, Loeber, Farrington, and colleagues assess the empirical status of life-course criminological theories (see, in particular, Chapter 2).

# 4

# THE METHODOLOGIES OF LIFE-COURSE CRIMINOLOGY

Most textbooks on scientific methodology tell us that our choice of method is dependent on the research question we want to answer. The research question, in turn, grows out of the researcher's interest and the philosophical underpinnings that more or less consciously inform the researcher's view of reality, science, and truth. That is the case in an ideal situation, where both the researcher and his or her research are completely free and autonomous, independent of any external influences or boundaries.

However, anybody with the slightest experience of conducting research – here, we are mostly concerned with the *social* sciences – knows that these ideal circumstances are extremely rare to occur (if they ever do). In the everyday life and work of social scientific research, the choice of method is contingent on a whole range of other factors. These include economical and staff resources, the practical question of getting access to relevant data, the quality of that data, demands and boundaries set by the financer, ethical considerations, and so on. In other words, it is almost always the case that one's choice of research method becomes a compromise between scientific ambition and practical possibilities and limitations.

These issues are relevant to all social research. However, they are likely to be even more relevant when it comes to longitudinal and life-course research, for several reasons. Conducting this kind of research often takes a lot of time (and sometimes include several generations of researchers), tends to be very expensive, and is methodologically quite complicated.

As longitudinal and life-course studies on crime and criminal careers have blossomed, the methodology behind this branch of research has developed and become increasingly sophisticated. Several important, methodological works have been published in the forms of books and articles, mostly on quantitative methods. Our purpose here is not to conduct an exhaustive review of these methods; such a review can, for example, be found in the great work by Biljeveld and van der Kamp (1998). Here, instead, we concern ourselves with a number of basic, core issues. Our aim is quite simple, and practical: to provide the reader with enough knowledge of longitudinal and life-course methodology, to enable you to understand the main methodological problems and possibilities in this kind of research.

## Why Study the Life Course?

Since life-course research is usually expensive, takes a lot of time and often creates (even more!) methodological issues than most other forms of research in social science, it is reasonable to ask the question: why do this form of research at all, and why has it become so prominent during the last few decades?

We have already, partially, discussed this issue but the basic answer is that, using this methodology, we can answer important research questions which other methods have trouble addressing. The foremost questions in this regard concern the issue of *continuity and change in behavior over time.*

So-called cross-section methodology, where researchers study a sample or a population at a single, specific moment in time, gives us the possibility to study individuals or groups of individuals when it comes to a whole range of variables (such as crime, peer relations, health, employment, and so on) and how these are related to each other. We commonly call these between-individual similarities and differences. Using life-course methodology, however, we can study the *same individual at repeated points in time.* Since we can study the relationship between the different variables at different points in time, we can also study whether the relationship between them is persistent or changes over time. It is possible, for example, that as long as the individual engages in repeated, serious crime, he or she will have a relatively unstable form of conventional work (if he or she has a job at all), have turbulent relationships with other people, have increasing problems with mental and physical health, etc. All this we can study using life-course methodology.

We can also study what happens when there is a change in one of the variables; is there a change in a person's criminal offending when he or she gets a more stable job, starts a romantic relationship, or becomes ill? Crucially, we can also – sometimes – study which change occurs before the other, i.e. does a person's criminal offending change as a result of him or her getting a job, etc., as Sampson and Laub argue, or is it the other way around – a person begins to decrease his or her criminal offending *and then* gets a job or starts a romantic relationship? This suggests two different theoretical processes, and thus two different answers to the question of what makes people cease their criminal offending, with important implications for policy and practice. Thus, we can begin to approach the difficult question of cause and effect, that is, the question of causality.

According to de Lange, four criteria in research in the social sciences should be fulfilled if we are to be able to draw causal conclusions:

> This research should i) demonstrate that the cause variable precedes the outcome variable in time, ii) show a significant statistical relationship between the presumed cause and outcome, iii) exclude possible alternative explanations, and iv) provide a professional theoretical interpretation of the relationship(s) under study. (de Lange 2005: 18)

As we will elaborate below, the first criterion above is probably the most important argument for using longitudinal research.

## Life-Course Research and the Longitudinal Method

Life-course research and longitudinal research are not necessarily synonyms. To state it simply, *life course* suggests a distinct research perspective, whereas *longitudinal* suggest a specific methodology which follows from the life-course perspective.

The aim of life-course studies is to study, understand, and explain one or more individuals' lives under a short or long time-span; some may focus on a specific stage of the life-course (e.g. 'What effect does the transition to adulthood have on the individual's future criminal career?'), whereas others take a more holistic approach ('How does criminal offending wax and wane across the life course?'). As we saw in the preceding chapters, the life-course perspective assumes that what happens at one time in life is contingent on – but not necessarily determined by – what happened at an earlier point in life. This theoretical assumption leads to methodological consequences, where life-course research must be carried out using longitudinal methodology.

### Prospective and Retrospective Designs

Longitudinal research can be of two kinds: prospective, and retrospective (Blumstein et al., 1986). *Prospective* longitudinal designs are forward-looking, in the sense that you take a sample of individuals, usually defined by age (a whole cohort, or a sample defined by some other criteria), and then follow that sample repeatedly and prospectively over their life course, or some part of it. As you go along, you make repeated measurements of the same factors or variables that you are interested in. So, for example, you take a sample of 8-year-old children and follow them to the age of 38, making new data collections every second year.

The primary advantage of the prospective design is obvious: you collect data on events relatively soon after they have occurred, and this way you manage to avoid the memory problem: it is more likely that an 18-year-old can provide a better picture of what his or her high school experience is like, than the same person would if he or she was interviewed at the age of 26. By using the prospective design, you also have control over the crucial dimension of *time*. You can identify what comes first: does drug use precede low attachment to the labor market in adulthood, or does low attachment to the labor market precede drug use? The Cambridge Study of Delinquent Development is an example of this prospective approach, where a sample of South London boys born around 1953 were enrolled in the study at eight years of age, with selection based on registers from six primary schools. They have then been continuously followed up using register data and interviews, beyond age 50 (Farrington et al., 2013).

The primary disadvantage of the prospective design is perhaps equally obvious: if you want to explore the life courses of a sample from age 8 to 38, it takes 30 years. If you want to make repeated measurements every other, or every third or fourth year, it consumes a lot of resources, both in terms of personnel and money. And not only that; by the time you have followed the sample to age 38, 30 years have passed, and that amount of time can do a lot to a society, and the sciences; what if the results you now have are no longer relevant. Not to mention the fact that you yourself get older!

The other design is *retrospective*, a design that looks backwards rather than forward. Typically, a sample is selected based on some criteria or other, such as adult inmates who serve time in a prison in a given year. Having done so, the researcher traces their backgrounds and past experiences, using register data and/or interviews. This was the design Wolfgang et al. (1972) used in their famous *Delinquency in a Birth Cohort*. They retrospectively chose all boys born in 1945 who were living in Philadelphia between 10 and 18 years of age, and then traced their criminal histories and backgrounds using register data.

The main advantage this design has is that it avoids the time-consuming step-by-step exploration of the unfolding of the lives of the sample. It is much more economical. There is, of course, a very problematic issue here as well, constituting the main disadvantage of the retrospective design. It has to do with the issue of time, in two ways.

Some studies only include official register data. This is perhaps more common in the Nordic and European countries, because the quality of their official records tend to be very good (Skardhamar and Lyngstad, 2011). However, the longer we go back in time, the more unstable the records usually become. In addition, the way data is collected, and the content of what is collected, can change: some data series cease, others start. There may be problems with the different data series' compatibility.

To give just one example, in a research project we, the authors, are working in (The Stockholm Life-Course Project), we want to trace the criminal histories of a

Swedish sample born in the 1940s and 1950s. In Swedish crime registers, we not only have to handle the problem of using two different sets of crime registers – police records, which are available until the 1980s, and the conviction records, which are available from the mid-1970s – we also have to take into account the sorting-out process that takes place within the police records, where individuals once recorded for crimes were sorted out if they were not recorded for a new offense, as the authorities only had the right to keep them for a certain amount of time. These records still exist at the Swedish National Archive, but must then be added on to the 'original' records to provide a full picture of their criminal histories. Other records – such as those kept by the social services – also change over time, with new variables replacing older ones, and so on. This makes a longitudinal analysis difficult, because at different points in time we may in fact capture, or measure, partly different things.

Second, if we do not – or not only – rely on register data, we are likely to rely on interviews in some way (we elaborate on life history interviews below). If we do these retrospectively, we may ask the interview participant to recall events and experiences that occurred a long time ago, making the crucial *sequencing of life events* difficult to pin down. Recalling what came first – starting to smoke marihuana or skipping school at the age of 15 – may be very difficult 30, 40 or 50 years later. In retrospective interviews, we also, of course, miss all the people who cannot be interviewed, since they may be dead.

## Quantitative and Qualitative Methods

Within the social sciences, there is a seemingly never-ending discussion and debate centered on this issue: should the social world be explored and explained quantitatively (e.g. using numbers and statistics), or qualitatively (e.g. using words and narratives, in the wide sense), or both?

This question has a partly philosophical basis concerning the fundamental features of the world (what the world 'is', or what exists) and how we can study those features, and what the researcher's task consists of. Quantitative methodology is historically tied to the philosophical branch of positivism and post-positivism, where the (somewhat simplified) stance is that the world exists independently of us and our understanding of it. The essential features can be counted in numbers (e.g. how high is the risk that a given individual reoffends after X years of abstinence?) and thus be studied with the help of statistical methods.

Qualitative methodology, on the other hand, is commonly associated with the traditions of constructivism, and symbolic interactionism. This tradition stresses the basically constructed nature of the social world where nothing (not very much, at least) is natural or static, but always contingent on the specific social and historical context. How people perceive, interpret, and understand the world is a big part of what *actually shapes* that world; what makes it come into being in a certain way rather than others.

This relatively stiff dichotomy of quantitative and qualitative methodology, and their associated philosophical underpinnings, is becoming less and less distinct, however – most prominently within life-course criminology, the dichotomy is being replaced by a kind of methodological pragmatism where the researcher simply chooses the method(s) that suit the research question and is possible to use, given the various practical boundaries of a given project. Maruna (2010: 127f) expresses this point clearly:

> Qualitative methods involve 'deep' immersion into a social scene that allows for awareness of situational and contextual factors that are often missed in [quantitative] research. They produce 'rich', 'holistic' data, as opposed to the focus on 'variables' … In its published form, qualitative analysis provides vivid illustration of phenomena, bringing social processes 'to life' for readers. Quantitative research does little of this, but has considerable strengths precisely where qualitative research is weak. Quantitative methods are transparent and do not rely on a 'take my word for it' approach. This work is therefore more replicable, precise (some would say 'objective'), and generalizable than qualitative research. Additionally, statistical techniques allow for the eliminating of confounding influences and better assess cause and effect relationships among variables. In published form, they produce findings that are notable for their clarity, succinctness, exactitude, and parsimony.

Criminal career research and life-course criminology in the 1970s and 1980s was dominated by influential, quantitatively driven studies. This is evident from several of the traditional key concepts: prevalence, offending frequency, duration, intensity, etc. (see Blumstein et al., 1986). Much of the most prominent work within the field has been done with quantitative data, including the pioneering studies by Wolfgang et al. (1972), Blumstein et al. (1986) and later studies such as the one by Piquero et al. (2007), to mention just a few. The field has also greatly benefited from developments in quantitative methodology, such as the one by Nagin (2005), who outlined a specific form of group-based modeling to understand criminal career trajectories in a new way.

## Two Forms of Quantitative Data

There are, you could say, two forms of quantitative data: official records (i.e. those that are collected and kept by the various authorities of a society) and specific quantitative data collected by the researcher within the frame of a given project. So, for example, your official employment history, health history, and whether you at some point in time have lived in a single household or not, that exists in many countries' official records.

Register data are therefore amazing. In most countries of the world, but particularly in welfare states such as Sweden and many other European countries, governmental and municipal agencies collect huge amounts of data on their citizens. Collecting and using these records (in many European countries, at least) is made simple by the fact that every person has a unique personal identification number. After getting ethical approval, researchers can be allowed access to these records.

Now, importantly, this data is collected for administrative purposes, which can entail a problem for the researcher: the purpose of the agency is not always compatible with the specific problem the researcher is interested in. Here, then, is a prime example of those forced compromises the researcher is forced to make when it comes to the research design, and the content of the data. The researcher is often forced to use variables and scales that constitute far from optimal operationalizations of the various constructs the researcher is interested in.

At the same time, the agencies' administrative records have one huge advantage: data are *dated*, and usually entered in to the register in a chronological order. This means that official register data has an *inherently longitudinal character*, even if it is collected by the researcher at a single point in time.

We noted above that whether or not you have lived in a single household often exists in official register data. But for life-course criminology it is a crucial question whether you experienced a 'good upbringing' or not, and that kind of official data usually does not exist. In general, that kind of data has to be gathered by the researchers, usually through more or less structured interviews, surveys, and tests specifically constructed for the specific study. The great value of doing this is that it can usually provide a much more rich description of the people you study and, in a much better way, covers the research questions and theoretical points of departure, than mere official records can.

One possible issue with this, very relevant in studies with a prospective design, is that what is considered a 'good' measurement of something can change over time. So, for example, in the research project we describe below (The Stockholm Life-Course Project, SLCP) 287 Stockholm boys born in the 1940s and 1950s were enrolled in a study, and underwent a large number of tests, including IQ tests (Terman-Merrill) and Rorschach tests. Today, the first of these measurements is considered a fairly okay, but not very good, indicator of a person's intelligence. The second form of test, Rorschach, the first follow-up study showed, is far too unreliable and imprecise to be used. This – what time does to a data-set – is an unsolvable problem, of course, but it is important to keep in mind when it comes to longitudinal studies with long follow-up periods.

Similarly, when researchers construct indicators of important theoretical constructs, they do so from a set of raw variables. The variables we need to use to construct something change over time, as society changes. For example, consider the issue of being 'well-adjusted' economically. In the 1980s, one such study tried to capture this by asking a whole bunch of specific questions, and then adding the answers to those questions together, forming an 'index'. Among other things, that battery of questions included a question about whether or not the respondent owned a VHS player (Sarnecki, 1985). Today, such a question is highly outdated, and if we were to conduct the same measurement of being 'well-adjusted' economically today, we would need to include other questions. The researcher, in other words, must continuously be conscious of the temporal dimension of his or her study, and how the relevance of certain questions, measurements, and variables may change as society changes.

## Qualitative Data: Process, Life History, and Context

While quantitative studies have contributed greatly to our knowledge of crime and the life course, some forms of qualitative method may help us to further understand, and explain the empirical social world within which people develop, continue, and cease criminal careers. What a detailed, context-sensitive qualitative approach loses in breadth, it gains in its depth and close attention to the nature of social life, along with its contingencies and complexities (Blumer, 1969).

Qualitative studies of criminal careers have always been important: consider, for example, Meisenhelder's early interview study (1977), which, based on interviews with a small number of property offenders, outlined the process of exiting a criminal career using social control theory. Still, it took until Sampson and Laub's (1993) first book on the Glueck data until qualitative analyses of criminal careers really took off. In life-course criminology, the life history interview has become a particularly important method. Among other things, this interview form reveals 'in the offenders' own words the personal-situational context of their behavior and their views of the larger social and historical circumstances in which their behavior is embedded' (Laub and Sampson, 2003: 58). This is something quantitative data can never achieve.

Consider the benefits Laub and Sampson (2003: 58f) see in life history interviews (we believe several of these benefits are valid for qualitative data in general):

- The life history method uniquely captures the process of both becoming involved in and disengaging from crime and other antisocial behavior.
- They can uncover complex patterns of continuity and change in individual behavior over time.
- Life histories reveal the complexity of criminal behavior.
- They are grounded in social and historical context.
- The life history method shows us the human side of offenders.

Now, a main strength of qualitative data is its capacity to uncover *processes*. In a few chapters we will get to the phenomenon of desistance, but we use it briefly here as an illustrative example. Kazemian and Maruna note that most studies of desistance measure it as static rather than taking a 'process view' of the phenomenon (Kazemian and Maruna, 2009: 279). By adopting a process view we take *changes* in offending into account, as well as 'the progression towards desistance' (ibid.).

We know that desistance – that is, a person ceasing his or her criminal career – in the vast majority takes the form of a process, in which the individual gradually leaves crime behind (Carlsson, 2014). It can also be a very dramatic, static event occurring at a single point in time (e.g. Cusson and Pinsonneault, 1986), but that seems to only rarely be the case. So when studying desistance, it is a challenge for the researcher who uses quantitative data to conceptualize it as a process. It is not impossible (e.g. Bushway et al., 2001), but very often quantitative studies end up with a static view of desistance, because it must be understood as the *absence of an observation* – when the individual's criminal offending (often measured by official records) is no longer present. There might, of course, be some indications of a desistance process at work in quantitative data: maybe the time between recorded offenses becomes longer? Still, the *meaning* of that observation is very unclear.

Here is where qualitative data, particularly life history interviews, are at their best. By interviewing (ex-)offenders in depth about their lives in and out of crime, going beyond the structured survey-like interview form, something like a story or *narrative* emerges. The idea underlying this perspective on the social world is the notion that we 'understand the occurrence of events by learning the steps in the process by which they came to happen' (Becker, 1998: 61). This doesn't necessarily imply linearity or continuity, but rather that, as Shaw (1930: 13) has noted, 'any specific act of the individual becomes comprehensible only in the light of its relation to … past experiences' and the individual projecting him- or herself into the future. Lines of action (or absence of action) 'can influence, in a dialectical fashion, the very forces or contingencies that condition later choices' (Ulmer and Spencer, 1999: 109).

So, in understanding the meaning of something – such as the processes of cumulative continuity, cumulative disadvantage, or the turning points of employment, military service, marriage, and residential change – we use qualitative life history interviews to study and understand them in the context of the surrounding processes of which they are part. That is, we see how they are contingent on social context, how the turning point emerges and how change is made possible. When we do these interpretations, we must however be aware that it concerns individuals' subjective experiences that are interpreted by this individual with the aim, consciously or unconsciously, to give the interviewer a certain image of him- or herself.

# Mixing Methods

Having read through the sections on quantitative and qualitative methodology, the reader may have asked him- or herself a question: there are obvious strengths and weaknesses with both quantitative and qualitative methods – so why not use both? That is a good question. To mix methods – i.e. using both quantitative and qualitative data to arrive at a deeper, more full understanding of a given research problem – is becoming more and more common within life-course criminology, and some of the most prominent and well-known studies in the field (e.g. Giordano et al., 2002; Laub and Sampson, 2003; Maruna, 2001) have done so. The strategy of mixing methods goes back to the Chicago School of sociology, where very quantitatively driven studies (e.g. Shaw and McKay, 1942) were complemented by life histories such as the one by Shaw (1930) about 'Stanley', the famous jack-roller. It has, however, been a controversial area:

> Because of the methodological paradigm struggles that arose in the last three decades and the lingering prejudices that resulted, the idea of combining qualitative and quantitative work has an aura of the exotic or even forbidden among criminologists today. (Maruna 2010: 124)

The underlying issue here is one concerning the philosophical assumptions that different methods are supposedly attached to. To repeat: quantitative analysis, it is said, assumes an objective reality that is possible to measure in numbers; qualitative analysis is said to assume a subjective reality that is constructed and made 'real' through people's perceptions and interpretations, a reality thus only possible to access by analyzing those interpretations. However, this harsh division between the methods is becoming more and more loose, being replaced by a form of methodological pragmatism where the researcher – as we mentioned above – chooses a method that (1) can provide data that answers the research question, and (2) is possible given the practical circumstances of the research project.

Several research projects adopt a mixed method strategy, and here we only illustrate the strategy with one famous example: Laub and Sampson's (2003) study, where they conduct a follow-up of the Gluecks' *Unraveling Juvenile Delinquency* study (1950), tracing the men up to age 70.

Collecting new data on criminal records, Laub and Sampson conduct a quantitative analysis and explore the men's recorded criminal careers up to age 70. Having done so, they use this data to select 52 cases from five groups of offenders: first, those who persistently engaged in violence and theft across the life course; two, nonviolent juvenile offenders who desisted in adulthood; three, violent juvenile offenders who desisted in adulthood; four, intermittent offenders with an onset of violence in adulthood; and five, intermittent offenders with an onset of violence in young adulthood.

Then, through close analysis of these 52 life histories, they delve deeper into the lived experiences of the men in the various groups. By doing so, they find the underlying processes and mechanisms at work in their age-graded theory of informal social control, but also realize the importance of human agency. Indeed, they go so far as to term it the missing link in understanding both persistence and desistance, and as such human agency provides a crucial piece of the puzzle of continuity and change in crime across the life course. This piece would not have been discovered were it not for their qualitative data analysis (in traditional, quantitative analysis human agency may have constituted a portion of the variance in the data that cannot be explained).

Let us leave you with an additional example. Let us say we find a quantitative, statistical relationship between being diagnosed with some form of cancer, and desistance from crime. That is, cancer diagnosis is predictor of desistance; when people get the diagnosis they are more likely to desist than before. This can be a simple co-variation between the two variables, so we have to make additional statistical tests where we control for various factors – such as age – to make sure that the two changes (in health, and criminal offending) indeed are connected to each other. Now, depending on what kind of quantitative data we have access to, we might not be able to say much more than this: other things controlled for (or 'held constant'), cancer diagnosis is a predictor of desistance from crime.

But *why* is cancer diagnosis a predictor of desistance? It could be due to a number of things. First, it could be that the simple 'shock' of the diagnosis makes the individual turn his or her life around. Or, it could be that the cancer diagnosis is an indicator of the individual's health problems, and people who have severe health problems are often not capable of committing crimes simply because their bodies are not up to the task. Or, third, it could be that the everyday life of the offender now changes in important ways: he or she must go through treatment, counseling sessions, and so on. These things can entail a strengthening social control that inhibits future criminal offending. Any of these three explanations – or a combination of all three and possibly additional ones! – are possible, but they all have one thing in common: the only way to find out is to undertake a qualitative analysis. You take a sub-sample of those you have studied quantitatively and ask to interview them, and ask them about it.

## Cross-Sectional and Longitudinal Research: The Main Differences

In this section, we return to the beginning of this chapter and the distinction between cross-sectional and longitudinal research, and develop this deeper by highlighting a number of methodological dimensions that distinguish a life-course study from a so-called traditional cross-sectional one (where all variables are examined at the same, one point in time). Returning to the beginning may seem somewhat strange, but we believe that another take on the distinction will make it clearer for you to understand what life-course research entails methodologically.

A cross-sectional study usually has two dimensions: individuals and variables. In a longitudinal study, as you now know, a *third* dimension is added: time.

In practice, this means that for every individual, not only do we collect data on traits, circumstances, and events, but also data on *when* these occur. This three-dimensionality in longitudinal data is described by Biljeveld and van der Kamp (1998) as a data box where every dimension is an axle: the box's axles are persons, variables, and moment, or time.

## The Persons

Every study that strives toward making generalizable conclusions has to handle the question about the representativity of the material. In quantitative studies, the sample is usually drawn from a well-defined sample population. Additionally, the sample must have a certain size for us to be able to get stable, statistically significant findings (the larger the sample, the better, for larger samples enable us to get stronger, statistical power, which in turn is almost necessary for statistical significance).

In so-called cohort studies such as the Swedish Stockholm Birth Cohort (Stenberg, 2013), you choose to study a whole population of persons, in this case every person born in Stockholm in 1953, and who resided in the city in 1963 (when the project was launched). In such cases, given that the attrition and missing data in the study is relatively small and random, it is possible to make claims about the studied population.

Now, a problem here is the issue of time: a cohort born in 1953 turned 60 in 2013 and only then could the researchers get a sense of how much of the cohort members' lives unfolded. To answer questions regarding, for example, the connection between juvenile delinquency and the risk of dying in different kinds of diseases, you may have to wait even longer. Thus, after many years of research, we may finally have an answer to our question about the relationship between crime and morbidity but do these findings apply to today's youth, or are they by now no more than historical documents?

When it comes to research about relatively rare phenomena, such as serious and persistent criminal offending, you either have to work with very large samples, or stratify your sample, so that the individuals who are especially interesting to the researcher (in our case, those with serious criminal offending) are overrepresented. The Pittsburgh Youth Study (e.g. Loeber et al., 1998) is an example of such a study. A difficulty for us in prospective longitudinal studies is that serious and persistent criminal offending distinguishes itself relatively late in life (e.g. after the age of 20). If we want to initiate our study before that, we have to over-sample the group of individuals who we believe will have a high risk of developing serious and criminal offending. It is not certain, either, that our choice of risk variables will be adequate in the long run.

Another problem is the question of attrition. Attrition is a problem for every type of research that in one way or another is dependent on the respondents' consent. The whole idea with longitudinal studies is that we, in some way, study individuals through time and place. We thus repeatedly measure the same respondents. So, a respondent may answer our questions at one time, but may change his or her mind (or tire, or die, leave the country, or move to an address we for some reason cannot find) the second or third time. We must remember that, for ethical reasons, we should not attempt to contact those who have already declined to participate. Thus, in longitudinal studies, the problem with attrition is usually larger than in cross-sectional ones and, at the same time, many of the longitudinal analyses we want to make are sensitive to attrition and missing data (Biljeveld and van der Kamp, 1998). There are, however, various methodological and statistical techniques for handling this issue.

## The Variables

A big problem in social science research is to outline the manifest variables so that they, in an adequate way, measure the latent ones, that is, the theoretical constructs that our study uses. How do we, for example, turn *antisocial potential*, *self-control*, or *informal social control* into something we can actually measure? After all, there exist no such universal variables, nor any universal agreement of how such a variable should be constructed and/or what it should include. So – how do we do it?

In less fancy words, we usually call this problem *the problem of operationalization*, and while we almost always encounter it, the reason as to why we do differs from study to study. If we conduct a self-report study, one reason why this problem occurs could simply be ethical: we cannot always ask what we want. However, much more common is the fact that we have to use data where the existing variables do not fully mirror the theoretical dimensions we want to include. One reason for this, of course, is that we often have to rely on data that is quite old, or in the case of register data, have been collected for a purpose other than the researcher's. At any rate, such issues lead to the inevitable fact of compromise when it comes to validity, e.g. Do we really measure self-control? Maybe we have to settle for studying one dimension, or simply one or a few *indicators* of the phenomenon we are after?

The problem of operationalization is likely to increase if the study has a longitudinal character: the same phenomenon (such as social adjustment, for example) must be operationalized differently at different ages. In the case of social adjustment, it is highly logical and relevant to include questions such as: 'Do you work and, if so, how many hours a week?' To ask the same question to a 13-year-old (or a 5-year-old!) would be somewhat strange. However, we still want to know how socially adjusted our sample was at the age of 13, so the problem does not go away. Thus, as we go along in our study, we have to be sensitive to the social process of aging and the flow of the life course, and re-operationalize many of our theoretical constructs to capture what is actually going on in their lives. Another problem concerns those contextual, social changes that we also have to consider: the times are changing. So, within our measure of social adjustment, we may want to include something that captures economic status. One way to capture this in 1985 or 1990 would be to ask whether or not the respondent has a mobile phone. Today, that question is essentially meaningless for any measure of status.

Additionally, the way we choose to formulate our questions and our interests in certain theoretical constructs and not others, may give rise to issues in long-term studies: what the researchers may have wanted to know when they initiated their research project, when the respondents were children or teenagers; when they are adults and time has passed, the questions we can now answer may not be considered relevant or interesting (although such words are *very* loaded with value judgments) by the science community or policy-makers. The reverse is also true, of course, that new research questions emerge, due to a new social and political climate, that nobody considered relevant when we initiated our study. In our own study, violence is a striking example of this. In Sweden, in the beginning of the 1960s, violence was considered a 'natural way' for young boys and men to solve conflicts. Theft, however, was a very serious crime and an indicator of a highly problematic background and high-risk life circumstances. Thus, among the older samples in The Stockholm Life-Course Project, we have practically no variables that capture use of violence in youth, but a large number of variables that attempt to capture theft. Since the 1960s, of course, there has been a change in how society in general and the criminal justice system in particular, perceives teenage violence. Today, it is a serious social problem and, on the individual level, an indicator of future problem behaviors.

There is no simple solution to this (and many other, related) problem of operationalization. However, a broad and encompassing data collection in the initial stage of the research project, where one also collects such data that do not feel immediately relevant, could make future analyses possible. At the same time, that kind of data collection may not be recommended for other reasons: first of all, data, in many ways, costs money and, second, the need for data always have to be weighed against individuals' personal integrity.

## The Time

Finally, the dimension of time is what distinguishes longitudinal and life-course studies from other branches of research. Now, above we mentioned that our measure of time can be retrospective or prospective, and that the number of 'waves' can range from one alone (and thus, fully retrospective) to 5, 10, 15, or more follow-ups. Here, we must decide how many follow-up waves we should do, and when we should do so. Ideally, of course, this should be decided based upon the project's research questions. If we are only interested in understanding continuity and change in crime during the pathway from adolescence to young adulthood, for example, it seems pointless to conduct a follow-up study beyond age 30. Instead, we should direct all our resources to get a close and detailed study as we can of the years between, say, 15 to 25. As always, however, and just as in the case with the other dimensions of the research project, we are likely to have to make a compromise between our ambitions and theoretical ideals, and our economic and other, practical conditions and requirements.

When studying criminal careers, observing teenagers and young adults every, or every second, year may be particularly useful, since criminal activity is relatively common during these years. If we want to study, say, their self-reported criminal offending, as often as one time every year would be ideal. Using longer time frames between observations when it comes to self-reported offending is possible but not desirable, due to the problems of memory recollection. The same goes for studying other facets of the criminal career, which often demand many observation periods, with short time lapses in between. One such issue concerns the onset of crime (see Chapter 6), another desistance (Chapter 8), and intermittency, where the individual temporarily ceases his or her offending before recidivating (see Chapter 7).

In our own research project, The SLCP, the number of observation periods have been relatively few: three or four, depending on which sample we refer to. The use of register data offers no problems here, but interviewing them does: at every observation period, we had to rely on the interview participants' retrospective accounts of longer periods of their lives, during which we had had no contact with them. The problem with this, of course, is that much of what interview participants tell about their past, may be affected by what has happened later in life. The past is, in a sense, always seen and narrated from the perspective of the present. In our interviews (which have been conducted on a smaller, strategically chosen sub-set of the sample) we have asked the interview participants to talk about their whole life courses. This makes it possible for us to compare their life histories as told at age 35 or 40, with life histories collected from them when they were in their 60s. We also have the possibility to compare their interviews to the more reliable register data (reliable in the sense that registers do not forget or mix up the timing of events).

One obvious advantage of not having too many observation periods where the sample is actively involved in the data collection (such as interviews or various forms of tests), is that they do not get tired of being examined and leave the study. Additionally, and importantly, the various observation periods can be assumed to be relatively independent from each other: it is unlikely that the interview participant or respondent remembers what s/he has said during the previous observation period, and, thus, feels no need to stick to a given life history or anything along those lines. However, in studies where the observation periods are many and occur frequently, studies have shown that there tends to develop a relation between the researcher and interview participant, which in turn may decrease attrition and missing data.

## The Stockholm Life-Course Project: A Case Study

As you have already seen, we use an authentic research project as our illustrative example. Our intention with this is to better aid the reader when it comes to grasping the main ideas, findings, and approaches of life-course criminology. In the coming chapters we include tables, diagrams, and interview extracts to illustrate the various facets of the criminal career. We introduce The Stockholm Life-Course Project (SLCP) here, however, because it has the same features as many life-course criminological studies. It is a study we are both actively involved in as researchers.

The SLCP is a mixed method, longitudinal research project, with the main purpose of exploring features of crime and the life course, including persistence, desistance, and intermittency. It consists of several different samples of individuals, but here we focus on the two 'core' samples: The Clientele Boys and the §12 Youth (young inmates of special youth institutions – Swedish form of reform schools). These are the ones we have studied most intensively, and the ones we have been able to interview.

## The 1956 Clientele Study of Juvenile Delinquents

The 1956 Clientele Study of Juvenile Delinquents ('The Clientele Study') was commissioned by the Swedish Parliament in the mid-1950s, due to the concern for the then increasing rate of juvenile delinquency in Sweden (see SOU, 1971:49 for further details). It was decided on by the Swedish government in 1956 (thus the name) and launched in 1959, with the main purpose of understanding the causes of delinquency. In total, 287 boys born in Stockholm 1943–51 were enrolled in the study; 192 of the boys had been recorded for at least one nontrivial offense (almost exclusively theft) prior to age 15, and constituted the delinquent group. The remaining 95 boys constituted a matched control group. They were matched on age, social group, family type, and neighborhood type, but had no known criminal history. To ensure that there were significant differences in *actual* offending between those recorded and not recorded for criminal offending by the police, Elmhorn (see SOU, 1969:1) conducted one of the first Swedish self-report studies of delinquency. She found that there indeed were considerable differences in actual offending between those recorded and not recorded by the police (boys who were officially recorded for at least one crime reported a significantly higher degree of involvement in crime than boys who were not).

Additionally, another 187 individuals (called *shadows*) were studied, however, only with the help of register data. The intention was to study possible interviewer effects that arose from participation in the study.

The idea was to compensate the low number of cases with the extensive and interdisciplinary studies conducted on each boy. The original study consists of around 2,000 variables and was reported in a series of state-official publications, authored by some of the most prominent Swedish psychiatrists, psychologists, and sociologists at the time, including people like Gösta Carlsson, Kristina Humble, and Gustav Jonsson (see SOU, 1971:49; SOU, 1972:76; SOU, 1973:25; SOU, 1973:49; SOU, 1974:31). Different teams (medical, psychiatric, psychological, social psychological, and sociological) collected a variety of data using an array of methods. For example, the sociological study included interviews with the Boys' parents, teachers, the Clientele Boys themselves, as well as register data, whereas the data in the psychiatric and psychological parts was obtained almost exclusively through judgments by the research personnel and different kinds of tests. The Boys' recorded and self-reported delinquency was also included.

Findings from the original study included a strong correlation between delinquency and important psychosocial and psychological variables (Sarnecki, 1985). For example, the researchers found a strong correlation between a 'laissez-faire' or erratic upbringing and delinquency. Similarly, low school adjustment/attachment was significantly related to juvenile delinquency. At the individual level, early conduct disorder and/or 'antisocial' potential were common risk factors. Other independent variables – social group, family type, and other 'standard' sociological variables – showed moderate correlations to delinquency (Sarnecki, 1985). In that sense, the original study's findings were (and are) consistent with much of the well-known risk factors for delinquency (Farrington and Welsh, 2007; Hirschi, 1969): factors 'within' the individual as well as social factors related to school, family, and peer life were associated with delinquency.

Every research project is inevitably dependent on the broader, intellectual context within which it is born. This context informs the research process in many ways, and The Clientele Study was no exception. Here, we only highlight three such elements of the initial study. First of all, the study only included boys. At the time this was a common research practice (e.g. Hirschi, 1969), as the rate of delinquency among girls was so low that it was not considered a social problem. However, in order to explain the causes of delinquency, it would seem equally beneficial to include those who show a relatively high degree of non-delinquent behavior (Messerschmidt, 1993).

Second, when it came to enrollment in the study, we noted above that the crime type was exclusively theft and not, for example, violence. The original researchers elaborated, as mentioned above, on this choice and argued that violence was not a particularly pressing problem; violence was considered a means boys used to solve conflicts. This, of course, must be understood as dependent on the social context of the time, when the main 'crime problem' was framed in terms of theft (see von Hofer, 2008). Since the early 1960s, a changed perception of teenage violence has occurred. Today, teenage violence is considered a serious social problem and at the individual level it is a problematic risk factor. In our study, due to this contingency, we have almost no data to explore the issue of violent boys, and violence careers.

Finally, some of the measures and examinations included in the original study reflect the intellectual research trends of the time: Rorschach tests were done in the psychological part of the study, and the psychiatrists examined the boys' skulls and documented any anomalous shapes or forms they found (*not*, we should add, in the vein of eugenics but in search of various forms of former head traumas). Rorschach tests have largely been discarded today and, while offenders' neuropsychological features are still regarded as important potential risk factors by some (Moffitt, 1993; Raine, 2013; Walsh, 2009), they are measured in other, more sophisticated ways. As some have pointed out, risk assessment methods and tools have developed considerably over time (Hoge et al., 2012), and tests made in the psychiatric and psychological parts of the original study may be somewhat outdated.

Around 20 years later, Sarnecki (1985, 1990) conducted a follow-up study of the Clientele Boys, who were now approaching middle-age. The delinquent group was then divided into two groups, D1 (n=131) and D2 (n=61). In the D1 group, every boy was known by the police to have committed at least one crime prior to age 15. In the D2 group, the boys were known by the police to have committed two or more crimes prior to age 15. Sarnecki collected register data on the 287 + 187[1] men's health (including mortality), education and employment history, criminal history, drug use, and household status, among other things. Sarnecki's main interest was social exclusion, or 'social maladjustment'. His findings mirror those of contemporary life-course criminology: in the group of serious juvenile delinquents (the D2 group) 30 percent were considered well or very well-adjusted as adults. For the D1 group, over half the group (55%) were considered living well-adjusted lives. That being said, he also found a striking degree of continuity in problem behavior over time: the risk of being socially maladjusted in adulthood was three times as high for boys being recorded for one crime prior to age 15 compared to those who were not recorded at all, and five times as high for boys with two or more recorded offenses.

Sarnecki compared the forecasts and diagnoses that were made in the original study with the examined men's social adaptation 20 years later. It turned out that the psychological tests made in childhood which were based on psychodynamic theory had the lowest prediction ability. The highest predictive value came from observations of the boys' actual behavior, not least those that were made by the teachers in the school environment. Sarnecki (1985) also noted that with the help of the risk factors that the researchers had access to when the individuals were under age 15, one could find the group of individuals with very high risks of very

---

[1] That is, the main population and the shadows.

serious maladjustment, including serious drug addiction. However, even in this group with very high relative risk, the proportion of serious drug users was not higher than 40 percent. A substantial proportion of individuals with high risk lives in childhood turned out to live well-adjusted lives 20 years later.

As part of this follow-up, Sarnecki and his research group also collected long, semi-structured interviews with 199 of the men. The focus here, aside from the individual's life history in a variety of areas, was on the contingencies of social adjustment and attitudes toward society, religion, parenthood, and other social institutions (Sarnecki, 1990). In the new follow-up we launched in 2010, we had access to not only data from the original study, but also the register and interview data Sarnecki collected in the 1980s. In our follow-up we collected new, extensive register data on all 287 men, including criminal records, health and medical records, employment history, relationship history, and many other things.

In the figures below, we show a number of descriptive trajectories for the D1, D2, and Control groups, ages 15 to 65 (mortality and crime) and 20 to 65 (physical and mental health). What we have done here is thus to single out individuals who have (a) no, (b) one, and (c) two or more recorded crimes prior to age 15. As you can see in Figures 4.1 to 4.4, there are marked differences between the groups in a variety of life domains; in terms of cumulative mortality, mean number of convicted offenses, and when it comes to indicators of physical and mental health, the D2 group seems to fare significantly worse than the other two groups.

In the next chapter, we return to the 187 delinquent boys (the D1 and D2 groups) and use another tool – that of risk factors – to explore their criminal trajectories in a slightly different way.

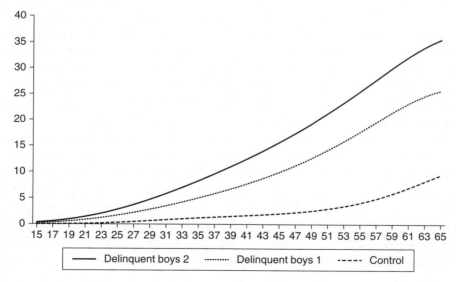

**Figure 4.1** Cumulative mortality rate for individuals in the D1 (n=131), D2 (n=61), and C (n=95) groups, ages 15 to 65

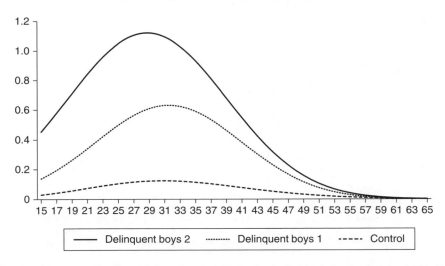

**Figure 4.2** Mean number of convicted offenses for individuals in the D1 (n=131), D2 (n=61), and C (n=95) groups, ages 15 to 65

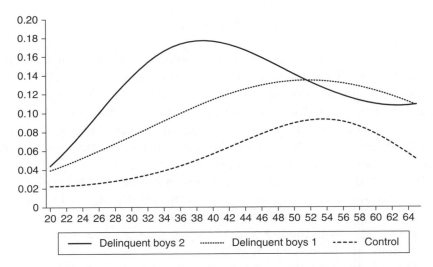

**Figure 4.3** Mean number of hospital admissions due to physical problems for individuals in the D1 (n=131), D2 (n=61), and C (n=95) groups, ages 20 to 65

In the new follow-up we launched in 2010, we also conducted new, long life-history interviews with a sub-set of the 199 men, aiming for depth rather than breadth, setting our goal to 30 interviews, that is, slightly more than 10 percent of the total original sample. In total, we conducted interviews with 30 men, drawing cases from the D1, D2 and control group to get variation. Some men we interviewed only once, but several men were interviewed twice, some three times, one four, and one five. The reasons for this were often practical, since it is difficult to do more than two interview hours in one sitting.

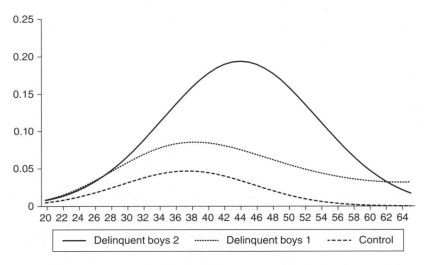

**Figure 4.4** Mean number of hospital admissions due to mental health problems for individuals in the D1 (n=131), D2 (n=61), and C (n=95) groups, ages 20 to 65

## The §12 Youth Group

The study was originally based on a Stockholm sample of women and men (n=420), born 1969–74: 298 were male; 122 were female. During 1990–4 they were subject to interventions by the Swedish social services under the Care of Young Persons (Special Provisions Act), for residential treatment in so-called 'youth homes', or '§12 homes' then operated by The Stockholm County Council.[2] Under this law, the State has the right to detain and treat young people involved in serious juvenile delinquency, substance misuse, and/or 'other socially destructive behavior'. Sarnecki (1996) constructed 'problem profiles' of the sample through a factor analysis. While other socially destructive behavior (such as truancy, promiscuity, prostitution, etc.) was the main reason for intervention when it came to the girls, the boys where mainly subject to intervention due to serious juvenile delinquency.

In a follow-up study made in 1998–9, when the sample was 24 to 29 years old, 132 of the 420 (31%) were interviewed. Due to practical reasons, no official publications were produced and thus closer documentation of this follow-up is missing. In 2010, we launched a second follow-up study on the original 420. Aside from collecting the same register data on all 420 as we did on the Clientele Men, we also contacted 118 of the 132 that were interviewed in the previous

---

[2] Today these homes are directed by The Swedish National Board of Institutional Care, which was founded in 1993 and took charge of the 'youth homes' in April 1994. It is (and was at the time of the initial study) considered a powerful intervention/sanction to be directed at juvenile delinquents in Sweden, including incarceration and severe restrictions.

follow-up. The remaining 14 had either died, or could not be located even after extensive searches. In total, life history interviews were conducted with 45 of the 118 (37%). Their structure followed the interviews we did with the Clientele Men. Twenty-five men and 20 women were interviewed, some only once but several people we interviewed multiple times. For this book we have only used the interviews we conducted with the men.

We did a descriptive sketch of the recorded criminal careers of the 420 using conviction data from The National Council of Crime Prevention (see Begler et al., 2011). In this sketch we outlined the age/crime curves of both the men and the women in the original study, beginning at age 15 and following them to age 35. For (1) any offense, (2) theft, and (3) violence both the men and the women followed the expected age/crime curve with a high prevalence in adolescence and then a steep decrease toward adulthood. When it came to drug-related convictions, however, the age/crime curve took a somewhat different shape, with a later peak and a slower decrease. Here, as expected, the level-difference between men and women was also smaller than for the other crime types (see Steffensmeier et al., 2005b).

Although a sample of serious juvenile delinquents, their recorded offending – at a group level – thus tends to take the typical form identified by criminal career research and life-course criminology. The same can be said about the Clientele Men.

## Retrospective or Prospective?

An interesting question emerges with The SLCP: is the research project retrospective or prospective? We do have repeated measures of the same (or at least very similar) constructs over time, but the time between the measurements is substantial, covering many years. This is sometimes the case in longitudinal research. In the original Clientele study, the researchers wanted to trace the boys' lives from the age of around 15, and all the way back to their birth. Simultaneously, in the 1980s follow-up, the men's lives were reconstructed from around age 40 all the way back to their childhood. In 2010, the interviews we conducted were similarly retrospective.

We would argue that The SLCP is thus both retrospective and prospective, even though we have several 'waves' of data collection at different stages in the participants' lives. The main advantage of this, is that it is possible to somewhat validate the men's life histories. For example, when it comes to their childhood experiences: do the men talk about them in the same way in 2010, as they did in the 1980s? That is an interesting question, and it turns out that by and large, they tended to do so. It does definitely not settle the question of how memories can blur the past, but it did give us some confidence as we went about analyzing the new interviews.

At the same time, our register data on crime, health, economic conditions, education, etc., are in themselves constructed prospectively, as these different conditions are registered by the authorities as they occur in time.

## What Do You Want to Know?

Life-course criminology is a research enterprise where longitudinal methodology is utilized in various ways: some use only quantitative data and try to uncover continuity and change in criminal careers by studying official records, specifically made tests, assessments, and/or self-report surveys. Others use qualitative life history interviews to explore the complexity and processual nature of human life. Some studies combine both quantitative and qualitative methods.

Every method has its strengths, but also its weaknesses. The basic question any potential life-course researcher should start with is: what do I want to know? Beginning with the research question is the scientific ideal and it gets you a long way. The next issue to pursue is whether a method or set of data already exists – or is possible to collect – to answer that question for you. If there is not, you rethink the research question somewhat.

If you, already at the outset, are faced with a given set of data, whether quantitative and qualitative, a good starting point is to explore the data: what are the characteristics of the sample? What information does it include? Has the information been collected prospectively or retrospectively? Answering these questions simultaneously provides you with the limits and possibilities inherent in the data. That was what we did when we first got our hands on the data that eventually became The SLCP; a research project we use in the subsequent chapters to illustrate and highlight important life-course criminological themes.

Being pragmatic is not always desirable, but in social research, and life-course research in particular, it is often the only possible way forward.

## Suggestions for Further Reading

Giele, Janet Z and Elder, Glen H. Jr. (1998) *Methods of Life Course Research. Qualitative and Quantitative Approaches*. Thousand Oaks, CA: SAGE.
This volume collects a number of influential (mainly sociological) life-course researchers and their takes on the methodologies of life-course research, including a chapter on integrating qualitative and quantitative data written by life-course criminologists Sampson and Laub.

Biljeveld, Catrien, C. J. H. and van der Kamp, Leo J. Th. (1998) *Longitudinal Data Analysis: Designs, Models, and Methods*. London: SAGE.

In this volume, the authors provide a thorough introduction to longitudinal data analysis.

Nagin, Daniel S. (2005) *Group-Based Modeling of Development*. Cambridge, MA: Harvard University Press.

In this book, Nagin introduces and outlines the technique of group-based modeling, which today is nearly a standard, quantitative method in the field of life-course criminology.

Atkinson, Robert G. (1998) *The Life Story Interview*. Thousand Oaks, CA: SAGE.

This is a brief introduction to the life story interview, probably the most common, qualitative life-course criminological method.

# 5

# RISK AND PREDICTION OF CRIMINAL CAREERS

Now we start the clock. Beginning in this chapter, we move through the different stages of the criminal career. Here is a good place to remind the reader that while these chapters are written to stand for themselves, they are also more than the sum of their parts: to get a sense of the sequentiality of crime and the life course – how each stage is contingent on the one that precedes it and unfolds toward and into the future – it may be beneficial to read them in sequence.

As we start the clock, we do so at the very beginning: with the phenomenon and concept of *risk*, and *risk factors*. We begin by defining risk factors and outlining the dynamics between risk and the criminal career. Finally, we turn to the heart of the enterprise of risk factor studies, namely, the possibility of making predictions of future criminal offending.

## Defining Risk Factors

In general, a risk is the probability that something (often considered undesirable) will occur in the future. Thus, we can talk about the risk of a car driver in Sweden having an accident in the next year, or cigarette smokers' increased risk of dying from lung cancer. In the latter case, cigarette smoking is the independent variable that occurs before the onset of, and is positively correlated to, the dependent variable (lung cancer). In other words, cigarette smoking is a risk factor for lung cancer.

Risk factors for crime can then be understood as 'events or conditions that are associated with an increased probability of disruptive or delinquent behavior' (Loeber et al., 2009: 293). These events or conditions can operate at different levels – such as the individual, family, or social – and a range of risk factors have been found to correlate with future criminal offending in previous studies. We go through these later in this chapter. For now, to grasp risk factors and the debate(s) surrounding them, it is important to look at a seemingly minor point in the above definition: risk factors are events or conditions that are associated with an *increased probability* of delinquency. In other words, risk factors are *predictive* of future criminal behavior. Straight away, then, we encounter the issue of time: a risk factor is something that is present in an individual's life *prior* to his or her onset of offending, and increases the probability that later offending will occur. This does not mean that they *cause* crime, but only that an individual exposed to a given risk factor is – compared to another, identical individual who is *not* exposed to that factor – at a relatively higher risk of offending.

Aside from being predictive of offending, risk factors also tend to come in *clusters*. What we mean by this is quite simple: social arrangements tend to mesh together. That is, problems in one sphere of life, such as the family, are often accompanied by problems in other spheres, such as the school. Risk factors are also very often *cumulative*. By using this term, we aim to capture the finding that a higher risk for criminal offending occurs when a constellation of risk factors are present; i.e. the more risk factors an individual is exposed to, the higher the risk of offending. Herrenkohl et al. (2000), for example, found that 10-year-olds exposed to six or more risk factors, were 10 times more likely to commit a crime (in this case, violence) by age 18, compared to 10-year-olds exposed to only one risk factor. Similarly, in a study by Farrington (2002), the percentage of violent boys with multiple problems increased with their risk scores, from around 1 percent of those with no risk factors to around 80 percent of those with at least seven risk factors (see also Appleyard et al., 2005; Atzaba-Poria et al., 2004; Stattin et al., 1997). Using The SLCP data, Sarnecki (1985) showed that boys who had grown up in families with many risk factors (such as an alcoholic father, poor supervision over the boy, poor emotional climate, insecure childhood conditions, low cultural standard, low social class, and low material standard) exhibited significantly greater risk of serious drug use before the age of 35, compared to individuals who grew up without, or only one of, these risk factors. In the high-risk group, the probability of serious drug use was 40 percent. In the low-risk group, less than 1 (!) percent.

Working like this – identifying, measuring, and studying risk factors and their relationship to subsequent crime – is central to a part of life-course criminology and criminal career studies known as the 'risk factor paradigm' (Farrington, 2007). It is an important field of research, but has not been accepted uncritically by all (Case and Haines, 2009).

It is important to note that at its most basic level, a risk factor can be understood as a factorized measure of an individual or social circumstance.

This factorization is made possible through a certain process of data collection, and the factor can then be shown to be statistically related to criminal offending (Case and Haines, 2009). The process of factorization is important, for it highlights the risk factor as a *construct*. This process may be highly complex (involving, for example, a diagnosis based on DSM-V), but the consequence is the same: some aspect of social life is turned into a number, which turns into values on a variable, or a value on an indexed set of variables. While the observed differences between two scores on the variable might be substantial and mirror actual differences in social reality, it is important to note that risk factors still are scientific *constructs*, and dependent on which questions are asked and which are not (Kemshall et al., 2006). Burgess makes a similar point early in the history of US sociology when he questions how intangible facts of life could be apprehended by statistics, giving the example of how affection would be measured between husband and wife, or qualities of personality such as charm and loyalty (Burgess, 1927: 111f; see also Blumer, 1956).

## Risk Factors and Criminal Careers

Typically, criminal career researchers are interested in risk factors that are predictive of onset of crime. Thinking in terms of crime prevention, this is a highly understandable and valuable focus; even the classical theorists of the 18th century argued that it is better to prevent crimes than to punish them (Beccaria, 1764/1983). Thus, if we can identify those risk factors that are most strongly predictive of onset of crime, we can direct interventions focused on counteracting or 'treating' those risk elements, and prevent the individual from engaging in crime at all (so-called secondary prevention).

Recently, however, criminal career studies and life-course criminology have moved beyond the search for early risk factors and also begun to study risk factors that are predictive of other features of the criminal career, such as persistence, or persistence in crime at different ages. Following the logic of a sequential unfolding of human life, it is likely that the risk factors that are predictive of onset may be different from those that predict recidivism and persistence. In this chapter, however, we are predominantly concerned with early risk factors.

It is now generally agreed that early risk factors influence the character of the subsequent criminal career, where those who score high are likely to have an earlier onset of offending (Stattin and Magnusson, 1995) and a longer criminal career characterized by more frequent and serious offending than those who score low (Piquero et al., 2007). Establishing this connection between early risk and the future criminal career is one thing – *explaining* it can be a very different task. Although life-course criminologists sometimes claim that they were the first to stress the need to distinguish between *causal* risk factors and those that are mere correlates (e.g. Farrington, 2007), this is not something new. On the contrary, a highly similar argument was made already by Hirschi (1969: 65):

> Sex, race, social class, neighborhood, mother's employment, the broken home, size of family, and so forth, are the stuff of which most empirical studies, textbooks, and theories of delinquency are constructed. These traditional variables share one thing in common: it is hard to know why they are related to delinquency if they are in fact so related.

Answering Hirschi's question – are the risk factors related to delinquency, and if so, *why and how*: are they causal or merely correlates? – is where theory comes in, and life-course criminological theories deal with early risk factors in different ways (see Chapter 3 for more details).

However, to continue our exploration, before we do anything else, we must outline the specific risk factors found to be predictive of criminal offending. As we start the life-course clock, we must do so while the mother is still carrying the child – in biology.

## Specific Risk Factors

So much risk factor research has been carried out that it is impossible to conduct a full review here. The description that follows is thus very selective and only supposed to cover the most central, empirical findings of the field. It is interesting to note, however, that the significant, predictive risk factors tend to be identical across contexts; those found most relevant in UK- or US-based studies, for example, are also often the most relevant in Scandinavian studies (see Farrington, 2003; Sivertsson and Carlsson, 2015).

### 1. Biological

Is crime inherited through genetics? The answer to this question is less evident than it may seem. Some studies suggest that around 50 percent of the variation in antisocial behavior in a given population can be attributed to genetics (Benson, 2013). This figure, however, is very tentative, and the specific risk factors in such cases are difficult to pinpoint. There is no such thing as a 'crime gene' or anything of the sort. The genetic influences on an individual's criminal offending seem to be the result of multi-genetic, and gene–environment interactions.

One such important interaction concerns the brain's neurotransmitters. Neurotransmitters are, simply put, biochemicals in the brain, which allow different cells of the brain to communicate with one another and as such influence how we feel, think, and perceive our environment. If a given neurotransmitter is improperly balanced (if we have too much or too little of it), we tend to feel, think, and perceive something in one way rather than another (that is, we may for example experience anxiety rather than feeling relaxed, see Benson, 2013). Neurotransmitters are influenced by both genes and the environment, and they come in many kinds but only a few of them seem to be related to crime: those involved in the dopaminergic and serotonergic systems.

The activity of the serotonergic system of the individual is considered to be hooked to Monoaminooxidas enzyme type A (MAO A) that de-compose mono-amines, including serotonin and dopamine. The enzyme encodes a gene with the same name as found on the X chromosome. Research on the relationship between the MAO A system and susceptibility to (violent) crimes in men, how-ever, shows the complexity of the relationship between genetic and environmental risk/protective factors. (Caspi et al., 2002). The Caspi et al. study shows that there is an interaction between low MAO A activity and expo-sure to child abuse in childhood. Individuals who have both low activity in the MAO A system and have been victims of child abuse are at significantly greater risk of committing violent acts than the other, although both low MAO A activity and child abuse in themselves may entail an increase in risk. This can also be expressed so that high MAO A activity protects individuals exposed to childhood traumas against developing a high propensity for violence.

Not all potential biological risk factors are inherited or genetically based. Some of the most important biological risk factors occur as the child lies and develops in the womb, or shortly after birth: prenatal and perinatal complica-tions, including low birth weights, complications during the pregnancy, the mother's drug use while pregnant, and poor nutrition, have all been shown to be related to subsequent onset of crime. The same applies to damage to the central nervous system (such as the frontal lobe) generated by traumatic violence or otherwise (e.g. Raine, 2013).

## 2. Psychological

Just as the biological and neurological disposition of the individual matters, so too does his or her psychological features. At this level, a considerable amount of research has been undertaken and one of the most influential studies in this regard is the Cambridge Study in Delinquent Development. At age 8 to 10, Farrington (2003) shows, a hyperactivity-impulsivity-attention deficit is inde-pendently and significantly predictive of future offending. This deficit manifests itself in the individual having poor concentration skills, restlessness, being daring and risk-taking, and suffering from psychomotor impulsivity. Similarly, low intelligence and low school achievement, displaying learning disabilities and anxiety, and early aggressiveness are strong predictors of an early onset of crim-inal offending (Lipsey and Derzon, 1998). These risk factors go very well in line with theories such as Moffitt's and Gottfredson and Hirschi's (in the latter case, as indicators of low self-control). It should be noted that some psychological risk factors may partly or completely have biological roots.

### 3. Family Risk Factors

In life-course criminology, for an understanding of the path that leads to onset of crime, family-based risk factors may be the most generally accepted. It is included as a crucial element of the individual's development of low self-control (Gottfredson and Hirschi, 1990), in the gene–environment interaction of the development of the life-course persister in Moffitt's taxonomy (1993), as well as in Sampson and Laub's (1993) control theory.

Individuals who come from broken homes, homes with a low socioeconomic status, or large family size have additional risk factors here, but, importantly, how the family functions seems to be crucial: poor parental supervision, harsh and/or inconsistent discipline, abuse/maltreatment/neglect, and family conflict are very strong predictors of future criminal behavior (Smith and Thornberry, 1995; Widom, 1989; in The SLCP, see Olofsson, 1971; Sarnecki, 1985). It is important to point out that the problems in parents' poor ability to bring up and supervise their children are often related to the parents' own problems such as crime, substance abuse, mental illness, and poverty. Numerous studies have shown that parental criminality is one of the most powerful predictors of an individual's future deviance (Farrington, 1996). In other words, family functioning is a significant 'contributor to the present and future behavior of youths' (Lab, 2014: 201), and its importance cannot be understated. The same can be said about the following set of factors.

### 4. Peer Factors

For a young person, peers have a powerful effect on his or her behavior, as well as on how he or she perceives the world (Warr, 2002). Research shows that proximity to, and association with, delinquent peers (and siblings) are strong predictors of future offending (McGloin, 2009). Of particular interest here – not least from a policy perspective – is the influence that gang membership exercises on the individual. This form of peer influence is strongly related to higher levels of offending, but this research, we must note, mainly comes from an Anglo-Saxon context, where the 'gang issue' may be more prominent than in, say, Northern Europe (e.g. Esbensen and Huizinga, 1993; for a European perspective, see Sarnecki, 2005).

### 5. School Factors

In 1969, Hirschi argued that schools and academic participation were important factors that kept the young person away from crime. We know that low academic achievement, low school attachment, dropping out and/or being suspended or expelled are significant risk factors (which tend to cluster together, in the sense that if you have one of these you are more likely to have one or several of the others as well). These factors all concern the individual's relation to his or her school.

School failure, measured in the form of incomplete grades from compulsory education, is one of the most powerful indicators of future persistent crime and serious drug abuse, according to Gauffin et al. (2013). Similarly, of all the predictors of future social adjustment among the boys in the older part of The SLCP, class teachers' assessments of the student's future had the greatest predictive value of future criminal offending (Sarnecki, 1985).

However, the school in itself may be a risk factor, following the logic of Rutter et al. (1979), who developed the idea of *effective schools*. Such schools are characterized by, among other things, effective classroom management, high teacher expectations, teachers as positive role models, positive feedback and treatment of students, good working conditions for the staff and students, and shared staff–student activities. A school that does not have any of these elements, may, in a sense, take less care of its students and, as such, not be able to exercise an effective social control upon them – in other words, it may be less effective in preventing an individual from engaging in crime.

On the other hand, well-functioning schools may, to some extent, be able to compensate for the disadvantages students from problem families would otherwise get in the school environment (Losel and Farrington, 2012; for a Swedish example, see Sandahl, 2014). As we saw in Chapter 3, this is one of the basic themes in Gottfredson and Hirschi's (1990) argument.

## 6. Neighborhood and Community Factors

Above the directly relational level (as in the individual's relation to his or her family, school, and peers), we have an additional set of risk factors: those that are located in the individual's local community and neighborhood. As we mentioned in Chapter 2, the importance of place was suggested and explored in the childhood of modern criminology by Shaw and McKay (1942). Since then, much research has been devoted to it, including influential studies by Bursik (1988), Wikström and Loeber (2000), and Sampson (2013). These and other studies have consistently shown that problems in the community – such as economic deprivation, disorder and incivility, poor neighborhood integration, the availability of firearms, and level of gang activity – contribute to individual deviance (Lab, 2014). Most likely, these factors' relationship to crime is *indirect*. That is, in line with Sampson and Laub's (1993) reasoning, a factor such as economic deprivation is connected to crime, but mediated by factors at a 'lower' level, such as low social control in the family or school.

## A Brief Summary and Discussion

To repeat, our review of specific risk factors has by no means attempted to be exhaustive, only instructive. As the reader may have noticed, a variety of risk factors in several domains of life have been shown to be predictive of future criminal offending. Remember, however, that risk factors tend to come in clusters – that is, problems in one sphere of life tend to be accompanied by problems in other spheres as well. So, to give a concrete example, an individual's concentration problems are likely to be correlated to a low school achievement and low school attachment may be connected to truancy, which in turn makes it possible for the individual to associate with delinquent peers. Rather than focusing too much on any specific risk factor, a holistic approach is likely to be more useful in understanding a young person's pathway into crime.

It could be argued, of course, that the manifest problem at one level is merely an indicator of a more latent problem at a 'deeper' level: association with delinquent peers can, for example, be an indicator of the psychological tendency of being risk-taking and sensation-seeking, which, in turn, can be an indicator of having a low at-rest heart rate (Raine, 2013). This chain of risk can be quite simple but, possibly, also quite complex, and the specific ways in which risk factors may interact – or merely be manifest symptoms of a latent, underlying factor – have just recently been given attention.

One more thing needs to be mentioned here, and it concerns the finding that family-, school-, and peer-related risk factors are very strong predictors of offending. The specific mechanism – that is, *how* these risk factors contribute to criminal offending – is a question for theory. Is low educational achievement an indicator of low self-control (Gottfredson and Hirschi's position), or antisocial behavior (Moffitt's take), or is it an indicator of low social control, where the individual considers there is nothing to lose by doing poorly in school (Sampson and Laub's position)?

Whatever theory we turn to, however, to be properly understood, we must begin by placing family-, school-, and peer-related risk factors within a general life-course framework. Simply put, in childhood and adolescence, the spheres of one's family, school, and peers tend to be dominant in one's everyday life; that is, life is to a large extent taking place and unfolding on those arenas. It is thus not surprising that problems in one or more of these spheres also predict offending. As we mentioned above, risk factors are *temporal* in nature: those predictive of offending at one stage in life might be insignificant or non-existent at another stage.

# Gender and Risk Factors

Extensive reviews of risk factor studies show that delinquent girls and boys tend to come from families characterized by conflicts and disruption, low incomes, large size, convicted parents, delinquent siblings, harsh discipline and poor parental supervision, suffer from mental health problems, attend schools where delinquency rates are high, more frequently than other adolescents drink large amounts of alcohol and consume drugs, and, much more often than non-delinquents, have experiences of victimization, including sexual abuse (Belknap and Holsinger, 2006; Odgers and Morretti, 2002; Rutter et al., 1998). There thus appears to be a considerable amount of commonality in risk factors across genders (see Rowe et al., 1995).

However, a more in-depth look shows that there are also gender-specific dimensions to such results. For example, we are often not dealing with the presence or absence of a risk factor, but rather the *severity* or *impact* of that factor. This is evident when it comes to (sexual) abuse as a potential risk factor for future offending. Smith and Thornberry (1995) found that documented child maltreatment prior to age 12 predicted both self-reported and official delinquency in both girls and boys. Here, differences between genders were not present (see also Moffitt et al., 2001). In a large study of 908 individuals, on the other hand, Widom found that girls with experiences of abuse or neglect were twice as likely to have an adult crime record (in Chesney-Lind and Pasko, 2013), a result also found among boys but much weaker when compared to girls (a finding replicated by Belknap and Holsinger, 2006). Studies show similar results for indicators of mental health as a risk factor for delinquency: it often strongly predicts offending in girls but not always for boys, and when it does predict offending across genders, it has a stronger predictive power for girls than for boys (Belknap and Holsinger, 2006: 51; Cernkovich et al., 2008; Gibbs, 1981).

When studies are based on high-risk samples, a greater number of risk factors tend to be more present among girls, and have a greater impact on girls than boys. This has been understood as a methodological problem of selection mechanisms, as agencies such as the criminal justice system and the social services can be seen as 'protecting' girls from environments considered dangerous or damaging (for a Swedish example of this argument, see Molero Samuelson, 2011). It has thus been suggested that these findings are not replicated in samples of general populations. However, a review by Farrington and Painter (2004) includes only large-scale community studies, and one of their main findings is that the distribution of risk factors across the genders is *non-symmetric* (girls and women tend to score higher, and on a greater number of factors, than boys do). Similarly, in a Scandinavian context, using data from the Stockholm Birth Cohort, Estrada and Nilsson (2009: 16) found that 'the small group of females who commit offenses repeatedly constitute a more highly selected (poorly resourced) group than the corresponding group of males'. There are thus good empirical reasons to believe that the relationship (that girls score higher, and on a greater number of factors) also holds for general populations.

Thus, girls and boys seem to share a majority of risk factors, but distinct *differences* between girls and boys also emerge, specifically concerning mental health and (sexual) abuse, which tend to be much more common risk factors for girls, but not non-existent for boys. Also, although the factors may be the same across genders, girls who engage in delinquency tend to have a *greater number* of risk factors than boys, and tend to *score higher* on most of those factors.

It can thus be assumed that in any given case – all else being equal – girls more than boys will constitute a more marginalized group, characterized by social exclusion and low economic resources (Estrada and Nilsson, 2012).

# Risk Factors and Prediction

The study of risk factors can be used in mainly two ways, one that is theoretical and one that is practical.

First, understanding what, how, and why risk factors affect the future criminal career can help us untangle the causal mechanisms involved when people engage in crime. Second, risk factors can be used to prospectively predict whether or not individuals will (1) engage in crime or not, and (2) if they will engage in crime, whether or not they have a risk of persisting in crime once they have started. The main policy implication here is that society can save costs with crime prevention strategies targeted at those individuals at risk of developing a long and voluminous criminal career. In other words – to cite the title of a well-known book – we can use risk factors to save children from a life of crime (Farrington and Welsh, 2007).

There is, however, also a well-known paradox inherent in the skewed crime distribution – while antisocial behavior in youth is the best predictor of anti-social behavior in adulthood, most antisocial children do not become antisocial adults (Robins, 1966). Therefore, we are predominantly interested in the potential possibility of prospectively identifying those who in the future will become what some call chronic offenders; that small segment of any offender population (usually between 5 and 10%) who will be responsible for more than 50 percent of all the crimes that population will commit and, thus, cost society a great deal of money and may harm not only others, but themselves as well.

This second way of using risk factors has a potentially profound impact on policy and intervention. In fact, many advocates of risk factor research argue that early risk factors perform exceptionally well in identifying future offenders (see, for example, Farrington et al., 2013). That may be true, depending on what we mean by 'exceptionally well'. Remember, what we are trying to do here is something that is very, very difficult: to predict the future, and not just any future, but the social future – a future which is filled with complexity, contingency, and coincidence.

When it comes to a given prediction, there are four possible outcomes (adopted from Lab, 2014: 195):

1. True positive: something is predicted to occur and it does (a successful prediction).
2. False positive: something is predicted to occur but it does not (a failed prediction).

3. True negative: something is predicted not to occur and it does not (a successful prediction).
4. False negative: something is predicted not to occur but it does (a failed prediction).

As the reader may suspect, outcomes 1 and 3 are the ones we want to achieve when we use various risk factors to predict individuals' future (non-)criminal careers. Consequently, 2 and 4 are the ones we wish to avoid, and for different reasons. In the case of a false positive, we may conduct a powerful and possibly damaging intervention in the life of an individual who will in fact not need it: based on our prediction, we think that s/he will engage in crime, but s/he will in fact not do so. Not only are we wasting money and time, but also we may in fact harm the individual and his/her perception of self. Lownkamp et al. (2006) show, for example, that the same type of treatment measures that provide recidivism-reducing effects on individuals with high risks can increase recidivism for individuals with low risks.

The most extreme consequence here is – in the vein of labeling theory – that the individual 'picks up' the image others have of him or her:

> One of the most crucial steps in the process of building a stable pattern of deviant behavior [i.e. persistence] is likely to be the experience of being caught and publicly labeled as a deviant. Whether a person takes this step or not depends not so much on what he does as on what other people do[.] (Becker, 1963: 31)

In other words, what Lemert (1967) calls a process from primary to secondary deviance may in fact be enforced by our intervention. This possibility, however, is not absolute: research suggests that it has less to do with whether or not we intervene, and more to do with *how* (as in, by what kind of intervention) we do so (Farrington and Murray, 2014).

A false negative is potentially just as damaging. Here, we are concerned with those individuals who, according to our risk factor analysis, are unlikely to engage in crime in the future, but who will in fact do so.

False positives and false negatives are thus an important, potential problem in life-course criminology. But this is all theoretical – how well *do* risk factors work as predictors of future criminal offending, when put to the test in empirical studies? It is to that question we turn now, before we summarize the chapter.

## Using Risk Factors to Predict Criminal Careers

While the issue is not fully set, a contemporary view shared by many is that the issue of false negatives, by and large, is not a problem, at least if we consider the development of long criminal careers (Farrington et al., 2013; Lab, 2014). In other words, the absolute majority of those individuals we predict to *not* develop persistent criminal offending will in fact not do so (exceptions exist, of course).

As we turn to the issue of *false positives*, we enter more problematic – and contested – ground. Research consistently shows that a large part of those prospectively identified to commit crimes in the future will in fact not do so (false positives). West (1982), the founder of the Cambridge Study in Delinquent Development, acknowledges that less than 50 percent of those who *had* a combination of three of the five early risk factors he observed in the study actually did engage in crime in later life. Stattin et al. (1997) found a nearly identical result: almost 46 percent of those categorized as high-risk had no recorded offending at the age of 18. Similar results are found in the majority of studies on risk factors and offending (Lipsey and Derzon, 1998; Spanjaard et al., 2012; White et al., 1990). When it comes to assessing long-term outcomes of risk factors, however, relatively little research has been conducted.

In an attempt at maximizing prediction using a cumulative childhood risk index, Farrington et al. (2013: 57) are able to predict as much as 88.5 percent of the adult offenders, and almost 30 percent of the high-rate chronic offenders. They conclude that 'childhood risk factors alone ... perform exceptionally well in identifying those who evince high rate offending trajectories'. In a similar test of prospective, long-term predictions using cumulative childhood risk factors, Laub and Sampson (2003) too find quantitative differences. Their conclusion, however, is quite the opposite. They state that 'persistent and frequent offending in the adult years is not easily divined from zeroing in on juvenile offenders at risk' (Laub and Sampson, 2003: 100).

What are at stake here are two different theoretical positions on the role and impact of risk factors on the criminal career. It is relatively easy to disentangle risk groups from one another, when criminal offending is studied *retrospectively*. When researchers do this, they first take a sample of individuals and group them together based on their criminal offending. So, we might end up with one group called 'high-frequent offenders', another one called 'classic desisters', and a third called 'intermittent offenders'. As we group these individuals together, and then explore how they scored on early risk factors, we are likely to see an association between criminal offending and risk. So, the classic desisters are, as a group, likely to exhibit lower levels of risk than the high-frequent offenders. This is how Farrington et al. proceed. But, remember, the individuals have been categorized *retrospectively*, once we know how their offending eventually unfolded. A social worker, a child psychologist, or a psychiatrist, who has the task of assessing a child's level of risk, does not have access to this data – only the risk scores. So to truly 'test' the predictive value of risk factors, we must do so prospectively; that is, we must categorize them not according to their future criminal offending but according to their *risk scores*. Having done so, we then study their subsequent criminal offending and compare the outcomes. That is how Laub and Sampson (above) proceed. When you do so, the predictive value of risk factors is much weaker.

In The Stockholm Life-Course Project, we tried to assess the predictive value of risk factors in this latter, prospective way. We were particularly interested in trying to predict any future high-frequent (what some would call 'chronic') offenders. Here is how we did it, and what we found out. We do not claim that this is the 'right' way to assess risk, nor that our findings are more representative or in any way important than are those of other studies; we merely want to show the reader how one can study the impact of risk on the criminal career.

## A Case Study: Testing Risk Factors' Predictive Value

In The Stockholm Life-Course Project, we used the 187 delinquent Clientele Boys to study the impact of risk factors (the results are reported in Sivertsson and Carlsson, 2015, and we base this section thoroughly on this paper). As you may recall from Chapter 4, the delinquent boys had originally been divided into two groups: D1 (boys with one recorded offense prior to age 15) and D2 (boys with two or more recorded offenses prior to age 15). While such a simple classification later in life led to marked differences in a variety of life domains, for this study, we wanted to approach criminal trajectories and the issue of prediction in a somewhat more intricate way.

### Constructing Risk and Risk Groups

We began by going through the quantitative assessments that were conducted in the original study, and trying to single out indicators of those risk factors that according to previous risk factor research seems to have the most impact on crime. Unfortunately, we were unable to account for the biological dimension of risk, as no such data were collected in the original study. This is the case for the vast majority of risk factor studies, so we are far from alone here, but it is still important to acknowledge that our risk factor analysis leaves out this potentially very important part.

In sum, we found indicators of risk at the individual, family, school, and peer levels. The indicators, and their specifics, are listed in Table 5.1.
Having done so, we followed the assumption of risk being cumulative, and constructed a number of risk groups. We dichotomized each index so that those scoring in the lowest quartile (i.e. high risk) were the ones characterized as having experienced risk in that particular dimension.

In Table 5.2, the risk dimensions have been added for every individual. Here it becomes obvious that risk should be viewed as a relative concept: within this sample almost half (46%) are characterized as experiencing no

**Table 5.1** The four dimensions of risk

| Dimension | Concept | Measures | Source | Scale | Missing | Missing % |
|---|---|---|---|---|---|---|
| Individual | Childhood temperament | Aggressiveness | Teacher interview | 1–5 | 3 | 1.6 |
| | Moral judgment | Mendacity | Teacher interview | 1–5 | 8 | 4.3 |
| | Destructiveness | Destructiveness | Teacher interview | 1–5 | 8 | 4.3 |
| | Social information processing | Attention and concentration problems | Teacher interview | 1–5 | 3 | 1.6 |
| | Sense of order | Sense of order | Teacher interview | 1–5 | 3 | 1.6 |
| | Depression | Emotional balance | Teacher interview | 1–5 | 3 | 1.6 |
| | Impulsivity | Motor restlessness | Teacher interview | 1–5 | 8 | 4.3 |
| | Intelligence | IQ (Terman-Merrill) | Test | Points | 0 | 0.0 |
| Family | Parental supervision | Supervision of parents | Home interview | 1–5 | 0 | 0.0 |
| | Caring | Caring | Home interview | 1–5 | 0 | 0.0 |
| | Consistency in the upbringing | Consistency in the upbringing | Home interview | 1–5 | 0 | 0.0 |
| | Punitive discipline | Punitive discipline | Home interview | 1–5 | 0 | 0.0 |
| | Togetherness/interaction between parents | Togetherness/interaction between parents | Home interview | 1–5 | 0 | 0.0 |
| | Congruency between parents | Congruency between parents | Home interview | 1–5 | 29 | 15.5 |
| | Emotional home climate | Emotional home climate | Home interview | 1–5 | 1 | 0.5 |
| | Antisocial father | Convicted father/stepfather | Records | 0–3 | 0 | 0.0 |
| | Poverty | Material standard of the home | Records | 1–5 | 14 | 7.5 |
| School | School performance in relation to capacity | School performance in relation to capacity | Teacher interview | 1–5 | 3 | 1.6 |
| | Adaption in school | Adaption in school | Teacher interview | 1–5 | 3 | 1.6 |
| | Attachment to school | Adaption to rules | Teacher interview | 1–5 | 3 | 1.6 |
| | Commitment to school | Ambition | Teacher interview | 1–5 | 3 | 1.6 |
| | Truancy | Truancy | Teacher interview | 1–5 | 11 | 5.9 |
| | Educational attainment | Average grades in reading subjects | Records | Points | 13 | 7.0 |
| Peers | Antisocial peers | Criminality among peers | Home interview | 1–5 | 22 | 11.8 |
| | Best friends criminality | Best friends criminality | Home interview | 1–5 | 44 | 23.5 |

risk. This should not be interpreted in absolute terms, especially considering the offender-based sample. Using this categorization only five of the delinquents (or 2.7%) experience high risk in all four dimensions. Due to the small proportions we combined the ones experiencing three and four risk dimensions into a high-risk group, which thus consists of 21 delinquents (11.2% of the whole sample). Considering the offender-based sample, it is reasonable to assume that those experiencing risk in only three dimensions are in a group consisting of high-risk individuals.

**Table 5.2** The prevalence of risk among delinquents

| No. risk dimensions | n | % | Cum. % | Risk group |
|---|---|---|---|---|
| 0 | 86 | 46.0 | 46.0 | 1 |
| 1 | 42 | 22.5 | 68.4 | 2 |
| 2 | 38 | 20.3 | 88.8 | 3 |
| 3 | 16 | 8.6 | 97.3 | 4 |
| 4 | 5 | 2.7 | 100.0 | 4 |
| Total | 187 | 100,0 | | |

## Criminal Offending

Now we have constructed our independent variable; that is, risk. Next, we must turn to our outcome, or dependent variable: criminal offending from age 15 to 59. Our source here was official crime records. The official police register of criminal records was available up to 1974, and the prosecution register from 1973 to 2009. We thus have two sources of recorded offending, due to the official restructuring of the Swedish crime statistics that took place at the time, and we therefore separate the trajectories. This is not a problem, as we are interested in comparing the groups on their *patterns* and not on the absolute incidence levels at every age.

From the overall concept of crime we excluded trivial offenses, such as driving without a license and not paying car taxes. Crime was further divided into different crime types: violence, theft, and narcotics. *Violence* includes acts recorded as threats, assault, manslaughter, rape, murder, and armed robbery, while *theft* includes larceny, grand theft auto, and shoplifting. *Narcotics* consists of illegal possession, distribution, production, and/or use of substances classified as narcotic.

We present the outcome with two features that are common in criminal career research, that is, prevalence and incidence (Piquero et al., 2007). Prevalence is calculated so that individuals who have had at least one recorded crime in a given age period are counted as one (1) and all the others as null (0). Incidence is calculated as the mean frequency of recorded offenses for all of the individuals during the actual age interval.

## Cumulative Risk and Crime Over the Life Course

We begin by comparing the four risk groups on prevalence and incidence outcomes counted on the whole studied life span, from age 15 to 59. As can be seen in Table 5.3, there are marked differences between the risk groups. Around 80 percent of the individuals in the high-risk group have been recorded for at least one non-trivial crime after adolescence, compared to around 40 percent of those with the lowest risk. Counted as incidence a person in the high-risk group has on average been recorded for 23 crimes, where the corresponding number in the low-risk group is around four crimes. For prevalence and incidence, a comparison between the four risk groups reveals an almost linear relationship. However, it is important to note that while there is a pattern that follows the assumption of a cumulative risk effect, almost 20 percent of the high-risk group are *not* recorded for a crime after age 15, whereas 40 percent of the low-risk group *are*.

**Table 5.3** Prevalence and incidence figures of different crime types by risk group (ages 15–59). Pearson Chi-Square test statistic on prevalence figures and Kruskal-Wallis test statistic on incidence figures **** = significant at the .001 level; * = significant at the .05 level

| | Low | | Medium-low | | Medium-high | | High | | Chi-Square |
|---|---|---|---|---|---|---|---|---|---|
| | N = 86 | | N = 42 | | N = 38 | | N = 21 | | df = 3, n = 187 |
| *Overall crime* | | | | | | | | | |
| Prevalence | 39.5 | | 50.0 | | 76.3 | | 81.0 | | 21.3*** |
| Incidence (S.d.) | 4.3 | (16.1) | 7.0 | (22.3) | 16.4 | (28.6) | 23.5 | (30.8) | 34.5*** |
| *Violent* | | | | | | | | | |
| Prevalence | 7.0 | | 19.0 | | 21.1 | | 52.4 | | 24.6*** |
| Incidence (S.d.) | 0.3 | (1.2) | 0.4 | (1.2) | 0.6 | (1.4) | 1.3 | (2.5) | 22.6*** |
| *Property* | | | | | | | | | |
| Prevalence | 14.0 | | 26.2 | | 47.4 | | 66.7 | | 30.0*** |
| Incidence (S.d.) | 1.2 | (7.2) | 3.0 | (10.8) | 6.2 | (13.8) | 7.8 | (12.9) | 34.3*** |
| *Narcotic* | | | | | | | | | |
| Prevalence | 8.1 | | 16.7 | | 26.3 | | 28.6 | | 9.4* |
| Incidence (S.d.) | 0.7 | (3.4) | 0.7 | (2.1) | 2.3 | (6.0) | 0.9 | (1.8) | 9.5* |

Figures 5.1 and 5.2 below show incidence trajectories of our four risk groups. Deceased individuals were censored after the age period when death took place. We illustrate the criminal histories in two separate charts, due to the

differences in counting crimes between our two registers. Figures 5.1 and 5.2 thus show the development in recorded incidence from age 15 to 23 (adolescence to young adulthood) and age 30 to 59 (adulthood) respectively, that is, the time periods where every individual in our sample is able to be recorded for a crime (i.e. exposure) given their year of birth and the records collected from the official police register of criminal records, and the prosecution register.

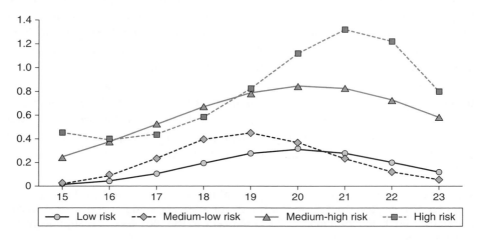

**Figure 5.1** Desistance from crime in four risk groups, ages 15–23. Mean number of recorded offenses/year and individual, among delinquent boys in the Clientele Study (Sivertsson and Carlsson, 2015). The groups have been divided into four risk groups based on 26 risk variables collected in their youth

In Figure 5.1 we see that from age 15 there is an increase in recorded offending in all four risk groups, up to late adolescence/young adulthood where they peak and thereafter decline. In terms of level, the high-risk group has the highest peak followed by the three other risk groups in the expected order. A difference to be noted is that the high-risk group's peak occurs somewhat later, at age 21, while the other risk groups peak at age 19 or 20.

As can be seen from Figure 5.2, there are overall marked differences between the four risk groups here as well, supporting the notion of a cumulative risk effect stretching into adulthood. The high-risk group has the overall highest incidence, followed by the three others in the expected order. Importantly, however, relatively large differences in recorded offenses become smaller with age. As they approach age 50, the four risk groups hardly differ at all. This declining pattern reflects the notion of desistance as the norm for every group of offenders, despite their level of childhood risk (Sampson and Laub, 2005).

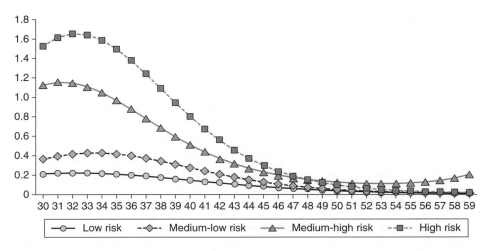

**Figure 5.2** Desistance from crime in four risk groups, ages 30–59. Mean number of recorded offenses/year and individual, among delinquent boys in the Clientele Study (Sivertsson and Carlsson, 2015). The groups have been divided into four risk groups based on 26 risk variables collected in their youth (ages 15–23)

## Predicting High-Frequent Offenders

Finally, we turn to our ability to prospectively identify those that in retrospect became the most frequent offenders in the sample. The high-frequent offenders are defined as the top 10 percent with the most recorded offenses per year alive from age 15 to 59. Table 5.4 shows how the high-frequent offenders are distributed among our four risk groups.

**Table 5.4** The association of risk in youth and high-frequent offending over the life span

|  | Low | Medium-low | Medium-high | High |
|---|---|---|---|---|
|  | N = 86 | N = 42 | N = 38 | N = 21 |
| High frequent offender (N=19) |  |  |  |  |
| Yes | 3 | 4 | 5 | 7 |
| No | 83 | 38 | 33 | 14 |
| *Percentage of risk group within high frequent offenders* | 15.8 | 21.1 | 26.3 | 36.8 |
| *Percentage of high frequent offenders within risk group* | 3.5 | 9.5 | 13.2 | 33.3 |

Seven out of the 19 high frequent offenders (around 37%) did belong to our high-risk group. That is, we can identify a third of the high-frequent offenders with childhood risk factors alone. The result almost replicates the percentage of predicted high-rate chronic offenders based on cumulative childhood risk factors in the Cambridge study (Farrington et al., 2013). Still, we should point out that over 60 percent of the high-frequent offenders did *not* belong to the high-risk group in youth and almost 16 percent belonged to the lowest risk group.

In line with previous research, the high-risk group, experiencing the worst conditions in at least three dimensions of risk (individual, family, school, peers), also turned out to consist of a higher proportion of adult offenders. On average, they also had a higher level of offending than the other three risk groups. The ordering between our risk groups further suggests that there is an association between cumulative childhood risk and adult offending. However, as expected, the between-group differences become smaller with age.

We prospectively identified a third of the high-frequent offenders from childhood risk factors alone. Still, three (16%) of the high-frequent offenders belonged to the group that did *not* stand out in any dimension of risk during youth. One of these actually became the most frequent offender within the sample. And, as noted in Table 5.3, almost 20 percent within the high-risk group were *not* recorded for any crime after age 15. These findings are illustrative examples of the problems of prospective offender identifications in criminal career research.

# Final Remarks

The study of risk factors is an influential sub-field of life-course criminology. As we have described in this chapter, there are myriad risk factors working at several levels, all the way from within the individual (biological, or neuropsychological factors) to the neighborhood or community within which that individual lives. The question is not whether or not risk factors are predictive of offending; we know that they, to varying extent, are. Instead, importantly, we need to understand *how* they are related to crime. Here is where theory must come in: we encourage the reader to ask him- or herself how a given risk factor would be interpreted differently, depending on which theory is used. Most risk factors discussed in this chapter are recognized by almost everybody, but the *mechanism* surrounding them are debated.

Additionally, what is at stake is whether or not perfect prediction is ever possible. Although risk factors are usually defined in probabilistic terms and thereby do not make offending a certainty, the driving logic of the early risk factor paradigm in theory seems to suggest that perfect prediction is actually possible. According to this view the issue of false prediction – the false positives and false negatives we outlined above – is one of operationalization and measurement accuracy.

However, it may be that perfect prediction can never occur. Sampson and Laub (2005: 179) suggest this, arguing that 'the continuous influence of randomizing events and human agency' that occur as people move along the life course, will make causal prediction impossible. In our case study, using data from The Stockholm Life-Course Project, we tried to illustrate this apparent tension; while risk factors have a clear predictive value, this value should not be overestimated.

## Suggestions for Further Reading

Case, Stephen and Haines, Kevin (2009) *Understanding Youth Offending: Risk Factor Research, Policy and Practice*. Portland, OR: Willan Publishing. A critical assessment of the 'risk factor research paradigm'.

Loeber, Rolf and Farrington, David P. (1998) *Serious and Violent Juvenile Offenders: Risk Factors and Successful Interventions*. Thousand Oaks, CA: SAGE. Quite a few years have gone by since this book came out, but it is still a very good overview of the field of risk factor research.

Sivertsson, Fredrik and Carlsson, Christoffer (2015) 'Continuity, change, and contradictions: risk and agency in criminal careers to age 59', *Criminal Justice and Behavior*, 42(4): 382–411. Sivertsson and Carlsson's paper is the basis upon which we try and illustrate a risk factor study in the last part of this chapter.

# 6

# ONSET OF CRIME

Onset of criminal behavior is perhaps the most studied phenomena in criminology. In classical criminological theory, onset is seen as the end result of social learning processes (Akers, 1985; Sutherland, 1947), low social and/or personal controls (Gottfredson and Hirschi, 1990; Hirschi, 1969; Reiss, 1951), drift (Matza, 1964), or certain adaptations to the experience of strain (Agnew, 1992; Merton, 1938), to mention just a few of the more well-known examples. Onset, in turn, is associated with processes of labeling (Becker, 1963), stigma (Goffman, 1963), and, as a result, secondary deviance (or, persistence) and continuity in the new behavior (Lemert, 1951), due to the societal reactions that onset tends to generate when detected by others.

Today, onset is also part of the conceptual apparatus of criminal career research and life-course criminology. Together with concepts such as persistence and desistance it frames the criminal career of any given offender: onset captures the initiation and beginning of the career, persistence accounts for the continuity of criminal behavior once onset has occurred, and desistance accounts for the change in offending toward cessation and the end of the career (Loeber and Farrington, 2012). As we move through these subsequent chapters, we introduce, review the research on, and discuss these fundamental concepts in life-course criminology. At first look, they appear strangely simple but, as we move in closer and study them in detail, they are very complex and contested.

## Defining Onset

As researchers, we try to capture and explain social reality through our concepts and methods. The researcher who uses the concept of onset usually does so in order to capture the initiation of the criminal career, that is, the first infraction of a criminal law committed by a person in his or her life. The number of criminal career studies where the concept does in fact capture this, however, is very low, if any such study exists at all. Blumstein et al. (1986: 21f) acknowledge the difference between what we can call *actual* onset, and *observed* onset:

> A person initiated criminal activity at some time ... The offender is assumed to begin criminal activity at some 'age of onset', $a_o$, but his official record does not reflect onset until some later time, at the point of his first arrest.

What we observe is thus not actual onset, but the individual's first known offending, according to one source or the other. These – the first infraction of a criminal law, and first known offending – can of course be identical, but that is unlikely: as we elaborate on below, studies that compare different measures of criminal careers, such as self-report data and criminal records, consistently find differences (DeLisi et al., 2013; Piquero et al., 2007; Thornberry and Krohn, 2000).

A simple answer to the question of when the criminal career begins is thus quite trivial: when the individual commits his or her first law-breaking infraction. Crime, according to this attempt, is an action that is punishable according to criminal law. The problem that occurs if we follow this definition is that for almost all of us, the criminal career would begin very early, since most children commit offenses that are equal to theft, robbery, and assault during their first years of life. We rarely, if ever, define these acts as 'crimes', of course.

In most countries, however, small children cannot be held responsible for their (criminal) actions in that way – they are assumed to lack the necessary capacity for impulse control, and the cognitive ability to consider the consequences of their actions, even in the (very few) cases where the resulting injuries are serious. But, as we have seen in the previous chapters, according to a number of theoretical traditions, these very early infractions may be of significant importance (e.g. see Moffitt's life-course persistent offenders). Usually, behavior of this kind – physical aggression around age 8 or 10, for example – at this early stage of life is often seen as a risk factor, indicative and predictive of what we can call *early onset*. Early onset, in turn, is predictive of a longer, and more serious, criminal career. Typically, onset is considered early when it occurs prior to the age of 14 (Tibbetts and Piquero, 1999). It may be useful to distinguish between other forms of onset as well, and once again – in the vein of life-course theorizing – they need to be defined by time. So, *adolescent onset*, is onset that occurs during the 'normative phase' of onset, i.e. the teenage years when any given population is in its most crime-prone phase (Theobald and Farrington, 2014). *Late onset*, in a general sense, is onset that occurs after the normative phase, that is, when it occurs toward the end of or after adolescence. We discuss late onset (and the notion of 'late-blooming') later in this chapter.

# Measuring Onset

In the well-known Cambridge Study in Delinquent Development (CSDD), Piquero et al. (2007) operationalize age of onset as age at first conviction.[1] Laub and Sampson (2003) proceed in the same way. Similarly, in the now classic study by Wolfgang et al. (1972: 130), onset refers to the event where 'a child designated delinquent was first taken into custody by the police'. In fact, in a large amount of life-course criminological studies, onset is measured in exactly this way.

The problem here is that only a very small proportion of all committed offenses is detected and recorded by the criminal justice system. Thus, serious crimes rather than petty crimes are recorded, crimes committed by a stranger are more often recorded than those that occur in intimate relations, and so on. Some crimes, or crimes committed at specific places, are detected purely through the actions and priorities of the criminal justice system, and the risk of apprehension is fully dependent upon how agencies such as the police, the tax authorities, the border control, etc., are prioritizing and acting in relation to a given crime, place, or 'type of person'. These issues are well-known within criminology in general. That being said, only a portion of all recorded offenses that come to the criminal justice system's attention will result in a suspected perpetrator, and an even smaller portion will result in a convicted offender – and it is only at these stages that we have a person tied to the crime. This, of course, is a necessary prerequisite for including it in a person's criminal career.

There is also another issue, connected to the above and rarely mentioned in criminal career research: individuals are not all equally likely to be 'designated delinquent'. For example, we know that some individuals – ethnic minorities, people with low SES, etc. – are more likely to be suspected and arrested by the police, and thus entered into the criminal justice system, than are others. We also know that those same individuals are more likely to be prosecuted and convicted. This is part of the criminological canon (see Becker, 1963: 12f) and has been empirically demonstrated not only in the USA but also in countries like Sweden (see Sarnecki, 2006). It follows from these empirical findings that some individuals risk getting entered into the criminal justice system earlier in life than others and that age of onset not only represents behavioral differences, but also to a considerable degree the practices of the criminal justice system and its associated agencies.

---

[1] We should note that Piquero et al. devote one chapter (7) to comparing different methods of measuring onset, but in the remaining parts of the study they rely on official records and convictions.

To come closer to the actual event of crime, criminal career researchers often use data that stems directly from the offenders in question, the predominant method being the self-report study. In the CSDD, Farrington (1989) systematically uses this tool and can thus compare self-report data with official, recorded offending. In The SLCP, we too have access to self-report data from the original study, but we have no self-reported follow-up data (aside from in-depth, life history interviews, which cannot be used in the same way as self-report data). Studies comparing self-report and officially recorded criminal offending, consistently show two things: first, the first officially recorded offense is often preceded by a number of actual criminal actions and second, in general, the age of onset usually occurs three to five years earlier in self-report studies than in official records (Theobald and Farrington, 2014). For example, in a study of 470 male delinquents in Montreal (LeBlanc and Fréchette, 1989), the average age of onset was 10.8 years according to self-report data, and 14.6 years according to official crime records. Similar results were found in The Pittsburgh Youth Study, a longitudinal study of over 1,500 boys (Loeber et al., 1998).

Now, it may seem that self-report data is a good cure to solve the problem of onset, and in many ways it is. Importantly, though, people's propensity to disclose their own criminal actions are contingent on a range of factors, one of them being issues connected to memory recollection. Within cognitive psychology, the well-known concept of telescoping attempts to capture the fact that people generally tend to perceive recent events as being more remote than they are, and distant events are more recent than they actually are (Neter and Waksberg, 1964). Connected to this tendency, is the fact that the self-report questionnaire may only cover the last 12 months (a very common strategy, and for good reasons), and the individual may have had an actual onset prior to this period but does not remember the timing of this event in a correct way. Some individuals include criminal activities that do not fit the time frame of the study, because they for various reasons perceive them as important. According to Andersson (2011), young people reporting their crimes are guided not only by actual crimes committed, but also by their self-image.

Empirically, retrospective, self-reported accounts of onset have been studied by Kazemian and Farrington (2005). They show that at age 32, the retrospective self-reports of offending were inadequate compared to contemporaneous ones; 41 percent of all prospectively admitted crimes were not accounted for in the retrospective self-report. Additionally, and crucially for our chapter here, the average, retrospectively self-reported age of onset was *four years later* than the average, prospectively self-reported age. Thus, depending on what purpose the researcher has in mind, retrospective accounts of onset should be dealt with very carefully. To the extent that it is possible, to get a good indicator of onset, a prospective self-report study is desirable.

# Research on Onset

Register-based studies show that the vast majority of people go through life without being recorded for any criminal offenses; in fact, before the self-report methodology took off during the 1950s and 1960s, the consensus, based on official crime records, was that crimes were committed by a small segment of the population and only individuals in that segment had a criminal career. Now, when we know that there are practically no people who are complete 'abstainers' in the sense that they never commit any crime, research has shown that among the vast majority of people, the criminal career is fairly short and relatively uneventful. In that sense, most people have an onset of crime, but it either coincides with or appears very near the termination of their career (that is, they only commit few and often not very serious crimes, typically during adolescence).

It is important to note that in research on onset, it is sometimes used as an independent variable, other times as a dependent one. In other words, it is treated as an outcome, where the presence of a condition or event (such as delinquent peers or a conduct disorder) increases the probability of onset. In such instances, onset is predicted from a number of risk factors. Other times, onset is treated as a risk factor in itself, where, for example, an early age of onset is seen as highly predictive of a subsequent, long and intensive criminal career (see Piquero et al., 2007; Stattin and Magnusson, 1995). Understandably, this makes the research on onset a bit tricky to review.

## Early Onset

When it comes to the existing research on onset, the main bulk of studies have focused on the predictors – and consequences of – early onset, and for good reasons. First, the link between early onset and future, persistent criminal offending is empirically relatively robust. Second, identifying and intervening in the lives of early onsetters is, according to many, an important task for policy-makers and practitioners, to adopt effective, preventive strategies (Farrington and Welsh, 2007).

Individuals who have an early onset of crime usually have a number of (other) problems, ranging from the biological to the social. Much of this research has thus been reviewed in the previous chapter on risk factors: the problems include poor neuropsychological development such as delayed cognitive and motor development, conduct disorder, low school achievement and truancy, bullying, running away from home, delinquent peers, coming from a family with low socioeconomic status, unemployment, substance use, social exclusion, and a criminal history.

Consider, as an example of this dynamic, an extract from one of our interviews in The SLCP:

**John:** I think the first part of my school years was very good for me. Nice and ... lots of friends and things like that. I did good in school, I was good and ... but then ... things spiraled in many areas. At home, socially, there were problems and I think that, in combination with all the hormones and ... it clashed pretty bad in school, for me, in fifth grade I think it was. And then I wasn't in school anymore, I didn't go, I was actually suspended in eighth grade.

**I:** **Do you remember the reason for that, you being suspended?**

**John:** Yeah, I had used Rohypnol. And I came to school and had to leave in an ambulance. There was a lot of ... fuss then.

**I:** **You got sick, so you had to go in an ambulance?**

**John:** Yeah, and then ... I was pretty rowdy then. This was just the thing that made it all topple over. But they had, what's it called, they decided to make me a bad example.

**I:** **What happened then?**

**John:** Well, I got ... they sent me to a youth institution, youth confinement.

Being sent to a youth institution, John's surroundings changed. He began experimenting with heavier drugs and experienced an increasing marginalization from the institutional fabric of society. Upon his release, John says, his criminal career 'really took off'. As John tells his life history, the problems, which eventually led to him engaging in crime and drug use, originated within his family, a traditionally highly secluded area.

In other words, an early onset of crime is usually only just one problem among many, and it is relatively common that criminal behavior emerges (or is detected) later than most of the other problems. Seen from this perspective, from a policy and prevention perspective, pinning down the exact time of onset may be less important than observing those risk factors (including crime) that may be indicative of future, persistent problems.

The concepts of the criminal career (onset, escalation, persistence, etc.) are linked and relational. So, if we look at onset, and an early age of onset in particular, we see that it is a predictor of later criminal career features. For example, in the CSDD, those boys who were first convicted of a crime between ages 10 to 13, up to age 56 had 9.2 convictions on average, while those first convicted between ages 14 to 16 only had an average of 6.1 convictions (Farrington et al., 2013).

Similar results emerged from The SLCP. Individuals who had a self-reported onset at age 11–12, were on average suspected for 27.6 crimes between ages

15 to 65. Those with a self-reported onset at age 13–14, on the other hand, were suspected for a mere 13.3 crimes, and those with a self-reported onset at age 15–16 for an average of only 4.7 crimes. Interestingly, however, those individuals who had a self-reported onset at age 17–18 had an average of 11.5 suspected crimes between ages 15–65. For this last group, we may have captured a number of so-called 'late-bloomers' (a phenomenon which we return to in a moment).

## A Brief Note on Adolescent Onset

As noted, while most of the research on onset has been conducted on early onset, this research has focused on a very small segment of any given offender pool. The vast majority of people who engage in crime, do so in adolescence. We know this from the many, representative self-report studies that explore juvenile delinquency and crime (in Sweden, these studies are conducted by The Swedish National Council For Crime Prevention). Why does crime increase so much in prevalence during adolescence?

The answers to such questions are largely to be found in theory. Moffitt, you may remember from Chapter 3, argues that those with adolescent onset have no history of antisocial behavior or high-risk circumstances, but when adolescence comes, many experience a kind of 'maturity gap' in the form of an inability to achieve adult goals and statuses due to their age. Delinquent acts, then, become a way of doing this: smoking, drinking alcohol, and committing (relatively minor) crimes. Others, such as Sampson and Laub (1993), would argue that the stage of adolescence is one where the young person 'breaks free' from and has a more negative attitude toward the social control of the family and other social institutions, including criminal law. Becoming 'free', in this sense, also frees the individual to engage in actions that are deemed illegal.

Importantly, in line with Moffitt's theory, we must also consider the meaning criminal behavior has for the one who engages in it, and how this meaning is contingent on life-course stages. In adolescence, and especially for boys, criminal behavior tends to be fun, exciting, status-generating, and an exhilarating experience (Carlsson, 2014). Young people who engage in many and serious crimes are, of course, often in vulnerable social positions. Engaging in crime also often entails risks of various kinds (being apprehended by the police, being victimized, etc.). Our point is not that crime is *only* fun, status-generating, and so on – our point is only that those aspects are much more prominent in adolescence than in adulthood. Many of the individuals who engage in crime during adolescence, cease to do so in the transition to adulthood. Why they do so will be part of our discussion in Chapter 8.

## Late, or Adult Onset

When adult onset is explored in longitudinal studies (see those by Eggleston and Laub, 2002; Zara and Farrington, 2009), the findings are often somewhat surprising: around *half* of all adult offenders have had an onset of offending in adulthood. Of course, a basic question to such findings is a clever one: when exactly is one considered an adult? In a study by McGee and Farrington (2010) an 'adult' was anybody at age 21 or older.

Now, a second question may be: how can we know that these individuals do in fact *not* engage in crime until adulthood? After all, register data may be a very shaky indicator of actual involvement in crime. Yes, this is true. So, to examine this issue, McGee and Farrington (2010) compare seemingly adult onsetters with their self-reported criminal offending, and find that around one-third of all adult onsetters in their study did, in fact, self-report frequent and relatively serious juvenile delinquency. They are thus not 'true' adult onsetters. The other two thirds, however, *were*.

In order to capture this phenomenon two concepts have been suggested by researchers: one is that which we have already introduced, adult onset, and the other is 'late-bloomer' (Krohn et al., 2013). The concepts are not equivalents, but rather reflect two different ways of conceptualizing and operationalizing criminal behavior that occurs later than what is normatively expected. Adult onset refers to individuals whose onset of criminal behavior occurs in adulthood (however we define that). When it comes to 'late bloomers', however, the situation becomes more complicated.

There are three characteristics of those offenders who 'bloom late': first, during adolescence, their rate of offending is 'substantively indistinguishable' from that of non-offenders (Krohn et al., 2013: 185); second, their criminal careers should only emerge after adolescence; and third, during the adult years, their offending patterns should reflect persistent, non-trivial involvement in crime.

The adult onset, or 'late-blooming' offender causes more trouble to some life-course criminologists than may appear at first sight. After all, note that neither Gottfredson and Hirschi's (1990) theory of self-control nor Moffitt's (1993) dual developmental taxonomy allow for such an offender to exist; they cannot explain its occurrence. Possibly, one could argue that these offenders have many of the same problems as persistent offenders have, but are also inhibited, nervous, and not influenced much by their peers in childhood and adolescence. These features, then, protect them from engaging in crime in their teens, but not from adult offending. Others suggest that adult onset, or late-blooming, may be due to changes in an adult individual's psychological and social circumstances, such as losing one's job, going through a divorce, or other negative life experiences (Laub and Sampson, 2003).

## 'Strategic Crimes'

An individual's first crimes are rarely serious ones (although they of course may be experienced as extremely serious by the victim): they tend to be petty thefts, threats, assaulting a peer at school, and similar actions. We also know that in the majority of cases, such crimes are committed by young people in groups of delinquent peers (Sarnecki, 2005; Warr, 2002). For those individuals who will develop a long, persistent criminal career, a common path is one of acceleration, or escalation, where criminal offending occurs more frequently and becomes increasingly serious. This development also, of course, increases the likelihood that the offender will be found in official crime records.

In general, the more serious offending an individual engages in, the worse is his/her future prognosis and the risk for a persistent criminal career. Register-based studies show, however, that some 'debut crimes' give a worse prognosis than do others. The Swedish National Council For Crime Prevention has conducted two studies where they investigated which recorded debut crimes gave the highest risk for persistence in crime. The first study (Brottsförebyggande Rådet, 2000) included people born during 1960, 1965, 1970, and 1975. The recorded crime that gave the worst future prognosis, was vehicle theft (in most cases, motor vehicles). The likelihood that an individual who had this crime as his/her first conviction would develop a persistent criminal career was 27 percent. For comparative purposes, we should note that if the first conviction was shoplifting, the risk of persistence was a mere 4 percent.

Additionally, robbery and theft (19 and 16%, respectively) were considered strategic crimes. Further, the study shows that for an individual who has vehicle theft as both his/her first *and* second conviction, the risk of persistence is 60 percent.

In the second study (Brottsförebyggande Rådet, 2011), they look at all convictions among 15–17-year-olds and find something seemingly banal, but actually quite interesting: the strategic crimes (that is, those that indicate future persistence) do not have to be the first recorded crime. It is enough that the individual is recorded for such a crime during *the first three years after having reached the age of criminal responsibility* (that is, age 15). In the 2000s, the three crimes that powerfully heighten the risk of future persistence are robbery, motor vehicle theft, and violence against someone in service (such as assaulting a police officer, firefighter, train conductor; basically, somebody in a uniform). In general, the new study supports the general life-course criminological finding that the perpetrators of these crimes also have extensive problems in other spheres of life, such as in school and relations with delinquent peers. The study further shows that even though certain crime types increase the risk for a long and serious criminal career, these individuals will later engage in a large variety of crimes; persistent offenders thus tend to have a low rate of specialization, on the contrary, they tend to be generalists (see also Piquero et al., 1999; Tumminello et al., 2013).

# Understanding Onset

As we noted at the beginning of this chapter, onset of criminal behavior is one of the most studied phenomena in criminology. In most classical criminological theory, onset is in one sense merely the consequence of the process that leads up to it. That is, in tracing the cause of onset, the researcher looks to the prior conditions that make onset possible, such as a weakening of social controls (Hirschi, 1969) social learning processes that facilitate the violation of law (Sutherland 1947), or the experiences of certain forms of strain (Merton, 1938). One could reflect on the great importance that central criminological theories ascribe to a concept that is so vague and difficult to both define and measure.

For other perspectives, the question of what leads up to onset is of minor importance. What is considerably more important for the development of a 'deviant' or criminal career, are certain actors' reactions to an individual's onset (e.g. Becker, 1963; Lemert, 1951). Indeed, many life-course criminological theories have one (or several) of these classic theories as their foundation.

The main contribution of life-course criminology when it comes to our understanding of onset has been to highlight two connected facts neglected by many of these classical theories. First, life-course criminologists note that onset of crime, for many individuals, is a feature of childhood and adolescence; thus, there must be features of these life-course stages that tend to 'produce' crime. Second, and perhaps even more importantly, life-course criminologists know that the phase of onset is not isolated; on the contrary, it is followed by something, such as persistence or desistance. The circumstances regarding these stages and transitions of the criminal career are of significant importance for an understanding and prevention of crime.

Within life-course criminology, the main work on onset has been done using quantitative methodology. Perhaps as a consequence of this, although Blumstein et al. (1986) discuss onset in terms of an *activation process*, onset is often conceptualized and measured as a single, static event. Criminal offending, however (including onset), is a process that unfolds over time, and for a student of criminal behavior, this is important to remember. Onset, as defined by Blumstein et al. (1986), is a descriptive concept: it concerns an individual's initiation of criminal behavior. There is nothing in this definition which suggests that it is to be considered a single event. As suggested by concepts such as 'late blooming', onset has often been considered as more of a 'phase' of the criminal career than as a discrete event, even though it has often been measured as such due to the way quantitative methodology tends to function (see Blumstein et al., 1986; Piquero et al., 2007). Similarly, to give one more example, inherent in the notion of risk factor research is an implicit conceptualization of onset as a process, since the risk factors in one way or another operate as mechanisms that facilitate criminal behavior (see Case and Haines, 2009).

# Suggestions for Further Reading

Gibson, Chris and Krohn, Marvin D. (2013) *Handbook of Life-Course Criminology*. New York: Springer.
In this updated and modern handbook, Part I and II deal with early circumstances and onset specifically, using a wide array of perspectives to approach the phenomenon of onset. The first chapter in Part III is concerned with late-blooming.

# 7

# CONTINUITY IN OFFENDING: PERSISTENCE

The criminal career begins with onset. For many offenders it ends soon thereafter: for any given group, prevalence in crime peaks during the teenage years when criminal offending is very common, and then it dramatically decreases. Between ages 20 and 29, the vast majority of offenders desist from crime and move into a conventional, adult life (Farrington, 2003). As Benson (2013: 123) notes, the

> vandalism, shoplifting, petty thefts, fist fights, illegal drug use, and drunkenness that are so common among teenagers that they are statistically normal become decidedly abnormal for a substantial majority of people after the age of 25.

Only a small portion of all offenders develop a persistent criminal career. These offenders, while they constitute somewhere between 5 and 10 percent of any given offender sample, will be responsible for around 50 percent of all crimes committed by that population and the major part of all serious offenses (Sarnecki, 1985; Wolfgang et al., 1972). In other words, following onset, they continue to commit many and serious crimes and over a relatively long period of time.

In this chapter, we unpack the theme of persistence in crime. We should note that it is in practice very difficult to separate persistence from desistance, as they in many respects are two sides of the same coin. As Sampson and Laub (2005) argue, most offenders, even persistent ones, eventually become desisters. We separate them in two different chapters, however, to give you a more in-depth examination of these two very interconnected phenomena. Although every chapter in this book is written in a way that should enable you to read only one or a few of them, and in the order you prefer, we suggest that this and the following chapter (that is, Chapter 7 and 8) be read together and in sequence.

# Understanding Persistence

A large portion of research and debate within the criminal career paradigm has centered on the phenomenon of persistence, and the persistent offender. There are several reasons underpinning this trend: first of all, for a long period of time, criminology paid remarkably little attention to the developmental implications of early antisocial and/or criminal behavior, and its stability across the life course (Sampson and Laub, 1997). When research in criminal careers began to emerge, and the significance of persistence became known, it thus did so with a bang. Second, persistent offenders are likely to cause much harm not only to themselves but also to other people and society at large. They will – importantly – consume much of society's resources in terms of time and money. From a policy and prevention perspective, early identification of the future persistent offender is thus highly desirable. Third, the persistent offender constitutes a part of the theoretical heart of life-course criminology: when Moffitt's dual developmental taxonomy is published in 1993, it becomes influential mainly through its systematic separation of two kinds of offenders: the adolescence-limited and life-course *persistent* ones. In the same year, Nagin and Land publish their first paper on what is called a mixed poisson model; a new way of analyzing longitudinal trajectories of behavior. Following this paper, they develop this technique further. These techniques, in the words of Savage (2009: 17),

> allow the analyst to assess whether there really are identifiable groups of life-course persistent or adolescence-limited offenders, as Moffitt proposed, and to look at correlates of persistent trajectories of offending.

As a result, during the next few years, research on persistence flourished. Before we turn to the findings of this research – and the main explanations of persistent offending – we must delve deeper into the phenomenon and concept of persistence.

## Persistence as Phenomenon and Concept

> What does it mean to persist in something? Does it mean to be doing a lot of some thing over a long period of time? A lot of some thing in a short period of time? A little of some thing over a long period of time? Or a little of some thing over a short period of time? (Piquero, 2009: 271)

Strictly, persistence can be conceived of as the continuation or repetition of a particular behavior, such as crime. That is, if we measure an individual's criminal activity at a number of different points in time, we find that the offender is engaged in crime at $t_1$, $t_2$, $t_3$, $t_4$, and so on.

Currently, however, there is no common, standard *operational* definition of persistence in crime. By operational definition, we mean a definition that tells us how to measure it. To give just one example, Wolfgang et al. (1987) defined persistent offenders as those individuals who had offended at least once as juveniles (below age 18) and at least once as an adult (after age 18). This way of operationalization is quite common; we also find it in Scandinavian studies, such as the one by Nilsson et al. (2013: 305) who conceive of 'persisters' as those who 'were recorded for a crime both during their youth and as adults'. Although such operationalizations capture the small segment of truly persistent offenders, they would also include an individual who, for example, has been recorded for nothing but two cases of assault, one at age 16 and one at, say, age 45. Is this offender truly a 'persister'? Many would probably say no.

To capture persistence in crime, however, we must also turn to the phenomenon itself: how, exactly, do we perceive the persistent offender? It turns out that the persistent offender is really not persistently criminal at all; when not imprisoned, hospitalized or in any other way incapable of offending, even

> persistent offenders do many things other than think about or commit offenses ... for much of the time, most offenders engage in everyday practices and routines that are similar to those of everyone else (Shapland and Bottoms, 2011: 257).

We should note that it is, of course, highly possible to commit offenses while in prison, treatment, or a hospital. What we refer to here is what has been called 'exposure time', i.e. 'time for which individuals are free on the street to commit crime' (Piquero, 2004: 108).

In Glaser's study of prison and parole systems he shows that 'almost all criminals follow a zig-zag path' (Glaser, 1964: 85), such that most individual criminal careers – in particular, persistent ones – are characterized by movements back and forth between periods of offending and non-offending. Even the more serious offenders are not 'persistently criminal' (Piquero, 2004: 105). Rather, they are 'casually, intermittently, and transiently' engaging in crime (Matza, 1964: 28).

So, for example, when Horney et al. (1995) examine month-to-month variations in offending in a sample of convicted felons, they find that changes in social controls turn offenders away from crime, even if only for short periods of time. In a sample of California parolees, Piquero et al. (2002) uncover similar patterns studying year-to-year changes in social controls, such as marriage, and offending (see also McGloin et al., 2007).

A concept closely connected to persistence is that of *frequency*. By frequency, Blumstein and his colleagues (1986) refer to the rate of an individual's criminal activity, that is, how many offenses he or she commits during a certain period of time. This rate they term Lambda, or $\lambda$. A small number of offenders have a very high rate of offending, while the majority have a very low. Offenders who persist in crime thus also, typically, show a relatively high frequency of offending.

Importantly, however, the rate of offending also changes *within* offenders as they move along the life course.

Persistence, then, is continuity but it is not static continuity; on the contrary, persistence in crime is a highly dynamic phenomenon that can include temporary waxes and wanes of criminal behavior.

# Explanations of Persistence

In Chapter 3, we made a distinction between two sets of life-course criminological theories: theories of population heterogeneity, or static theories, and theories of state dependence, or dynamic theories. Here, this distinction becomes relevant once more. In this section, we review the answers to 'why do some offenders persist in crime?' given by the arguably four most central theorists of persistence: Moffitt, Gottfredson and Hirschi, Sampson and Laub, and Farrington.

## Population Heterogeneity and Persistence

Theories of population heterogeneity, remember, suggest that some people – to put it bluntly – are more prone than others to do crime. It is among these individuals we will find the persistent offenders. The two most prominent theories here are the one outlined by Moffitt and the one developed by Gottfredsson and Hirschi. They both agree that the persistent offender can be identified – and thus distinguished from those who will desist from crime in the transition to adulthood – by early personality traits.

Moffitt's claim, we remember from Chapter 3, was that persistent antisocial behavior was caused by a combination of neuropsychological risks and a criminogenic environment. The interaction between the individual and his or her environment leads to traits and characteristics such as impulsivity, low verbal skills, low cognitive abilities, and low self-control. These in turn lead to an early and serious onset of antisocial behavior. In explaining persistence, she argues that the factors that lead to onset in childhood, persist into adulthood and *directly* cause problems in adulthood as well. So, for example, children who are ill-tempered in childhood tend to be hot-tempered as adults as well, leading to an increased risk of continuity in crime. Moffitt calls this process contemporary continuity.

These early problems also have an indirect effect on later offending: 'early individual differences may set in motion a downhill snowball of cumulative continuities' (Moffitt, 1993: 683). To continue our example of tantrums, or being ill-tempered in childhood – having tantrums in childhood is predictive of lower stability when it comes to social relations in adolescence, which, in turn, are predictive of having lower stability in social relations in adulthood.

Now, being able to acquire work and develop stable, conventional social relations are two important reasons as to why individuals are able to desist from crime. If people do not have access to these relations, or are unable to create them, continuity in crime is a likely outcome. Consider the words of Fredrik, an offender around the age of 40 whom we interviewed in depth during our work in The SLCP. Having a long history of antisocial and criminal behavior, he was reflecting on his future:

> **Fredrik:** You know ... even if I want to quit, I think like, what would life be like, for someone like me? I should work, form a family. I should go straight, every day, every week, every month. That's what, you know, that's what guys my age do. I couldn't do that. I can't function like that. I just know that I can't. I could never live up to those, never settle like that. I would go crazy.

Danny, a man with a background very similar to Fredrik's, provided us with a narrative along the same lines:

> **Danny:** I got out [from prison] there, when I was 24, I had that long stretch, several years. Then I was out for about a year, and then I got three more years. Got out again. But I had no place to live, no job, nothing. So I continued [to do crime], basically.

In Fredrik's and Danny's respective narratives, we see the dynamics of Moffitt's argument emerge; individual antisocial behavior couples with the social, cumulative continuity of exclusion and marginalization brought about by their engagement with crime and drugs.

Now, it is important to note that Moffitt's notion of persistence not only refers to persistence in crime. As you may recall, for Moffitt's life-course persistent offenders, criminal behavior is merely one manifestation of their underlying, antisocial disposition. If life-course persistent offenders do not die premature deaths (this group's mortality rate is very high compared to a normal population), they may commit criminal actions pretty much through their entire lives. However, it is more likely that the specific manifestation of their antisocial tendency changes with age. That is, they may desist from crime but persist in other forms of antisociality, such as excessive drinking, gambling, and so on.

Gottfredson and Hirschi's (1990) account of persistence is different. Their explanation of criminal behavior across the life course is that 'individual differences in self-control are the chief determinant of stability in waywardness from childhood to adulthood' (Lilly et al,, 2011: 395). This low self-control is the causal factor leading to crime, a factor which is stable over time and situations, and those with low self-control thus consistently display higher levels of offending than those with high self-control (i.e. *inter-individual* stability).

That being said, everybody follows the age/crime curve, that is, they decrease their criminal offending as they age (i.e. intra-individual stability). For Gottfredson and Hirschi, this is what persistence is: persisters consistently offend at a higher rate than do others, but with increasing age they all move toward a state of desistance.

## State Dependence and Persistence

In contrast to theories of population heterogeneity, theories of state dependence do not assume that some people – due to relatively static traits and characteristics – are more prone than others to do crime. On the contrary, theories of state dependence consider human life as always in the making. While early experiences may be important, the *primary* explanation for continuity in criminal offending is to be found in the social situations and circumstances people encounter as they move along the life course.

The most well-known account of persistence within this strand of theories, is that of *a cumulative disadvantage* presented by Sampson and Laub in a publication from 1997. 'The idea', they note, 'draws on a dynamic conceptualization of social control over the life course, integrated with the one theoretical perspective in criminology that is inherently developmental in nature–labelling theory' (Sampson and Laub, 1997: 135).

The basic argument is built upon the notion of an event chain that effectively takes the shape of a downward spiral, thus seemingly very similar to Moffitt's notion of cumulative continuity. Sampson and Laub, however, place much more emphasis on crime and antisociality as a *social* behavior. Indeed, they note, behavioral stability may rather reflect stability in the response of others, than the 'time-invariance of an individual trait' (Sampson and Laub, 1997: 154). Taking aggression as an example, they argue that

> aggression is a social behavior that, by definition, involves interpersonal interaction. Moreover, aggression and conduct disorder often generate immediate and harsh responses by varying segments of society compared to most personality traits ... aggression tends to foster physical counterattacks, teacher and peer rejection, punitive discipline, parental hostility, and harsh criminal justice sanctions. The common feature to all these responses is retaliation and attempts at control and domination. (Sampson and Laub, 1997: 144)

In other words, the 'trait' that Moffitt sees as a direct, causal factor leading to persistence in crime (aggression), is seen by Sampson and Laub as a social behavior that gets its significance and stability primarily through the reactions of others. Having said that, individual differences in criminal propensity do still come out as significant when this model is tested. But, and this is the key of Sampson and Laub's persistence argument, our theory [of persistence] invokes the causal role of prior delinquency in facilitating adult crime through a process of 'cumulative disadvantage' ... committing a crime has a genuine behavioral influence on the probability of committing future crimes. In other words, crime itself – whether directly or indirectly – causally modifies the future probability of engaging in crime ... Although this role is potentially direct, *we emphasize a developmental model where delinquent behavior has a systematic attenuating effect on the social and institutional bonds linking adults to society* (e.g. labor force attachment, marital cohesion). (Sampson and Laub, 1997: 144, emphasis added)

In the case of any given individual's life course, this process of cumulative disadvantage primarily takes place within four key institutions of social control: the family, school, peers, and state sanctions. Antisocial behavior, say aggression, in itself cuts off ties to conventional society, alienating the individual from family, school, and conventional peers. Additionally, official sanctions may increase this alienation even more. For example, Hagan (1991) finds that middle-class boys who escaped the negative consequences of arrest, did not suffer in adult outcomes of adjustment due to their involvement in juvenile delinquency. 'Avoiding the snares of arrest and institutionalization' can thus give the individual 'opportunities for prosocial attachments ... in adulthood' (Sampson and Laub, 1997: 152).

Now, crucially for Sampson and Laub, they must provide us with a tool in order for us to be able to distinguish the desisters from the persisters. That is, why do *some* offenders engage in a process of cumulative disadvantage, and not others? This is a matter of structural (dis-)advantage and resources. They cite Clausen (1993: 521), who notes that 'early advantages become cumulative advantages; early [problem behaviors] lead to cumulative disadvantages'.

Notice the almost total absence of any links to conventional society in the narrative of Tomas below. Like Danny and Fredrik above, he is a man with a long criminal record who was interviewed as part of The SLCP. Here he describes what a typical day was like for him, when he was 'on the scene':

Tomas:    I was out all night and slept all day. A regular day was like, you got into town. You went to Plattan [a big square in Stockholm] in the afternoon, where everybody met. And this was the beginning of the 90s, all the bad guys hung out there. And there were a lot of people, gangs, there. And there was always somebody who had money and drugs. One day it was me, another day it was somebody else. You hung out, used drugs, maybe somebody went home. But we always stayed out, maybe we robbed somebody in the evening, a couple of robberies. That's how it was. And then maybe you went out and did some burglaries if you hadn't gotten enough money from the robberies, until four or five in the morning when the Central Station [train station] opened. Then you went and had breakfast somewhere, and then you slept. Like that, it just rumbled on.

In other words, early life problems and circumstances (such as juvenile delinquency) tend to 'knife off' future life chances and possibilities, thus limiting access to conventional arenas. This is thus very similar to Moffitt's notion of cumulative continuity, but Sampson and Laub locate their juvenile delinquent in a larger, structural context where those born into a disadvantaged environment with weak resources and family problems will be significantly more likely to engage in crime – which paves the way for continued criminal behavior due to this downward spiral. As a consequence, this small but serious segment of offenders will be unable to encounter any possible turning points that lead other offenders out of crime.

Leaving Sampson and Laub now, Farrington's attempt at explaining persistence can be found in his Integrated Cognitive Antisocial Potential (ICAP) Theory (Farrington, 2005). The core construct of the theory is *antisocial potential* (or AP, see Chapter 3), meaning an individual's potential to commit antisocial acts, including crime and delinquency.[1] In any given population and at any age, the distribution of AP is highly skewed; few people have a very high level of AP, the majority have a relatively low level. However, AP will be high if children are not attached to (prosocial) parents or they come from disrupted families (broken homes). AP will also be high if people are exposed to and influenced by antisocial models, such as delinquent peers, for example in high-crime schools and neighborhoods (Farrington, 2005: 79).

Now, whereas the distribution of AP in any population is fairly stable and consistent over time, it is quite dynamic and subject to change at the individual level; getting a job, getting married, having children, and residential changes are life events that affect an individual's AP, because these tend to change an individual's strain and socialization processes. These, in turn, affect criminal offending (i.e. make the individual desist). Consequently, the other way around, if an individual's antisocial potential *remains* high, he or she is likely to persist in offending. This is how Farrington accounts for persistence, or continuity. The likelihood that an individual will encounter life events that affect AP is contingent upon the individual's prior (antisocial) history. It is less likely, for example, for an individual to get a job if s/he has never been employed and has a massive criminal record. This is thus similar to Sampson and Laub's turning point argument, but Farrington does not locate the catalyst for persistence in interaction (as Sampson and Laub do), but within the individual.

Similarly to Moffitt, Farrington can account for the fact that many of those who persist in crime eventually desist but still live quite marginalized lives

---

[1] Note that the core construct is at the individual level; antisocial potential is an individual trait, and thus different from Sampson and Laub's location of the core construct (which is located in the *interaction between* the individual and his or her environment).

characterized by deviance in other ways. As the individual gets too old, too tired, and too worn to find crime rewarding – and is less likely to find him- or herself in situations where s/he is exposed to possibilities to engage in crime – s/he may stop committing criminal acts. That individual's antisocial potential may remain high, however, which makes him or her engage in excessive drinking, developing a gambling problem, etc.

Farrington thus situates his theory somewhere between that of Moffitt and Sampson and Laub's. He argues that the core catalyst for criminal offending and persistence, antisocial potential, is located within the individual, much as Moffitt does (the life-course persistent offender's core catalyst for offending is his or her antisocial behavior). However, an individual's antisocial potential is more dynamic and subject to change due to life events (and here he approaches Sampson and Laub).

## Distinguishing Explanations of Persistence

Having gone through a number of major theories' attempts at explaining persistent criminal offending, the attentive reader surely notes that they, to a considerable degree, agree on a number of critical issues, especially when it comes to the processual nature of persistence. In all theories, even self-control theory, persistence emerges through a set of cumulative, linked events: one factor or event leads to another, which leads to a third, a fourth, and so on. Truancy tends to lead to low school attachment, which leads to low grades, leading to low labor attachment in adulthood (because without good grades it is difficult to engage in higher education, which makes it more difficult to get a good job), which is a predictor of crime in adulthood. Similarly, truancy in childhood may lead to more time to interact with delinquent, older peers, which increases the risk for early onset of crime, which can lead to a number of disadvantages later in life. Social life is messy and complex, with many processes and events unfolding in a parallel fashion and sometimes intersecting, and in any given case, persistence in criminal behavior is likely to be a result of several such processes.

But, the attentive reader may ask again, what is the causal mechanism behind truancy in the first place? For Gottfredson and Hirschi, it is low self-control. For Moffitt, it is the future life-course persistent offender's tendency to engage in antisocial behavior from an early age, a tendency rooted in the unfortunate interaction between genes and environment. For Farrington, it is antisocial potential. These three, then, locate the core catalyst for offending *within* the individual. For Sampson and Laub, on the other hand, the causal factor is found in low, informal social control – a factor working *outside* of the individual. This is the core difference, and it is a big one.

# Drugs and Persistence

The four theories we have discussed so far have laid a kind of base or foundation for us to work with. If you are doing work in life-course criminology and deal with persistence you are bound to, consciously or not, position yourself with or against one or several of these theories.

Now we move on, going deeper into the research field of persistence. A central, predictive factor of persistence is drug use. Many individuals use drugs, such as marihuana, for recreation and do not develop an addiction (Becker, 1963), but some do. Many of the risk factors we outlined in Chapter 5 are predictors of crime, and that includes the (criminal) act of using drugs. Drug use, however, and especially *hard* drugs such as amphetamine or heroine, is in turn a predictor of future criminal involvement. It is, in the words of Hussong et al. (2004), a *snare*, contributing to persistence and hindering desistance. It can be understood as one element within each of the theories we outlined above.

The user typically finds him- or herself in a context where the activity of consuming drugs is forbidden and punishable. This leads him or her to associate with others who are in the same position, on the outskirts and margins of society. In these peer groups, crime is often present. As this process goes on (and the individual may begin to develop an addiction), ties to society begin to weaken and perhaps even break, leaving the individual relatively isolated from the conventional fabrics of society: 'Drug use and its lifestyle concomitants', Schroeder et al. (2007: 213) note, 'bring together a host of distinct social network dynamics that uniquely complicate desistance processes'. Consider the effect of drugs in the narrative of Oliver, from The SLCP. He has 45 registered crimes and among them, 22 drug-related, four frauds, and two thefts. He is the only child of his family, with an alcoholic father and a mother who had a job as a social worker. Today, he lives alone and suffers from lung disease, which he says was brought on by his 'lifestyle.'

> **Oliver:** I had a relatively normal life until I was sixteen, seventeen. Then I got onto the drug scene. And those were the years people spent forming a family, making a career, all that. And when I began to wake up I was around forty and, well, then it was too late.
>
> **I:** It was too late?
>
> **Oliver:** Yeah, how the hell am I going to find a woman and form a family? I am pretty tired and torn, show me a woman who wants that. Somehow I have lived, while life has run away from me.

The snare of drugs is thus not only a physical and psychological one, but importantly, a social one as well. Adding to this social dynamic, there is also a strong, structural element here: the 'War on Drugs' in many Western societies. Today, many drug offenses, not only in the Anglo-Saxon countries but also in countries like Sweden, can lead to harsh prison sentences. Such severe state sanctions, we know from Sampson and Laub (1997) and others, tend to increase the offender's process of cumulative disadvantage and lead even further into the downward spiral.

Drug use is thus a critical component in the process of persistence. In fact, a recent Swedish life-course study (Nilsson et al., 2014) suggests that the crime problem may actually be a drug problem; those who persisted in crime beyond the transition to adulthood were almost exclusively those who were engaged in serious drug use.

## Gender and Persistence

In Chapter 5 we concluded that boys and girls share many of the risk factors for future criminal offending. When it comes to gender differences in persistence and the long-term consequences of problem and criminal behavior, we know much less. This has several reasons, one being that many life-course studies only include males. Another reason is that those studies which do include females rarely have sample sizes large enough to permit analyses of females (e.g. Bergman and Andershed, 2009; Giordano et al., 2002). Very few of these studies follow women further than young adulthood (Estrada and Nilsson, 2012). To give you an idea of the impact this has had on the field, consider those crucial 5 to 10 percent of any given offender population who emerge into 'chronics'. They consist of males only, but that is due to the structure and content of the longitudinal data sets used to arrive at this result – they do not include females (Soothill et al., 2003; Tremblay et al., 2004). It is possible, however, that a similar, small number of high-frequent, persistent female offenders exists.

Some processes into crime, we argued in Chapter 5, may be gendered (such as being sexually abused) but others may be more generic. 'Attention to such experiences [sexual abuse]', Giordano (2010: 23) writes, 'in combination with other more traditional [factors and processes] may be required to round out our understanding of the mechanisms involved'. This also seems to be the case in the relatively small number of studies on gender and persistence. Gaarder and Belknap (2002), to give just one example, find support for this notion when analyzing a sample of life histories from women transferred to adult courts because of engaging in serious offenses such as robbery and assault.

A repeated finding is that high-frequent, persistent offending is much more common among men than among women (e.g. Piquero, 2001; Wiesner and Windle, 2004). Indeed, in a cohort study by Soothill et al. (2003), they find that whereas 4.7 percent of the male offenders could be regarded as persistent, only

0.4 percent of the females exhibited such an offending pattern. Other studies show similar gender differences (DeLisi, 2002; Steffensmeier and Allan, 1996), including a Swedish cohort study by Estrada and Nilsson (2012), who find that whereas 11 percent of the males persisted in offending, only a tenth (1.3%) of the females did so.

Moffitt (1993) suggests that most female antisocial behavior is adolescence-limited and that the life-course persistent offenders are almost exclusively male (Moffitt, 2006), but the theory does allow for adolescence-limited female offenders to get 'caught' in the snares of drug use or labeling, resulting in continuity in offending. In a thorough review of persistent female criminal offenders, Goldweber et al. (2009) find that for these women, delinquency begins relatively early and is more serious, frequent, and consistent than average female offending, 'progresses through adolescence, and is then *truncated more abruptly* in adulthood compared to persistent male offenders' (p. 229).

In a life-course study titled 'Does it cost more to be a female offender?' Estrada and Nilsson (2012) explore the childhood circumstances and adult living conditions of criminally active men and women up to 48 years of age. What they find is that the female offenders have experienced more disadvantaged childhoods than their male counterparts, and that involvement in crime seems to cost significantly more for females, in terms of social exclusion. For example, at age 48, 61.8 percent of the persistent female offenders were categorized as socially excluded, compared to 39 percent of the male persisters (Estrada and Nilsson, 2012, Table 4). Persistence, then, seems to cost more for females than for men. Why is this so?

Even if both boys and girls share many of the same risk factors, the authors argue, it may, to put it bluntly, 'take more' to become a female offender. They do not 'only' come from 'broken homes' but often from rather more serious social problems involving long-term poverty, drug addicted and alcoholic parents, physical and emotional neglect, sexual abuse, etc. (Estrada and Nilsson, 2012: 198). As they move along the life course, they are likely to experience much more negative consequences of their criminal involvement than male offenders; female offenders experience a form of double stigmatization 'as they break not only the law but also the norms and expectations associated with their femininity' (p. 198f). As we saw above, drugs are a strong predictor of persistence and the vast majority of all persistent female offenders are drug users, adding to the 'Street Woman Scenario', seen as central for female criminal offending (Daly, 1992). Indeed, Estrada and Nilsson (2012: 212) conclude:

> When controls are included for differences in childhood conditions and drug abuse, female offenders do not differ from the corresponding male offender categories, which are to say that if we compare female offenders with male offenders presenting similar backgrounds and experiences of drug abuse, we see more similarities than differences between the two groups. In short, the same factors seem to produce the same long-term outcome for males and females.

Once again, then, males and females show many similarities in persistence, but also (at group level) a number of distinct gender differences.

# The Importance of Intermittency

We began this chapter by stating that the phenomenon of persistence, while it seems simple enough, is actually quite difficult: even the most persistent offenders are not really persistent, in the strict sense. Crime is a sporadic activity even for these offenders, and offenders thus engage 'intermittently' in criminal behavior.

Before we end this chapter, we therefore highlight a highly related concept, which emerged within the criminal career literature on persistence and desistance toward the end of the 1980s and early 1990s. Since a criminal career often includes stops and starts, desistance researchers were faced with a puzzle: should this phenomenon of stops and starts in itself be named? For Piquero (2004: 108), intermittency is 'a temporary abstinence from criminal activity during a particular period of time only to be followed by a resumption of criminal activity after a particular period of time'. Intermittency thus refers to the intermediate phases of the criminal career, occurring after onset but prior to actual desistance (Carlsson, 2013).

Barnett et al. (1989) were among the first to identify this empirically, based on time between recorded offenses. The intermittent group of offenders initiated their offending around the normative age of 16, were convicted several times and seemed to desist around the age of 20 – but reappeared in the criminal records some seven to ten years later and started to reoffend. Several studies have followed, conceptualizing intermittency in the same or a very similar way (see D'Unger et al., 1998; MacLeod et al., 2012; Nagin and Land, 1993).

'Drifts' or 'lulls' in offending are likely to occur due to the nature of the social world, full as it is with its complexity, coincidences, and contingencies – and this last note is of importance. Remember, our task as life-course criminologists is to understand within-individual continuity and change in criminal offending. Our concepts are only as good as the actual explanatory power they have.

It is with intermittency that we link persistence and desistance (which is the topic of our next chapter). By studying intermittency closely, we can track and examine the ways criminal behavior waxes and wanes in an individual's life over time: do periods of non-offending become more or less durable as time goes by? Does a longer period of non-offending reduce the risk of future recidivism? This way, we can begin to untangle offenders' initial moves toward desistance.

Research on intermittency has mainly been quantitative in nature, but a small number of qualitative studies have been done. As offenders age, the time gaps between offenses increase (see Raskin, 1987, among many others). In a similar vein, findings in recidivism studies have repeatedly shown that the longer an individual's period of non-offending is, the less likely it is that recidivism will occur (Blumstein and Nakamura, 2009; MacLeod et al., 2012; Zamble and Quinsey, 1997). To account for this within-individual change over time, Carlsson (2013) conducts a qualitative study of intermittency processes in The SLCP and suggests that it may be fruitful to distinguish between two forms of intermittency.

One form of intermittency is where the offender for a significant period of time 'holds up', takes a 'time-out', experiences a temporary 'burn-out', or takes a 'break'. These episodes seldom occur as abruptly as the word 'break' suggests, but are rather gradual processes of temporarily decreasing (and ceasing) offending. This form of intermittency is not characterized by any changes in the areas of lifestyle, routines, or identity. We can see this in an extract from the interviews with Mark and George in Carlsson's study:

I:      Were there times [back then] when you thought that you wanted to quit?

Mark:   No but I wanted to hold up. When I got out of prison, I didn't want to go right out on the same track again, but that was for many reasons. I wanted a time out, you know, and do some work, make some legit money, and then go back [here, Mark is referring both to 'going back to prison', and to what can be called 'a criminal life']. I didn't want to go straight from prison, because I had seen people getting out, being out for a couple of weeks, doing parties and burglaries and drugs, and then come back, getting an even harsher punishment [because of the Swedish parole system]. I wanted to get out for a while, be fresh and in good health. But then the drugs and that life started to suck me in again, because that's who I was.

He went through several such phases of 'holding up' and, as can be seen in this extract, these phases were not attempts at achieving any substantial change in life. Similarly, in the case of George:

George: I began early, I began ... then I held up for a while, during the 1980s, was married and started to study, went to vocational school and became a carpenter.

I:      Right.

G:      Then I got divorced, opened my business again [started to reoffend], so I did another stretch there. I wasn't satisfied the way I lived, so I moved between different worlds, in a way. But I never tried to, you know, to stop, not back in those days. I was still young, in a way, still in the game. Those phases just kind of happened.

We see George 'holding up for a while' during the 1980s when he got married, started to study, and became a carpenter. However, he describes a parallel process here, where he was 'moving between worlds … still in the game'.

While the men do talk about 'holding up' or 'taking a time-out', these narratives can also be characterized as narratives of 'rumbling on', 'staying in the game', 'not being done yet' – narratives of continuity. It constitutes a natural part of offending for most offenders with a criminal career stretching into adulthood. This form of intermittency seems to occur relatively early in life, typically prior to the age of 40.

The second form of intermittency is best understood as incomplete, unsuccessful or aborted attempts to desist from crime. The main difference here is the will to desist, that is, a change in human agency. It is often accompanied by a change in values and desires, and attempts to change one's lifestyle, routines, and everyday life. It is characterized by longer periods of non-offending and less serious offenses. But, attempts to enter conventional roles are combined with difficulties and this is eventually what makes it impossible for them to enter or remain engaged in them, even if they want to. This 'strain' of conventional life is part of what makes them relapse into criminal offending. Consider the examples of David and Fred here, interview participants in Carlsson's (2013) study, who discuss their inability to engage in conventional relationships:

> **David:** There were some relations then, on the drug scene, but I mean, they were doomed, even if both wanted it to work. If there're drugs in the picture, the relationship will never work. Amphetamine has that sex drive thing too, so you destroy your sex life, in a way, so it's, I don't want any relationships. And also, I feel I enter some kind of trap. I feel un-free. Even if I wanted a relationship, you know, being a man and all, I know that it would never work. Because I'm that fucked up, I have no normal upbringing, my life hasn't been normal.

Fred described a similar life course process:

> **Fred:** That [his inability to maintain relationships] has followed me through life, basically, relationships and traditional family life … after a couple of years they make me feel claustrophobic. There have been many short ones. I mean, I can see that my years growing up have structured my life in a way that I can't live like a regular person. I have been drawn to addictions and kicks the whole time, I have always gone back to that. But, as I tried to stop, I managed to be crime-free longer and longer.

The distinct form of intermittency thus tends to change over time, as the offender moves along the life course. The first form tends to precede the second one in time and they thus constitute different phases of the criminal career. A 'will to change' often emerges through a set of interconnected life-course processes that include not only changes in social control and routine activities, but also processes of aging and maturation. Intermittent offending patterns can thus entail qualitatively different underlying processes: to 'hold up' is very different from 'attempting to change', to 're-start' one's offending is very different from 'failing to stay away' or 'relapsing'. The offender who holds up and 're-starts' is an actor acting according to his or her intention and will (Matza, 1964), the offender who 'fails to stay away' cannot, for one reason or another, overcome the obstacles associated with desistance and conventional life. This second form of intermittency typically entails more distinct changes in lifestyle, desires, and values, and is characterized by longer periods of non-offending and less serious offenses.

Carlsson's outline of intermittency processes is of course only one way to approach the phenomenon and it is likely that qualitative, future studies of intermittency will counter his argument, refine it, and by doing so, develop our understanding further (see King, 2014 for a critical discussion of Carlsson's argument).

Intermittency is thus a slightly different way of approaching the phenomenon of persistence, or continuity in offending. It is quite an interesting concept because, as you can see from the above discussion, it closely examines the dynamics of criminal offending and discovers minor changes, ripples, and lulls in offending that otherwise might go unnoticed.

It thus seems likely that periods of non-offending in an individual's criminal career become more durable as time goes by. Intermittency is then closely tied to desistance, since the latter is likely to emerge from the later phases of an intermittent offending pattern. As people age they – at least to a greater extent than earlier – tend to move toward non-offending. To account for this movement is thus, by and large, to account for the emergence of desistance.

# The Implications of Persistence

Persistence in crime is a controversial theme in life-course criminology, because any discussion of persistent offenders comes with questions of policy, punishment, and interventions. In Chapter 1 we outlined the political dimension of a measurement called Lambda, or $\lambda$. The central question was, might some offenders persist in offending at a near constant rate regardless of age? Gottfredson and Hirschi (1986) considered the idea that some offenders commit crimes at a constant rate to be 'an academic myth' (Hagan, 2010: 110). In line with Gottfredson and Hirschi's (1990) theoretical position and empirical illustrations of the age/crime curve, all offenders de-escalate and eventually cease their offending with age. On the other hand, some criminal career researchers argue that the non-zero rate of $\lambda$ might be real and profound (Moffitt, 1993).

It is here that we enter politically contentious issues. While we have showed that persistence in crime is not equal to constancy in Lambda, we have also gone through a number of studies which demonstrate that a small number of offenders ('chronic offenders') in a given population account for the majority of crimes committed by that population as a whole. They commit many and serious crimes, and do so over a rather long period of their lives. This would then seem to justify the strategy of selective incapacitation (i.e. the strategy to, through imprisonment, prevent particularly dangerous individuals from committing new crimes). Gottredson and Hirschi are highly skeptical to the fruitfulness of that idea. Their position instead suggests that interventions be focused on reducing overall participation in crime (that is, policies focused on the general population). The criminal career advocates agree with this, but are also open to the possibility of a more restrictive, concentrated focus on the 'chronic' offenders. 'So far', Blumstein et al. (1988: 7) note, 'the evidence on both approaches is sufficiently inconclusive that neither is clearly preferable, and pursuit of either should not preclude interest in the other.'

We return to and develop this further in the next chapter, as we study the various forms of treatments that can support offenders' ways out of crime.

# Suggestions for Further Reading

Savage, Joanne (2009) *The Development of Persistent Criminality*. Oxford: Oxford University Press.
This volume constitutes a long and thorough examination of persistence, both as phenomenon and concept, and includes methodological reflections.

Piquero, Alex R. (2004) 'Somewhere between persistence and desistance: the intermittency of criminal careers,' in Shadd Maruna and Russ Immarigeon (eds), *After Crime and Punishment: Pathways to Offender Reintegration*. Devon: Willan Publishing. pp. 102–27.
Carlsson, Christoffer (2013) 'Processes of intermittency in criminal careers: notes from a Swedish study on life courses and crime', *International Journal of Offender Therapy and Comparative Criminology*, 57(8): 913–38.
Nagin, Daniel S. and Land, Kenneth C. (1993) 'Age, criminal careers, and population heterogeneity: specification and estimation of a nonparametric, mixed poisson model', *Criminology*, 31(3): 327–62.
These three papers all deal with the phenomenon of intermittency, but from different perspectives; Piquero discusses the phenomenon and concept of intermittency, whereas Carlsson explores it from a qualitative perspective. Nagin and Land's paper is one of the first expositions of intermittency, using a quantitative model.

# 8

# DESISTANCE FROM CRIME

The term criminal desistance means, quite simply, that an individual who has previously engaged in crime, ceases to do so. Once again, however, as we have seen when it comes to onset and persistence – two concepts that, in theory, look pretty nice and simple – desistance as a concept comes with a set of complications, contradictions, and choices that need to be made by the empirical researcher who considers using it.

In contemporary life-course criminology, the research field of desistance has been given much attention, perhaps because it deals with something that is both highly relevant from a policy-maker's perspective, as well as empirically and theoretically challenging for researchers.

## Defining Desistance

When people who, once they have started, stop committing acts defined as criminal, they have desisted from crime (Kazemian and Maruna, 2009). That seems simple enough but this conceptualization is deceptive, because, as we saw in the previous chapter, in a sense, people cease their offending all the time. Maruna (2001: 23) illustrates the problem eloquently:

> For example, a person can steal a purse on a Tuesday morning, then terminate criminal participation for the rest of the day. Is that desistance? Is it desistance if the person does not steal another purse for a week? A month? A year? … Suppose we know conclusively that the purse-snatcher … never committed another crime for the rest of his long life. When did his desistance start? Is not the voluntary termination point or concluding moment the very instant when the person completes (or terminates) the act of theft? If so, in the same moment that a person becomes an offender, he also becomes a desister. That cannot be right.

In other words, it is difficult to pinpoint what desistance is and when it occurs. Just as in the case of onset, the issue is simple to handle when we work with recorded crime data. Desistance could, then, be defined as the absence of any further recorded crime. One problem, of course, is that as long as the individual is alive, s/he may be recorded for new crimes. Given the frailty of human nature, if we adopt an extremely strict notion of desistance we may in fact not know with certainty that a person has desisted from crime until s/he is deceased (Maruna, 2001). How long we should wait before we may say that an individual is a desister, is thus a difficult question to answer.[1]

Now, the problem of pinpointing the moment of desistance may actually be a problem in itself, because it suggests a specific idea of how we think that desistance occurs. There are mainly two ways to conceive of desistance: as a static event, or as a process (Kazemian and Maruna, 2009). In much of the literature, desistance is often directly or indirectly conceived of as a static event, since it is measured by the absence of an observation, that is, the absence of criminal offending in register data or other quantitative materials (see, for example, Estrada and Nilsson, 2009). In those studies, individuals are categorized as 'persisters' or 'desisters' in an either/or fashion (but see Bushway et al., 2001). In an elegant review of research on desistance Devers (2011) argues that, until the 2000s, life-course criminology was not particularly interested in understanding desistance in any sophisticated way. On the contrary, she claims that, even during the 1990s, to desist from crime was simply one half in a strict dichotomy of persistence or desistance.

Although some offenders do abruptly and dramatically cease their offending (see Cusson and Pinsonneault, 1986), desistance from crime in the vast majority of cases takes the form of a process where individuals gradually decrease and cease their criminal offending.

Consider LeBlanc and Fréchette's (1989) distinction between four *processes* of this kind, where the individual decreases his or her criminal offending, without fully terminating it:

1. De-escalation: the severity of an individual's criminal offending decreases (i.e. s/he still commits crimes, but less serious ones).
2. Deceleration: the individual frequency of an individual's offenses decrease as the individual commits less offenses per time-unit.
3. Reaching a ceiling: the individual reaches a peak in criminal offending, and although his/her offending may not immediately decrease it may now stay at the same level (in terms of frequency and seriousness).
4. Specialization: the individual begins to focus on committing one form of crime, such as drug-related crimes, making the total amount of crimes committed per time-unit start to decrease, due to the fact that the crimes s/he does commit result in larger rewards.

---

[1] A similar problem can be found in medicine: how long, after treatment, should an individual be free of symptoms before s/he can be considered cured of cancer?

These are just four ways of attempting to capture the dynamic of change in criminal offending that tends to occur as the individual progresses along his or her criminal career. Because, remember, no matter where along the life course an individual is, the meanings and implications of a specific stage are likely to impact on his or her criminal offending.

If we accept a processual view of desistance – that is, as something that unfolds gradually – we also approach it differently. By conceptualizing desistance as a process, we thus take changes in offending (such as de-escalation) into account. This processual view of desistance has sometimes been connected to qualitative studies of criminal careers (e.g. Laub and Sampson, 2003; Maruna, 2001), but is also mirrored in studies based on recorded offending, for example in the fact that the average number of months between recorded offenses increase with age (Farrington, 2003; Raskin, 1987; Shover, 1996), thus suggesting an emerging desistance process.

When viewed as a process, we do not leave the subject of desistance once the individual has ceased his or her offending. Instead we follow him or her beyond that stage and pay attention to the *maintaining* of desistance, that is, how the individual maintains a 'crime-free' life, including the 'lulls' or 'drifts' that occur along the crime–non-crime continuum, and what those lulls or drifts might be attributed to.

## Desistance: The Basics

Life-course criminology often takes credit for having been the first to notice that the vast majority of people who engage in crime cease to do so. As we saw in Chapter 2, this is not true: in modern criminology, it was noticed by (among others) David Matza as early as 1964. Where life-course criminology has made a significant contribution, however, is in understanding why, how, and when desistance (does not) occur.

As mentioned previously, most people who engage in crime have careers that are very brief, and limited to a few (very often trivial) crimes in adolescence. In Chapter 7, we discussed that relatively small number of offenders who develop a persistent criminal career. Having said that, the vast majority of these offenders too are very likely to desist sooner or later. In other words, at group level, desistance from crime seems to be the norm; there are extremely few, if any, 'chronic' criminals in the strict sense of the word.

An important – and possibly unsolvable – problem is what kind of behavioral change we refer to when we talk about desistance, and when we can call someone a 'desister'. As we stated above, if we adopt an extremely strict notion of desistance we may not know whether or not a person actually has desisted from crime, until s/he is deceased (Maruna, 2001). In a way to address this question, recent explorations in criminal career research (e.g. Blumstein and Nakamura, 2009) suggest that one reason to think of somebody as a 'desister' is when his or her risk of committing another crime is equal to that of a non-offender at the same age. This risk decreases over time as the offender ages and the amount of time without contact with the criminal justice system increases. That is, with time, the predictive value of having a criminal history when it comes to future criminal offending approaches zero.

## A Note on False Desistance

Criminologists sometimes use the term *false desistance*. We do this to capture a relatively basic but deeply problematic aspect of studying desistance: in some cases, individuals only *seem* to have desisted from crime whereas they actually have not. For example, if we study recorded offenses we may observe that an individual suddenly seems to cease his or her offending. This may not be the case, however: he or she may continue to engage in crime but avoid detection (and thus will not be recorded for an offense). Or, the individual may simply have died. In that case, it is not fruitful to speak of desistance; had s/he lived, s/he may have continued to do crime.

While it is very difficult to manage our data to control for those who persist in crime but avoid detection by the criminal justice system (we would need prospective self-report data to do so), it is less difficult to control for mortality: all we need to do is couple our data on recorded offenses with data on mortality. When an individual dies, we simply 'take out' those people from the data. That way, they remain in the analysis as long as they are alive, but do not cause any noise in the data when they are deceased.

A third scenario is not only possible, but also even more difficult for us researchers to handle. It is connected to the problem Maruna identified above, and how we define desistance; more specifically, how long an individual must be crime-free in order to be defined as someone who has desisted from crime. Let us imagine that an individual frequently engages in crime but then ceases to do so for, say, 10 years. At this stage, we collect our data and we define him or her as a desister. Maybe a month or a year later, the individual re-starts his or her criminal career. The only thing we can do to counter this problem, is to (1) be aware of the limits and problems in our definition(s) of desistance, and (2) try to collect prospective data to continuously re-evaluate how we have categorized the individuals in our sample.

## Explaining Desistance

In Chapter 3, we reviewed a number of the dominant theories of crime and the life course, and in that chapter much of the theoretical achievements of understanding desistance are described. Here, we go through the element of desistance, as explained by some of those theories, before we push the topic of desistance further.

To help you grasp these theories, we use an actual empirical finding from The SLCP and as we go through the theories, we will see how they each try and account for what we observe. Consider the below age/crime curve for the four risk groups in The SLCP (which you may already have encountered as Figure 5.2 in Chapter 5).

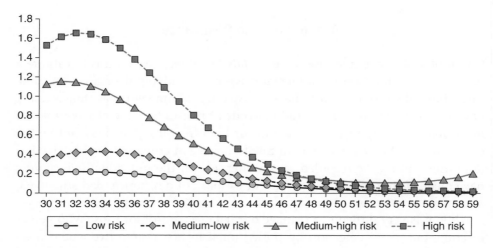

**Figure 8.1** Desistance from crime in four risk groups, ages 30–59. Mean number of recorded offenses/year and individual, among delinquent boys in the Clientele Study (Sivertsson and Carlsson, 2015). The groups have been divided into four risk groups based on 26 risk variables collected in their youth

In short, as you can see, we show the crime curves in adulthood for a group of boys who were originally delinquent (officially recorded for an offense). We have divided them into four risk groups based on how they scored on 26 risk factors, assessed at ages 11–15. We show what is termed incidence, that is, the mean number of recorded offenses per year and individual. The two low-risk groups cluster together at a lower level of offending, while the two higher risk groups seem to offend at a higher rate. However, crucially, they all seem to move toward a state of non-offending with increased age. In fact, around age 45, the four groups become difficult to separate and a few years later they are practically indistinguishable from each other. This empirical finding is far from unique; in fact, most criminal career studies find similar patterns (e.g. Loeber, 2012).

How then, are we to explain what we see? All theories we have discussed in this book claim that they can account for it, and they do so in very different ways.

Beginning with Gottfredson and Hirschi (1990), we saw in Chapter 3 that the fundamental, causal factor for desistance is age – everything else is just spurious and white noise in the data. Whereas low self-control in conjunction with suitable targets and opportunities for crime accounts for onset, aging out of crime is what really happens when people desist. Here, they refer to Matza's notion of maturational reform. Desistance is thus nothing but maturational reform, and 'maturational reform is just that, change in behavior that comes with maturation' and the aging of the organism (Gottfredson and Hirschi, 1990: 136). Now, whereas our risk factor index captures much more than the individual trait of self-control, Gottfredson and Hirschi would argue that parts of our index (such as childhood temperament, impulsivity, destructiveness, and moral judgment) are good indicators of self-control. These in turn are the actual causal factors that make the same individual score high on other factors (such as delinquent peers, low school achievement, and so on).

Thus, there is a lot of information in the risk factor index that may make the categorization somewhat unreliable with regard to self-control alone. That being said, the empirical data goes in line with the theory: self-control is largely stable throughout life and gives rise to the stability postulate. While criminal offending decreases with the process of aging, the group with lower self-control will continuously offend at a higher rate than the group where self-control is higher. As you can see, this explanation fits the data quite well, at least until around age 45.

Now, although Gottfredson and Hirschi have received much critique, they are a good starting point for us here. Their sole explanatory variable, age, might not be all we need to understand desistance, but the importance of age – as a biological and social process – as an element in the desistance process cannot be understated. Turning to Moffitt's developmental taxonomy, as you may recall from Chapter 3, her explanation of how and why the adolescence-limited offender desists is based on the very process of aging.

For Moffitt, the basic cause of criminal offending for the adolescence-limited offender, is the individual's 'maturity gap'; crime becomes a tool to gain access to a desirable resource (adult status). In the transition to adulthood, this maturity gap ceases to exist, and thus, the individual no longer has any need for criminal activity. Since his or her criminal offending has been sporadic and minor, it has not accumulated any negative social or psychological consequences – and s/he has no substantial problems of leaving crime behind. According to Moffitt, exterior pressure is put upon the individual to desist from crime: criminal behavior is not compatible with the features of adulthood and the social role of the adult. In other words, desistance from crime becomes a normative act in two senses: first, as something the vast majority of offenders do; and second, as something that is expected from the individual by society. This goes for many of the offenders in our empirical example above as well, especially those in the three lowest risk groups.

What about those offenders that we encountered in the last chapter, namely, those that for some time *persist* in crime? These offenders, according to Moffitt, belong to the category of life-course persistent offenders and some of them do indeed engage in crime until they die prematurely (as we saw in previous chapters, the mortality rate among persistent offenders is significantly higher than what is expected in a normal population).

Now – despite the name of the category – those offenders that do not die may desist from crime but, when they do, they are unlikely to enter and live the rest of their lives within the institutional fabric of conventional society. Age is important here too: sooner or later, even the highly persistent offender will be too old to engage in most forms of crime. S/he thus leaves the act of crime behind, but for these individuals crime has always been only one manifestation of an underlying, antisocial tendency – the life-course persistent offender who ceases to do crime, is now likely to engage in other antisocial behaviors (excessive drinking and alcoholism, developing a gambling problem, etc.). If we study our high-risk group in the empirical data above, Moffitt would argue that this is what we see.

Switching from Moffitt's explanation of (non-)desistance to the age-graded theory of informal social control, as developed by Sampson and Laub (1993) and Laub and Sampson (2003), we now arrive at a very different notion of what desistance is and how it works.

For Sampson and Laub, the basic cause of criminal offending is the same for all persons, namely, low social control. Some offenders fare worse than others – due to social and individual circumstances, and the process of cumulative disadvantage that may result from (serious) criminal offending – but they are all moving along the life course and the criminal career, following the age/crime curve, toward desistance. This is what we see in the criminal career patterns for our four risk groups above.

Desistance from crime occurs as the individual becomes embedded in a stronger net of social control, due to the social institutions of military service, employment, and relationship formation. Sampson and Laub term these *turning points*, but it is important to remember that they are not turning points in themselves. A turning point constitutes a change in the life course, which in turn constitutes a change in the individual's offending. It is not employment, marriage, military service, residential change, or other changes in themselves that bring about desistance but rather the way such changes under certain circumstances can bring about *other* changes, which are theoretically understood as central for desistance processes to emerge (Carlsson, 2012). The changes brought about by a turning point tend to be an increase in social control, a change in routine activities, and a cognitive change in the individual's self-image (we return to this later). Consider, as an example of Sampson and Laub's outline of the desistance process, this extract from a life history interview with David, one of the men in The SLCP with a lengthy criminal record and a long history of drug use.

I:       If I've understood you correctly, when you were with her, you didn't do drugs and crime as much?

David:    I didn't do it at all. Because she made demands, I was on heroin then, too. So she said, it's either me or the drugs. I was madly in love, so I chose her. 'If you quit, I'll be there for you 100 percent', she said. And I mean, I was lying at home in detox, and had a relapse, and when she found out about that, I started doing amphetamine instead. I did a month of that, and then she made me quit that, and when I turned to alcohol, she made demands there too. But it was harder to quit that.

I:       It was harder to quit alcohol than amphetamine?

David:    It was harder because I had to have *something*.

In David's narrative of his change process, we see the importance of social control: his partner forces him to quit. We also, however, see the processual nature of desistance. He does not fully stop using drugs (or engaging in crime) but he has initiated a process of change.

Thus, while the most common turning points take the form of military service, employment, and relationship formation, the notion of turning points is larger than that; anything that has this effect on the individual (and leads to or toward desistance) could be termed a turning point.

We know that the vast majority of people who engage in crime cease to do so in the transition to adulthood. For Sampson and Laub, this is not surprising: the transition to adulthood tends to be the very stage where the individual does his or her military service, begins to work, and/or forms more longstanding romantic relationships; that is, encounters these turning points. For those who have begun to engage in serious crime – and/or live their lives at the fringes of conventional society – the likelihood that they will be exposed to such turning points, however, is much lower; the process of cumulative disadvantage prevents them from such possibilities. This may explain the relatively higher trajectory of the two high-risk groups compared to the lower ones in our empirical example above. At group level, the individuals in the lower risk groups have not become so socially excluded that they cannot make the transition into desistance; for the high-risk groups, however, social exclusion and cumulative disadvantage hinders them from leaving crime behind. But still, they eventually do, and this fact could be problematic for Sampson and Laub – how do people desist from crime without exposure to institutional turning points? We return to this below.

In Farrington's ICAP Theory, much is similar to Sampson and Laub's argument, but with one important difference: in Chapter 3, we noted that the core of Farrington's theory of crime and the life course is antisocial potential (AP). The nature of AP is age-contingent:

levels of AP *vary with age*, peaking in the teenage years, because of changes within individuals in the factors that influence ... AP (e.g. from childhood to adolescence, the increasing importance of peers and the decreasing importance of parents) ... Also, *life events affect AP*; it decreases (at least for males) after people get married or move out of high crime areas, ant it increases after the separation from a partner. (Farrington, 2010: 261f, emphases added)

In other words, an individual's antisocial potential may decrease, as in the case of getting a job, getting married or perhaps making a residential change to a neighborhood with fewer criminal opportunities (what Sampson and Laub would call turning points). This dynamic can lead the individual away from crime, since the ties we have to conventional institutions – such as family, school, religion – embed us in social bonds that prevent us from engaging in crime. Such life events, then, lead to desistance in the broad sense of the term; since desistance in the vast majority of cases takes the shape of a process, these life events triggers a process of de-escalation, deceleration, etc. We would thus expect our high-risk group to consist of more individuals with a high antisocial potential, compared to the other groups, and based on the early risk factor assessment that seems to be the case. The time-varying dimension of antisocial potential is thus mirrored in the decrease in crime that we can see for all four groups.

For Giordano et al. (2002), however, such explanations of desistance miss one important dimension. The initial move toward a conventional life is not accounted for, but rather attributed to chance or luck due to the scaffolding of the environment, as the individual 'happens' to engage in employment or a 'good marriage' (see, for example, Laub et al., 1998). 'Nonetheless', Giordano et al. argue,

individuals themselves must *attend* to these new possibilities, discard old habits, and begin the process of crafting a different way of life. At the point of change, this new lifestyle will necessarily be 'at a distance' or a 'faint' possibility. Therefore, *the individual's subjective stance* is especially important during the early stages of the change process. (Giordano et al., 2002: 1000, emphases added)

In other words, offenders tend to vary in their 'openness' to change and their receptivity to certain catalysts, or 'hooks for change', such as higher education, employment, or relationship formation. These 'hooks' are important not only as sources of social control but also because they provide blueprints for how to maintain one's change and be able to replace one's former self with a new one (Maruna, 2001). Returning to our empirical example one final time, it is likely that almost all offenders sooner or later will want to desist from crime. However, they are not equally likely to be exposed to the potential hooks for change. The high-risk group, for example, is likely to be much more socially excluded and marginalized than the low-risk group. However, even the majority of offenders in the high-risk group will want to desist from crime and thus actively seek out opportunities to do so. This may account for their decreased criminal activity.

# Desistance and Human Agency

Although Giordano et al. (2002) do not explicitly use the concept, their main argument is centered on a concept and notion that has taken center stage in much contemporary research and discussions of desistance: the important, but highly dubious, concept and phenomenon of human agency that we briefly encountered in Chapter 1.

To repeat, the guideline of human agency holds that people 'construct their own life course through the choices and actions they take within the opportunities and constraints of history and social circumstances' (Elder, 1998: 4). In its simplest form, human agency thus entails 'attempts to exert influence to shape one's life trajectory' (Hitlin and Elder, 2007: 183). For the last 15 years or so, human agency, conceived of in one way or another, has been deeply influential to life-course criminology and studies on desistance from crime (to mention just a few recent examples, see Carlsson, 2014; Healy, 2013; King, 2014). Developing a human agency committed to change, it is said, is perhaps even *the* most important predictor for desistance (Lebel et al., 2008).

But what, more specifically, is agency? When we say that an individual exercises his/her human agency – what do we mean by that? In fact, one common critique of human agency (as a concept) may be closely connected to our incapability of pinning down what we mean: that agency is used as a form of residual category which the researcher utilizes when a behavior cannot be explained by the common, sociological determinants (see Matsueda, 2006).

Here, we thus begin to enter deep waters: as King (2014) notes, agency is a vague and at times elusive concept. When empirical research tries to understand the role agency plays (or does not play) in the desistance process, the operationalized version of agency tends to be relatively simplistic, which naturally leads to contention. Can agency be captured in empirical reality? Can it perhaps even be measured in numbers? If so, it seems reasonable to break down the concept into dimensions – but what dimensions? In empirical research, the attempts range from 'the ability to initiate self-change' (Thoits, 2003), 'self-efficacy' (Gecas, 2003), Clausen's (1993) 'planful competence', to Alexander's (1992) 'moments of freedom' and 'effort', and beyond.

No matter what we include in our definition and conceptualization of agency, we may usefully consider agency, in a general sense, as our intentional attempts at influencing our current and future life situation. But what makes our agency change over time? That is, what makes us, at one point in time, intend to engage or persist in crime, and what makes us, at another point in time, want to desist? Here, life-course criminology offers different answers: some suggest a thoroughly social mechanism, where social experiences 'foster new definitions of the situation ... and a blueprint for how to succeed as a changed individual' (Giordano et al., 2002: 1607). Others argue that 'intentional self-change is understood to be more cognitive, internal, and individual' (Paternoster and Bushway, 2009: 1106).

Now, even highly persistent offenders tend to develop a human agency aimed toward desistance; that is, with time they want to desist from crime. To want to do it, and to actually do it, however, can be two very different things: while internal, cognitive changes may be a crucial condition of possibility for desistance to occur, it is (at least, very rarely) enough:

> it is important to underscore that choice making takes place against a backdrop of structural contingencies and constraints. Choices are bound, that is, never completely divorced from the social systems (macro-level, immediate social networks) within which they unfold .... If individuals are sufficiently advantaged, a show of agency is not necessary (since things typically fall into place). Conversely if individuals are sufficiently disadvantaged, a show of agency is not nearly enough. (Giordano, 2010: 32).

In other words, to desist, the offender need not only develop a human agency committed to change, but also find him- or herself in a situation (or create one) where his or her will aligns itself with the structural opportunities that are needed to successfully do it. Next, we pursue the importance of human agency further.

## The Dynamics of Agency and Identity: Pro-Social Blueprints

The importance of agency is not limited to an individual's capacity to act and through that action push oneself in one direction rather than another. Intimately tied to agency, are the research findings uncovered by Maruna (2001). By interviewing a large number of desisters and persisters, Maruna aims to 'identify the common psychosocial structure underlying [ex-offenders'] self-stories, and then to outline a phenomenology of desistance' (2001: 8). Maruna conducts his analysis against the background of a strange empirical finding in the data: whereas some offenders had desisted from crime and others persisted, he *cannot* differentiate these individuals based on any psychological, social, or criminal history. If there are any differences between desisters and persisters, they are not to be found in 'the usual suspects' of risk factors.

All of us have a life story or narrative that we live by; this narrative is fundamentally important, because it tells us (and others) who we are, where we come from, and what our future looks like. Similar to Giordano et al. (2002), Maruna thus delves deeper into the offenders' cognitive self-understanding of their lives by studying how they narrate their past, present, and future.

By closely studying how the desisters and persisters narrate their lives, Maruna is able to distinguish between two forms of scripts: redemption scripts and condemnation scripts. Thus, the desisters tended to narrate their lives in terms of 'making good'; they were able to make sense of, and find purpose in, the 'bleakest of life histories' (Maruna, 2001: 10).

We find this theme echoed in many of the life history interviews we conducted with the Clientele Men in The SLCP. Consider the extract below, from our interview with Ulf, who had a tough upbringing filled with what we would call early risk factors. He engaged in frequent and serious crime in adolescence, and struggled during the transition to adulthood:

I:    Yes, that [changing one's life] is difficult, I can imagine.

Ulf:    Yes, that's depending on what kind of will you have, and how deep in trouble you are. You know, some people, they can't handle the loneliness, they have to go out and stuff like that. And that, it's damn easy to fall into, you know. But I have the view that, and I had that already when I was doing it [crime], how shitty it is. But there was like no ... I couldn't keep it together. I had no job, no permanent place of living, I didn't have any stuff like that. I had nothing safe to hold on to. But then, when I managed to get that, everything started to shape up, and I did it all on my own. I won't, I can't say that anybody has helped me or anything, it was ... It has worked out, I've had to fight a lot for it, on my own, but that's just good because, I've made it.

As you can see, Ulf's narrative highlights the complex interaction between agency and social structure that is needed in order for desistance to occur. However, applying a narrative perspective, we can read Ulf's story as a form of 'making good', resisting the marginalization he finds himself in, where the struggle to desist takes the form of a kind of redemption: 'I've made it.'

For Maruna, narratives such as these not only suggest a change in action, but also in identity: to successfully desist from crime, (ex-)offenders must also redefine themselves as persons: 'to desist from crime, ex-offenders need to develop a coherent, pro-social identity for themselves' (2001: 7).

What about those who persisted in crime, then? Maruna's analysis suggests that the narratives these individual tell, are very different: whereas the desisters could be understood in terms of narrating redemption scripts, the persisters speak in line with a form of condemnation script: these individuals speak of themselves as 'doomed to deviance' (p. 74). They cannot change their behavior, due to being poor, lacking an education, being drug-dependent, or stigmatized by others. We find this illustrated in The SLCP data as well:

Tim:    It's pretty hard to score a job when you have bad papers [i.e. a criminal record] and things like that, even if you'd want to. Once you're in that chair [frequently selling and using drugs], that label sticks to you the whole way.

Another example of this form of narrative comes from John:

John:    I got no help from my parents to grow up to become a young man, you know, I became an irresponsible teenager. So I had to do it all on my own. But by then it was too late.

I:      Can you expand on that?

John:   Well, you know. Who the hell would want to hire a 62-year-old ex-addict? An ex-addict who can't stay away? I know I wouldn't.

In such narratives, we see not only the limited number of possible actions (and thus, kinds of future) the offenders perceive, but also a specific cognitive self-image. Thus, for Maruna, offenders who manage to desist go through a qualitative, cognitive transformation that can keep them 'straight', even when circumstances are rough.

Now, if you are skeptic to Maruna's argument, you may argue that the problem the persistent offender faces, is one of cognitive distortion. That is, the offender need only to change his or her way of thinking, and everything will fall into place. In cognitive interventions, crime-producing patterns are often discussed in such terms (e.g. Barriga and Gibbs, 1996). However, Maruna is quick to point out that

> [t]he obstacles that interviewees say prevent them from making good are not delusions or figments of their imagination. Making an honest living is not easy for a poorly educated, poorly connected, working-class ex-convict with a massive criminal record, weak family ties, and no savings. (2001: 73).

In other words, the individual's cognitive self-image is very much molded by his or her social and economic circumstances.

Now, a crucial dimension remains: desisters and persisters narrate their lives in such different ways, but narrative also is connected to action. A life story is thus not only a story, but can also 'provide rough indicators of the internal self-story that the person ... *lives by*' (Maruna, 2001: 49f, emphasis added). How we perceive of ourselves, our past, present, and future, impacts on how we act and how we do not act in a given situation. The desister's redemption script is thus not only a way of making sense of oneself and one's place in the world; it also provides the desister with a concrete, realistic blueprint for how to live a lawful life. It is thus tightly connected to human agency. This dimension of the desistance process, as you might have suspected, is almost entirely missing in the explanations given by Sampson and Laub, Moffitt, and Gottfredson and Hirschi.

## Gender and Desistance

While the basic causes for offending may be similar across genders (Steffensmeier and Allan, 1996), the pathways into crime might differ (Belknap and Holsinger, 2006; Opsal, 2012). It follows from such findings, that women's criminal careers may look different as well. As we saw in the last chapter, male and female persisters were characterized by both similarity and difference (Block et al., 2010; Estrada and Nilsson, 2012). This goes for desistance too: whereas the basic processes of, for example, relationship and family formation and work are likely to be the same (e.g. Giordano et al., 2002; Opsal, 2012), considering that these institutions are gendered, there may not only be gender similarities but also a number of differences when it comes to desistance. That is, the desistance process, as we have outlined it above, has not been insensitive to gender: by and large, the explanations we have reviewed claim to be able to explain desistance among men as well as women (for example, while Sampson and Laub's study does not include women, other researchers have tested their theory on samples including both genders). Gottfredson and Hirschi (1990), for example, argue that the age/crime curve is invariant; females offend at a much lower rate than men do, but their criminal careers too can be explained as a result of low self-control, opportunities to engage in crime, and the aging process. In this regard, they are no different from men.

In this section, we need to highlight the issue of gender and point out a number of important differences. According to Gunnison (2014: 78), empirical research on female desistance is 'historically sparse' and when it has been conducted, it has mainly been done using qualitative data. This may be true if we compare the total number of life-course criminological studies of desistance to the number including women. As we have noted previously, a majority of longitudinal studies include men only. However, today, a number of desistance studies include women as well.

One of the most powerful predictors of desistance has been what some have called 'The Good Marriage Effect' (Laub et al., 1998). Following the logic of control theory, a 'good marriage' fosters desistance through the exertion of social control and structuring of routine activities. We saw this exemplified above (p.131), in the life history of David from The SLCP. However, whether or not this also is the case for female offenders is less clear. For example, Giordano et al. (2002) find that marital attachment does not seem to be a predictor of desistance, other than for a subset of both men and women. Doherty and Ensminger (2013) examine desistance among male and female African Americans and find no marriage effect on desistance for women. Gunnison (2014), however, finds a small marriage effect for females. Bersani et al. (2009) use data from The Netherlands and the Criminal Career and Life Course Study to explore whether there is a difference in the marriage effect due to gender. They find that 'marriage is more beneficial for men; however, marriage is also associated with a decrease in the odds of a conviction for women' (p. 19). One explanation for this, the authors suggest, is that while criminally active men tend to 'marry up', criminally active women often 'marry down', due to the differences in criminal involvement across gender: 'women', they note, 'are more likely to come into contact with criminal men' than vice versa (p. 19).

A different, but somewhat interconnected gendered factor of desistance, is the notion of pregnancy and parenthood. In the literature, becoming pregnant is one of the most prominent promoters of desistance from drug use for females (e.g. Yamaguchi and Kandel, 1985). It is important, however, to remember the life-course theoretical theme of timing here: *when* the pregnancy occurs is likely to be important. Rutter (1994), reviewing the literature on teenage pregnancy, suggests that becoming pregnant during one's teenage years is likely to have a negative effect on females' trajectories. That being said, Giordano et al. (2011) find that both women who *want* to become pregnant, and women who actually *do* become pregnant, are more likely to desist from crime. Similarly, Graham and Bowling (1995) conduct life history interviews with a number of female ex-offenders and find that becoming pregnant and having children had a powerful effect on their desistance processes. Women, Graham and Bowling find, endure not only practical consequences of becoming a parent, but also emotional ones. Opportunities to engage in crime decline significantly, and the consequences of criminal behavior become much more negative and salient for mothers.

The female offender is often considered deviant in more ways than one: not only is she a woman, she is also an offender (Chesney-Lind and Pasko, 2013; Messerschmidt, 1993), and the stronger the stigma is, the stronger the personal and social problems associated with it tend to be (Goffman, 1963). Additionally, the social control of women and men in Western societies looks very different (Ericson and Jon, 2006). For example, offending is rarely an effective way of 'doing femininity', irrespective of age, since women's opportunities and pressures to conform to and maintain the social order is gender-specific. Byrne and Trew (2008: 249) find that being perceived by both oneself and others as a 'bad mother' may be a 'worse transgression of femininity than being a criminal'. This transgression is age-graded, in the sense that the transgression might be considered worse at some stages in the life course than others, with subsequent implications for the woman's life.

# The Implications of Desistance

So far in this chapter, we have gone through a number of attempts at capturing the phenomenon of desistance, defining the concept, and then the perhaps most influential explanations that attempt to untangle the process of desistance. Let us now return to a question we began to discuss in the last chapter, namely, society's conscious efforts at trying to help active offenders desist from crime.

We have already shown that the most effective interventions are bound to be informal. That is, we should not expect official interventions – sanctions, treatments, programs, etc. – to result in more than moderate changes on people's future offending. Important changes in the life course tend to occur along the pathway from adolescence to adulthood and beyond: the 'turning points' of higher education, relationship and family formation, employment, and so on. These and other, similar changes in life are the most crime-inhibiting interventions we know of.

Channeling individuals away from crime is often a very difficult task, especially when it comes to more serious offenders. While it is crucial to facilitate the reintegration of offenders who attempt to change, any intervention needs to have in mind that the road toward desistance is often long and the 'participants often unwilling' (Laub and Sampson, 2003: 292). As you may have suspected already, it is rather rare that interventions aiming to foster a desistance process are discussed as possible turning points in life-course criminology (see Devers' 2011 review as an example). To give you an example, some treatment programs are designed to prepare offenders to do legitimate work and legitimate employment is one of the most important turning points in desistance research, but Devers also notes that the 'effects of employment programs are modest and limited' (Devers, 2011: 13).

At the same time, though, for a long time, desistance has been a central theme in research on punishment and treatment. This field of research has primarily been interested in what interventions lead people to not engage in any criminal activity at all in the first place (e.g. preventing onset) or cease criminal offending (Sherman et al., 1998). In treatment research, it has long been considered that a complete cessation of criminal offending is not the only criteria for an intervention to be considered a success or not. Considering what we know about desistance processes, if an individual's offending de-escalates (or, indeed, ceases to escalate) or if s/he ceases to commit serious crimes but persists in other crimes, as a result of an intervention, it is not unreasonable to consider the intervention a success (not least based on the fact that interventions rarely have dramatic effects in behavioral change, see Lab, 2014).

When various forms of interventions are evaluated, if they are evaluated at all, they often follow the treatment group for only a short period of time. This makes it difficult to draw conclusions of the, if any, effects of – often very powerful and serious – interventions. In Sweden, this is the case for, for example, young offenders sentenced to special youth homes. Since many interventions have long-term goals (the individual is supposed to undergo a lasting, personal change), it is plausible that the intervention may be successful but that desistance from crime may take time to occur. Even though the question of causality becomes much harder to answer the more time goes by, it is a feature of social life that some effects become clear only with the passing of time. It is partly because of such and similar findings that many evaluations have a longitudinal character (in fact, some criminological life-course studies have been launched as evaluations of various interventions aimed at individuals at a high risk for persistent criminal offending).

The perhaps most famous longitudinal treatment evaluation was a follow-up of the Cambridge Somerville Youth Study, commissioned in 1936 and launched 1939 (Cabot, 1940). The study included around 500 boys aged 5 to 13, sentenced to institutional care in eastern Massachusetts. The sample included a treatment group and a control group, and the treatment group underwent extensive treatment (among other things, medical and psychiatric treatment). In the short run, the evaluation showed no treatment effect at all. In the long run, however, the treatment was proven to have had a clear negative effect, amplifying the treatment group's problem behavior (McCord, 2007). This study is a criminological classic, partly because it was the first study that alerted us to the fact that well-meaning forms of interventions against criminal and antisocial behavior can be harmful, and partly (which is crucial in this context) that evaluations of treatment interventions should have a longitudinal character.

In The SLCP, we did an attempt at such a follow-up, using the younger §12 Group. The group, as we described in Chapter 4, consists of people born in 1969–74 who, during the early 1990s, were subject to intervention by the social services due to social problems, drug use, and serious criminal history. The intervention in question was in most cases a three-month-long compulsory placement and treatment at so-called youth homes. All individuals were not admitted and did not undergo treatment, however, primarily due to space limitations at the homes in question. The two groups (the admitted, and the not-admitted) are by and large similar in terms of social problems and background, but, we must stress, they were not constructed according to any Randomized Controlled Trial (RCT) standards.

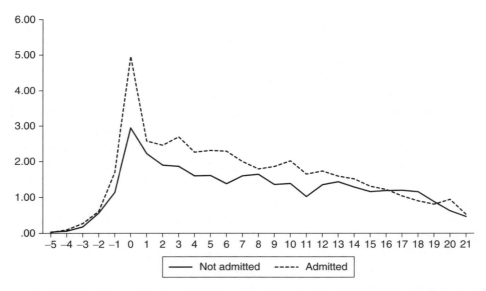

**Figure 8.2** Mean number of convictions five years prior to, and 21 years after being subject to intervention by the social services. The sample is divided into those who were admitted (n=752) and not admitted (n=475) to treatment at special youth homes

In Figure 8.2, you can see the average number of convictions per individual for the admitted and not-admitted group from five years prior to them being subject to intervention, up to 21 years after admission, having controlled for mortality. We see how criminal offending (using this indicator, at least) increases in both groups up until admission (Year 0), and then starts to fall. The decrease, however, is likely to be a statistical effect of 'regression to the mean' and the fact that the sample grows older. As we study any possible long-term outcomes, we see that their curves are substantially similar. Based on this data, and without making any further controls for other factors, we may thus conclude that, for this sample, being admitted to a special youth home had little, if any, effect on desistance processes.

## Interventions and Desistance

Given what we now know about persistence, desistance, and the life course, it is important to remember two interconnected things. First, whether or not interventions are successful is less likely to depend on early life circumstances than on the present social and material situation of the offender; a present which nevertheless – through processes that unfold in space and time – may be related to factors, events, and processes that occurred in early life. Second, the meaning of interventions and life changes are age-graded. We should thus be sensitive to the fact that official programs or interventions that target adolescent offenders may need to be different from programs directed to adults (e.g. Uggen (2000) finds that employment has a crime-inhibiting effect among older, but not younger offenders).

When society, through its various governmental and non-governmental agencies, intervenes in an individual's life, it can facilitate desistance if the intervention in question increases the individual's embeddedness in the conventional, institutional fabric of society. Such intervention increases the individual's opportunities for prosocial development, and decreases the likelihood of continuous, antisocial development. This, then, means that intervention centered on incapacitation, such as prison or being sentenced to institutional care, can have powerful effects in terms of increased control and almost no opportunities to engage in crime. In the short run. In the long run, large quantities of research have shown, the effects of incapacitation are bound to be the opposite (for an overview, see Lab, 2014). Through incapacitation, the individual is isolated from those (perhaps few) prosocial sources that s/he has access to, such as work, education, family, friends, and so on. The number of potential turning points, or hooks for change, decrease dramatically. It is, for example, much more difficult to get a job if you are recorded for a crime (Backman, 2012; Blumstein and Nakamura, 2009), and it is very difficult to maintain close ties to family, keep your apartment or house (if you have one), and so on. We should note, though, that at least in the short run, if incapacitation is coupled with education, work training, or treatment, it has shown a small but significant increased probability of desistance (Brottsförebyggande Rådet, 2001). Evaluation studies, although we must stress again that their follow-up period often is relatively short, also suggest that such combined interventions are more likely to result in positive (that is, prosocial) development for the offender.

## Suggestions for Further Reading

Giordano, Peggy C., Cernkovich, Stephen A. and Rudolph, Jennifer L. (2002) 'Gender, crime, and desistance: toward a theory of cognitive transformation', *American Journal of Sociology*, 107(4): 990–1064.
In this seminal paper, Giordano and her colleagues outline a theory of desistance, using both quantitative and qualitative data. Together with the other two suggestions we list here, it is one of the most influential statements on desistance to date.

Laub, John. H. and Sampson, Robert J. (2003) *Shared Beginnings, Divergent Lives. Delinquent Boys to Age 70*. Cambridge, MA: Harvard University Press.
Laub and Sampson follow up the Boston Boys to age 70, interviewing 52 of the original, delinquent boys, and develop their theory of age-graded informal social control.

Maruna, Shadd (2001) *Making Good. How Ex-Convicts Reform and Rebuild Their Lives*. Washington, DC: American Psychological Association.
Using life story interviews with male offenders in Liverpool, Maruna re-defines the process of desistance into one of maintenance. In doing so, he distinguishes between two forms of narrative scripts that impact on and help shape the offenders' future life trajectories.

# 9

# LOOKING BACK, LOOKING FORWARD

As you may have noticed, this book has to a large extent been looking back at the field of life-course criminology: how did it rise to fame? What central ideas, studies, methods, and theories make up the field? What are the implications of life-course criminology?

By now we have traveled a long way. At the same time, we actually have a very long way to go. If this was a journey through an unknown city, we have only been able to show you the biggest landmarks, the largest streets, and the most important parts of the town's infrastructure. In writing a book of this kind, we have had to make choices: there is so much going on in life-course criminology right now, what to include, what to leave out? We chose to include those parts of the field that we felt you would need to have if somebody were to put a newly published paper in life-course criminology in your hands and asked you not only to read it, but also to grasp the context within which it was written and the possible significance of the article; that is, to truly understand it.

In this final chapter, we do something that any experienced life-course criminologist (and you, having read this far) know is a very delicate thing: some attempts at glancing into what might happen in the future. We end the chapter with a brief conclusion.

## The Futures of Life-Course Criminology

As you will see, there is good reason to name this section The *Futures*, not *future*, of life-course criminology. The field has not one but many future trajectories.

# The Need for New Life-Course Studies of Crime

As we repeatedly have stressed in this book, life-course research comes with a long list of problems. It takes a long time before interesting results can emerge, it costs a lot of money, there are a number of methodological issues you would not have to deal with if you were to instead do cross-sectional research, etc. Despite this, life-course research has become well-established in criminology by now, and its strengths – not least the possibility to reach causal conclusions – greatly outweigh its weaknesses. There are thus strong reasons to believe that the field will continue to grow and expand.

At the same time, intriguingly, as we write this in the beginning of 2015, relatively few, new life-course criminological studies are being launched (but see Wikström, 2005). One reason for this may be that they cost a lot of money to initiate. Today, many agencies, organizations, and foundations that hand out research grants prefer to hand out money to more, but smaller projects than before.

However, launching new life-course studies is important: society is undergoing changes, thus changing the people who live in them, and results from studies based on older cohorts may have a limited validity for new generations.

As you may know by now, in Scandinavia and countries such as The Netherlands, governmental agencies collect large and reliable records of the entire population. These give researchers the opportunity to – using relatively simple, cost-effective methods – compare different cohorts with each other and, that way, capture the importance of social change from a life-course perspective.

# The Study of Criminal Transmissions

At the same time, though, many of the well-known life-course studies in criminology have now been up and running for so long that the people making up the original samples have become parents and, in some cases, grandparents. Many criminological theories (if not all) and empirical findings stress the importance of upbringing and family factors for an individual's pro- or antisocial development. Thus, since many of the older life-course studies now include children and grand-children, criminology is now able to study the intergenerational transmission of criminal behavior from a life-course perspective (e.g. Auty et al., 2015; Besemer and Farrington, 2012). This includes both vertical transmission (e.g. from parent to child) and horizontal transmission (e.g. between siblings).

# The Expansion of Qualitative Studies of Crime and the Life Course

Even though studies based on longitudinal register data give us essential, criminological knowledge, they are unlikely to give us the equally important, deep insight into the processes underpinning and driving persistence, intermittency, and desistance. To understand these processes, we need to talk to (perhaps even observe) the people who live them. Many traditional life-course studies of crime include both register data and prospectively collected, relatively structured interviews. Few of these studies, however, include qualitative life history interviews where the interview participant narrates his or her life relatively freely, giving the data the depth needed for analyses of the sort conducted by Maruna (2001), Calverley (2012), or Carlsson (2014). Many more studies of this kind are needed and, we think, are in the process of being planned or launched as we write this. The most interesting life-course studies of today, we argue, consist of a mixed method approach.

## Forms of Crime, Types of Offenders

As you know by now, the 'offending' and 'offenders' studied in life-course criminology are often limited to 'everyday crimes' such as interpersonal violence, theft, vandalism, robbery, and illegal drug-use and drug-dealing committed by white working-class men in big cities, such as Philadelphia, Boston, London, Copenhagen and Stockholm (Farrington, 2005). In this regard, life-course criminology has not been very different from the type of 'mainstream' criminology that dominated the field between, say, 1920 and 1960 and mainly focused on the more 'traditional' and visible crimes and gave little attention to crimes of the powerful, or crimes committed by females.

Exceptions have emerged, of course, with studies in white-collar crime and criminal careers (Weisburd and Waring, 2001), fencing as a criminal career (Steffensmeier and Ulmer, 2005a), and the possible importance of features such as gender (Carlsson, 2013; Opsal, 2012) and ethnicity for desistance processes (Calverley, 2012; Elliott, 1994). Still, however, there are many more possible expansions of life-course criminology here. For example, consider the possible criminal careers of individuals in hooligan gangs, extreme far right and far left groups, and (other) forms of terrorism. In order to understand a given phenomenon, it is often fruitful to broaden one's scope of what the phenomenon may consist of.

## Life-Course Criminology Beyond Crime?

An individual may cease committing actions that are defined as punishable in criminal law but still engage in behaviors which by many are regarded as 'deviant', i.e. drink excessive amounts of alcohol, develop a gambling problem, and so on. Considering the possibility suggested by several static theories – that criminal behavior is merely one expression of a more basic, underlying construct, such as low self-control, which during one stage in the life course manifests itself as crime – this is an important question. One way to approach this issue is to expand the life-course criminological enterprise and, as some have already done, take the offender's life situation as a whole into account, including elements such as unemployment, physical and mental health problems, and (other) features of social exclusion and marginalization.

The criminological and political interest often lies in finding answers to what gets people 'out of crime'. But, just because people eventually desist from crime does not mean that they are no longer socially, economically, and psychologically marginalized. We find this notion echoed in Shover's (1996: 145f) account of persistent offenders:

> Most of those who stay out of prison are 'successes' in only the narrowest, most bureaucratic meaning of the term non-recidivism. Most ex-convicts live menial or derelict lives and many die early of alcoholism or drug use, or by suicide.

The true challenge might not only be to make offenders desist from crime; it might also be to increase the living conditions and life standards of social groups where material resources are weak. If we manage to do that we are also likely to reduce crime, and shorten the criminal careers of even the most persistent offenders. To do that requires that the life-course criminological enterprise broadens its scope to include studies where the dependent variable is not crime but, as some have already done, attachment to the labor market, mental and physical health, and other indicators of social exclusion.

## Intervening in the Life Course

We previously mentioned the classic longitudinal follow-up study of the Cambridge Somerville Youth Study (McCord, 2007). Generally speaking, not many other long-time follow-up studies have been done of interventions directed toward individuals with a high risk for future, persistent criminal activity. This is highly unfortunate for, as mentioned previously, many of these interventions have *long-term* behavioral change as their goal.

What this means is that, in one way, the intervention aims at achieving lasting change in behavior. In another way, however, it also means that it may take a considerable amount of time for the behavioral change to occur. When society intervenes, Sherman and Harris (2014) show, something interesting but rather unexpected can happen, of which we know very little: the intervention can have powerful, long-term and unexpected effects on individuals who are not the offender in question, but still involved in a given criminal event (such as a spouse, friend, or relative).

Studies that evaluate the long-term effects of society's various forms of interventions are another and – to us – very important, desirable development of life-course criminology.

# Crime, Criminology and the Life Course

As we hope you have come to understand, there is a huge bulk of knowledge gaps and interesting research questions that emerge when you begin to study the whole life course with regard to crime and deviance. This, we believe, is one of the core reasons as to why life-course criminology has risen to fame in such a relatively short period of time. For a long time, the criminological study of crime in many ways entailed the cross-sectional study of juvenile delinquency (Cullen, 2011). When life-course criminology began to develop, and the whole life course suddenly emerged as a possible field of study, much of what once was considered self-evident truths, uninteresting, or simply 'not a problem' themes on the margins of the discipline, turned upside down and became the focus of intense study, theorizing, and problematization.

In this book, we have tried to unfold the field of life-course criminology for you. As you have probably noticed, while there are important debates going on within the field, there is also much that many agree on when it comes to the onset, persistence of, and desistance from crime. If there is one thing that all the theories, studies, and analyses have in common, it is this: what happens in the future is contingent on (but not determined by) what is happening right now, and on what has happened before. Below we list six general conclusions about crime and the life course that we believe are quite familiar to you by now (we take the first five of these from Farrington, 2005: 5f):

1. The prevalence of offending peaks in the late teenage years, between ages 15 and 19.
2. The peak age of onset of offending is between 8 and 14, and the peak age of desistance from offending is between 20 and 29.
3. An early age of onset predicts a relatively long criminal career, and the commission of relatively many crimes.
4. There is considerable within-individual continuity in offending and anti-social behavior from childhood to the teenage years and into adulthood.
5. A small fraction of the population (the 'chronic offenders') commit a large fraction of all crimes.
6. At the same time, however, there is also considerable within-individual change in offending over time, not least in the transition from adolescence and into adulthood. That is, the vast majority of all offenders who engage in crime cease to do so.

As you can see, the conclusions are quite empirical and descriptive. The big debates in the field are centered on the underlying processes that make these empirical patterns emerge, that is, they are theoretical. Is crime the product of neuropsychological dispositions interacting with an unforgiving environment, or is it the result of interactional processes of social control? Is human nature relatively static, or is it dynamic? Do people, in fact, exercise their human agency when influencing their future pathways, or are changes in trajectory merely the result of situational and social factors? Can something be done to help lead people out of crime, or is desistance from crime primarily done by a process of aging out?

We are still arguing about these and other, related questions (indeed, not even the two authors of this book are in full agreement). At this point, we thus leave it up to you to seek out your own answers and, possibly, form new questions.

# REFERENCES

Agnew, Robert (1992) 'Foundations for a general strain theory of crime and delinquency', *Criminology*, 30 (1): 47–88.

Akers, Ronald (1985) *Deviant Behavior: A Social Learning Approach*. Belmont, CA: Wadsworth.

Alexander, Jeffrey C. (1992) 'Some remarks on "agency" in recent sociological theory', *Perspectives*, 15 (1): 1–4.

American Psychiatric Association (2013) *Diagnostic and Statistical Manual of Mental Disorders, Fifth Edition (DSM-5)*. Arlington, VA: American Psychiatric Publishing.

Anderson, Nels (1923) *The Hobo*. Chicago, IL: University of Chicago Press.

Andersson, Lina (2011) *Mått på brott? Självdeklaration som metod för att mäta brottslighet*. Stockholms universitet, Kriminologiska institutionen.

Appleyard, Karen, Egeland, Byron, van Dulmen, Manfred H.M. and Sroufe, L. Alan (2005) 'When more is not better: the role of cumulative risk in child behavior outcomes', *Journal of Child Psychology and Psychiatry*, 46 (3): 235–45.

Atkinson, Robert G. (1998) *The Life Story Interview*. Thousand oaks, CA: SAGE.

Atzaba-Poria, Naama, Pike, Alison and Deater-Deckard, Kirby (2004) 'Do risk factors for problem behaviour act in a cumulative manner? An examination of ethnic minority and majority children through an ecological perspective', *Journal of Child Psychology and Psychiatry*, 45 (4): 707–18.

Auty, Katherine M., Farrington, David P. and Coid, Jeremy W. (2015) 'Intergeneration transmission of psychopathy and mediation via psychosocial risk factors', *British Journal of Psychiatry*, 206 (6): 26–31.

Backman, Christel (2012) *Criminal Records in Sweden. Regulation of Access to Criminal Records and the Use of Criminal Background Checks by Employers*. Göteborg: Göteborg University.

Barnett, Arnold, Blumstein, Alfred and Farrington, David P. (1989) 'A prospective test of a criminal career model', *Criminology*, 27 (2): 373–88.

Barriga, Alvaro Q. and Gibbs, John C. (1996) 'Measuring cognitive distortion in antisocial youth: development and preliminary evaluation of the "How I Think" questionnaire', *Aggressive Behavior*, 22 (5): 333–43.

Beccaria, Cesare ([1764]/1983) *An Essay on Crimes and Punishments*. Boston, MA: Branden Publishing.

# REFERENCES

Becker, Howard S. (1960) 'Notes on the concept of commitment', *American Journal of Sociology*, 66 (1): 32–40.

Becker, Howard S. (1963) *Outsiders: Studies in the Sociology of Deviance*. New York: Free Press.

Becker, Howard S. (1970) 'The self and adult socialization', in Howard S. Becker (ed.), *Sociological Work: Method and Substance*. New Brunswick, NJ: Transaction Publishers. pp. 289–303.

Becker, Howard S. (1998) *Tricks of the Trade*. Chicago, IL: University of Chicago Press.

Begler, Erik, Carlsson, Christoffer, Kinell, Emmy and Sivertsson, Fredrik (2011) *Lagförd brottslighet bland flickor och pojkar som varit föremål för socialtjänstens särskilda insatser åren 1990-1994: En longitudinell studie till och med 35 års ålder*. Unpublished Paper, Department of Criminology, Stockholm University.

Belknap, Joanne and Holsinger, Kristi (2006) 'The gendered nature of risk factors for delinquency', *Feminist Criminology*, 1 (1): 48–71.

Benson, Michael H. (2013) *Crime and the Life Course: An Introduction*. London: Routledge.

Berger, Ronald J. and Quinney, Richard (2005) 'Part 3: Education and work. Introduction', in Ronald J. Berger and Richard Quinney (eds), *Storytelling Sociology. Narrative as Social Inquiry*. Boulder, CO: Lynne Rienner Publishers. pp. 176–80.

Bergman, Lars R. and Andershed, Anna-Karin (2009) 'Predictors and outcomes of persistent or age-limited registered criminal behavior: a 30-year longitudinal study of a Swedish urban population', *Aggressive Behavior*, 35 (2): 164–78.

Bergman, Lars R. and Magnusson, David (1990) 'A pattern approach to the study of pathways from childhood to adulthood', in Lee Robins and Michael Rutter (eds), *Straight and Devious Pathways*. Cambridge: Cambridge University Press. pp. 101–15.

Bersani, Bianca E., Laub, John H. and Nieuwbeerta, Paul (2009) 'Marriage and desistance from crime in the Netherlands: do gender and socio-historical context matter?', *Journal of Quantitative Criminology*, 25 (1): 3–24.

Besemer, Sytske and Farrington, David P. (2012) 'Intergeneration transmission of criminal behavior: conviction trajectories of fathers and their children', *European Journal of Criminology*, 9 (2): 120–41.

Biljeveld, Catrien, C.J.H. and van der Kamp, Leo J.Th. (1998) *Longitudinal Data Analysis: Designs, Models, and Methods*. London: SAGE.

Block, Rebecca C., Blokland, Arjan A.J., van der Werff, Cornelia, van Os, Rianne and Nieuwbeerta, Paul (2010) 'Long-term patterns of offending in women', *Feminist Criminology*, 5 (1): 73–107.

Blokland, Arjan A.J. and Nieuwbeerta, Paul (2005) 'The effects of life circumstances on longitudinal trajectories of offending', *Criminology*, 43 (4): 1203–40.

Blumer, Herbert (1956) 'Sociological analysis and "the variable"', *American Sociological Review*, 21 (6): 683–90.

# REFERENCES

Blumer, Herbert (1969) *Symbolic Interactionism. Perspective and Method.* Berkeley, CA: University of California Press.

Blumstein, Alfred and Nakamura, Kiminori (2009) 'Redemption in the presence of widespread criminal background checks', *Criminology*, 47 (2): 327–59.

Blumstein, Alfred, Cohen, Jacqueline and Farrington, David (1988) 'Criminal career research: its value for criminology', *Criminology*, 26 (1): 1–35.

Blumstein, Alfred, Cohen, Jacqueline, Roth, Jeffrey A. and Visher, Christy A. (eds) (1986) *Criminal Careers and Career Criminals.* Washington, DC: National Academy Press.

Bottoms, Anthony H. (2006) 'Desistance, social bonds, and human agency: a theoretical exploration', in Per-Olof H. Wikström and Robert J. Sampson (eds), *The Explanation of Crime. Context, Mechanisms, and Development.* Cambridge: Cambridge University Press. pp. 243–90.

Brim, Orville and Kagan, Jerome (1980) *Constancy and Change in Human Development.* Boston, MA: Harvard University Press.

Brottsförebyggande Rådet (2000) *Strategiska brott.* Rapport 2000: 3. Stockholm: Brå.

Brottsförebyggande Rådet (2001) *Kriminell utveckling: tidiga riskfaktorer och förebyggande insatser.* Rapport 2001: 15. Stockholm: Brå.

Brottsförebyggande Rådet (2011) *Strategiska brott bland unga på 00-talet.* Rapport 2011:21. Stockholm: Brå.

Burgess, Ernest W. (1927) 'Statistics and case studies as methods of sociological research', *Sociology and Social Research*, 12: 103–20.

Bursik, Robert (1988) 'Social disorganization and theories of crime and delinquency: problems and prospects', *Criminology*, 26 (4): 519–52.

Bushway, Shawn D., Piquero, Alex R,. Broiday, Lisa M., Cauffman, Elizabeth and Mazzerolle, Paul (2001) 'An empirical framework for studying desistance as a process', *Criminology*, 39 (2): 491–515.

Bushway, Shawn D., Piquero, Alex R. and Krohn, Marvin D. (2003) 'Desistance as a developmental process: a comparison of static and dynamic approaches', *Journal of Quantitative* Criminology, 19 (2): 129–53.

Byrne, Claire F. and Trew, Karen J. (2008) 'Pathways through crime: the development of crime and desistance in the accounts of men and women offenders', *The Howard Journal of Criminal Justice*, 47 (3): 238–58.

Cabot, Richard (1940) 'A long-term study of children: the Cambridge-Somerville Youth Study', *Child Development*, 11 (2): 143–51.

Calverley, Adam (2012) *Cultures of Desistance.* London: Routledge.

Carlsson, Christoffer (2012) 'Using "turning points" to understand processes of change in offending: notes from a Swedish study on life courses and crime', *British Journal of Criminology*, 52 (1): 1–16.

Carlsson, Christoffer (2013) 'Processes of intermittency in criminal careers: notes from a Swedish study on life courses and crime', *International Journal of Offender Therapy and Comparative Criminology*, 57 (8): 913–38.

# REFERENCES

Carlsson, Christoffer (2014) *Continuities and Changes in Criminal Careers*. Dissertation. Stockholm University: Department of Criminology.

Case, Stephen and Haines, Kevin (2009) *Understanding Youth Offending: Risk Factor Research, Policy and Practice*. Portland, OR: Willan Publishing.

Caspi, Avshalom, McClay, Joseph, Moffitt, Terrie E., Mill, Jonathan, Martin, Judy, Craig, Ian W., Taylor, Alan and Poulton, Richie (2002) 'Role of genotype in the cycle of violence in maltreated children', *Science*, 297 (5582): 851–54.

Catalano, Richard F., Park, Jisuk, Harachi, Tracy W., Haggerty, Kevin P., Abbott, Robert D. and Hawkins, J. David (2005) 'Mediating the effects of poverty, gender, individual characteristics, and external constraints on antisocial behavior: a test of the Social Development Model and implications for developmental life-course theory', in David P. Farrington (ed.), *Integrated Developmental and Life-Course Theories of Offending. Advances in Criminological Theory, Vol. 14*. London: Transaction Publishers. pp. 93–123.

Cernkovich, Stephen A., Lanctot, Nadine and Giordano, Peggy C. (2008) 'Predicting adolescent and adult antisocial behavior among adjudicated delinquent females', *Crime & Delinquency*, 54 (1): 3–33.

Chesney-Lind, Meda and Pasko, Lisa (2013) *The Female Offender: Girls, Women, and Crime* (3rd edn). London: SAGE.

Clausen, John (1993) *American Lives: Looking Back at the Children of the Great Depression*. New York: The Free Press.

Cohen, Lawrence E. and Felson, Marcus (1979) 'Social change and crime rate trends: a routine activity approach', *American Sociological Review*, 44 (4): 588–608.

Cullen, Francis T. (2011) 'Beyond adolescence-limited criminology – choosing our future: the American Society of Criminology 2010 Sutherland Address', *Criminology* 49 (2): 287–330.

Cusson, Maurice and Pinsonneault, Pierre (1986) 'The decision to give up crime', in Derek Cornish and Ronald V. Clarke (eds), *The Reasoning Criminal: Rational Choice Perspectives on Offending*. New York: Springer-Verlag. pp. 72–82.

D'Unger, Amy, Land, Kenneth C., McCall, Patricia L. and Nagin, Daniel S. (1998) 'How many latent classes of delinquent/criminal careers? Results from mixed poisson regression analyses', *American Journal of Sociology*, 103 (6): 1593–630.

Daly, Kathleen (1992) 'Women's pathways to felony court: feminist theories of lawbreaking and problems of representation', *Southern California Review of Law and Women's Studies*, 2 (1): 11–52.

De Lange, Annet (2005) *What about Causality? Examining Longitudinal Relations between Work Characteristics and Mental Health*. Dissertation: University of Amsterdam.

DeLisi, Matt (2002) 'Not just a boy's club: an empirical assessment of female career criminals', *Women and Criminal Justice*, 13 (4): 27–45.

# REFERENCES

DeLisi, Matt, Neppl, Tricia K., Lohman, Brenda J., Vaughn, Michael G. and Shook, Jeffrey J. (2013) 'Early starters: which type of criminal onset matters most for delinquent careers?', *Journal of Criminal Justice*, 41 (1): 12–17.

Devers, Lindsey (2011) *Developmental and Life-Course Theories. A Research Summary*. Bureau of Justice Assistance: U.S. Department of Justice.

Doherty, Elaine Eggeleston and Ensminger, Margaret E. (2013) 'Marriage and offending among a cohort of disadvantaged African Americans', *Journal of Research in Crime and Delinquency*, 50 (2): 104–31.

Dunham, Warren H. and Knauer, Mary E. (1954) 'The juvenile court in its relationship to adult criminality', *Social Forces*, 32 (3): 290–6.

Eggleston, Elaine P. and Laub, John H. (2002) 'The onset of adult offending: a neglected dimension of the criminal career', *Journal of Criminal Justice*, 30 (6): 603–622.

Elder, Glen H. (1974) *Children of the Great Depression: Social Change in Life Experience*. Chicago, IL: University of Chicago Press.

Elder, Glen H. (1998) 'The life course as developmental theory', *Child Development*, 69 (1): 1–12.

Elliott, Delbert S. (1994) 'Serious violent offenders: onset, developmental course, and termination', *Criminology*, 32 (1): 1–22.

Ericson, Kersti and Jon, Nina (2006) 'Gendered social control: "a virtuous girl" and "a proper boy"', *Journal of Scandinavian Studies in Criminology and Crime Prevention*, 7 (2): 126–41.

Esbensen, Finn-Aage and Huizinga, David (1993) 'Gangs, drugs, and delinquency in a survey of urban youth', *Criminology*, 31 (4): 565–89.

Estrada, Felipe and Nilsson, Anders (2009) *Criminality and Life-Chances: A Longitudinal Study of Crime, Childhood Circumstances and Living Conditions Up To Age 48*. Report 2009: 3. Stockholm: Department of Criminology.

Estrada, Felipe and Nilsson, Anders (2012) 'Does it cost more to be a female offender?', *Feminist Criminology*, 7 (3): 196–219.

Ezell, Michael E. and Cohen, Lawrence E. (2005) *Desisting From Crime: Continuity and Change in Long-Term Crime Patterns of Serious Chronic Offenders*. Oxford: Oxford University Press.

Farrington, David P. (1977) 'The effects of public labelling', *British Journal of Criminology*, 17 (2): 112–25.

Farrington, David P. (1989) 'Self-reported and official offending from adolescence to adulthood', in Malcolm W. Klein (ed.), *Cross-National Research in Self-Reported Crime and Delinquency*. Netherlands: Kluwer. pp. 399–424.

Farrington, David P. (1996) 'The development of offending and antisocial behavior from childhood to adulthood', in Peter Cordella and Larry Siegel (eds), *Readings in Contemporary Criminological Theory*. Boston, MA: Northeastern University Press. pp. 107–22.

Farrington, David P. (2002) 'Multiple risk factors for multiple problem violent boys', in Raymond. R. Corrado, Ronald Roesch, Stephen D. Hart and

# REFERENCES

Josef K. Gierowski (eds), *Multi-Problem Violent Youth: A Foundation for Comparative Research on Needs, Interventions, and Outcomes*. Amsterdam: IOS Press. pp. 23–34.

Farrington, David P. (2003) 'Developmental and life-course criminology: key theoretical and empirical issues. The 2002 Sutherland Award Address', *Criminology* 41 (2): 221–55.

Farrington, David P. (2005) *Integrated Developmental and Life-Course Theories of Offending. Advances in Criminological Theory, Vol. 14*. New Brunswick, NJ: Transaction Publishers.

Farrington, David P. (2007) 'Childhood risk factors and risk-focused prevention', in Mike Maguire, Rod Morgan and Robert Reiner (eds), *The Oxford Handbook of Criminology*. Oxford: Oxford University Press. pp. 602–41.

Farrington, David P. (2010) 'Life-course and developmental theories', in Eugene McLaughlin and Tim Newburn (eds), *The SAGE Handbook of Criminological Theories*. London: SAGE. pp. 249–70.

Farrington, David P. and Murray, Joseph (eds) (2014) *Labeling Theory. Empirical Tests*. New Brunswick, NJ: Transaction Publishers.

Farrington, David P. and Painter, Kate (2004) *Gender Differences in Risk Factors for Offending*, Home Office Findings 196. London: Home Office.

Farrington, David P. and Welsh, Brandon (2007) *Saving Children From a Life of Crime*. Oxford: Oxford University Press.

Farrington, David P., Piquero, Alex R. and Jennings, Wesley G. (2013) *Offending from Childhood to Late Middle Age: Recent Results from The Cambridge Study in Delinquent Development*. New York: Springer.

Gaarder, Emily and Belknap, Joanne (2002) 'Tenuous borders: girls transferred to adult court', *Criminology*, 40 (3): 481–517.

Gauffin, Karl, Vinnerljung, Bo, Fridell, Mats, Hesse, Morten and Hjern, Anders (2013) 'Childhood socio-economic status, school failure, and drug use: a Swedish national cohort study', *Addiction*, 108 (8): 1441–9.

Gecas, V. (2003) 'Self-agency and the life course', in J.T. Mortimer and M. Shanahan (eds), *Handbook of the Life Course*. New York: Kluwer. pp. 369–88.

Gibbs, Jewelle T. (1981) 'Depression and suicidal behavior among delinquent females', *Journal of Youth Adolescence*, 10 (2): 159–67.

Giordano, Peggy C. (2010) *Legacies of Crime. A Follow-Up of the Children of Highly Delinquent Girls and Boys*. Cambridge: Cambridge University Press.

Giordano, Peggy C., Cernkovich, Stephen A. and Rudolph, Jennifer L. (2002) 'Gender, crime, and desistance: toward a theory of cognitive transformation', *American Journal of Sociology*, 107 (4): 990–1064.

Giordano, Peggy C., Seffrin, Patrick M., Manning, Wendy D. and Longmore, Monica A. (2011) 'Parenthood and crime: the role of wantedness, relationships with partners, and SES', *Journal of Criminal Justice*, 39 (5): 405–16.

Glaser, Daniel (1964) *The Effectiveness of a Prison and Parole System*. Indianapolis, IN: Bobbs-Merrill.

# REFERENCES

Glueck, Sheldon and Glueck, Eleanor T. (1930) *Five Hundred Criminal Careers*. New York: Alfred A. Knopf.

Glueck, Sheldon and Glueck, Eleanor T. (1934) *Five Hundred Delinquent Women*. Cambridge, MA: Harvard University Press.

Glueck, Sheldon and Glueck, Eleanor T. (1934) *One Thousand Juvenile Delinquents*. Cambridge, MA: Harvard University Press.

Glueck, Sheldon and Glueck, Eleanor T. (1950) *Unraveling Juvenile Delinquency*. Cambridge, MA: Harvard University Press.

Goff, Colin and Geis, Gilbert (2011) 'Edwin H. Sutherland: the development of differential association theory', in Francis T. Cullen, Cheryl Lero Johnson, Andrew J. Myer and Freda Adler (eds), *The Origins of American Criminology*. Brunswick, NJ: Transaction Publishers. pp. 37–62.

Goffman, Erving (1961) *Asylums*. London: Penguin.

Goffman, Erving (1963) *Stigma. Notes on the Management of Spoiled Identity*. New York: Simon and Schuster.

Goldweber, Asha, Broidy, Lisa M. and Cauffman, Elizabeth (2009) 'Interdisciplinary perspectives on persistent female offending: a review of theory and research', in Joanne Savage (ed.), *The Development of Persistent Criminality*. Oxford: Oxford University Press. pp. 205–30.

Gottfredson, Michael and Hirschi, Travis (1986) 'The true value of lambda would appear to be zero: an essay on career criminals, criminal careers, selective incapacitation, cohort studies, and related topics', *Criminology*, 24 (2): 213–34.

Gottfredson, Michael and Hirschi, Travis (1990) *A General Theory of Crime*. Stanford, CA: Stanford University Press.

Gottfredson, Michael and Hirschi, Travis (1995) 'National crime control policies', *Society*, 32 (2): 30–6.

Graham, John and Bowling, Benjamin (1995) *Young People and Crime*. London: Home Office Research.

Gunnison, Elaine (2014) 'Desistance from criminal offending: exploring gender similarities and differences', *Criminology, Criminal Law, and Society*, 15 (3): 75–95.

Hagan, John (1991) 'Destiny and drift: subcultural preferences, status attainments, and the risks and rewards of youth', *American Sociological Review*, 56 (Oct.): 567–82.

Hagan, John (2010) *Who Are The Criminals? The Politics of Crime Policy from the Age of Roosevelt to the Age of Reagan*. Princeton, NJ: Princeton University Press.

Healy, Deirdre (2013) 'Changing fate? Agency and the desistance process', *Theoretical Criminology*, 17 (4): 557–74.

Herrenkohl, Todd I., Maguin, Eugene, Hill, Karl G., Hawkins, David, Abbott, Robert D. and Catalano, Richard F. (2000) 'Developmental risk factors for youth violence', *Journal of Adolescent Health*, 26 (3): 176–86.

Hirschi, Travis (1969) *Causes of Delinquency*. New Brunswick, NJ: Transaction Publishers.

## REFERENCES

Hirschi, Travis and Rudisill, David (1976) 'The great American search: causes of crime, 1876–1976', *The ANNALS Of The American Academy Of Political and Social Science*, 423 (1): 14–22.

Hitlin, Steven and Elder, Glen H. Jr. (2007) 'Time, self, and the curiously abstract concept of agency', *Sociological Theory*, 25 (2): 170–91.

Hoge, Robert D., Vincent, Gina M. and Guy, Laura S. (2012) 'Prediction and risk/needs assessments', in Rolf Loeber and David P. Farrington (eds), *From Juvenile Delinquency to Adult Crime. Criminal Careers, Justice Policy, and Prevention*. Oxford: Oxford University Press. pp. 150–83.

Horney, J.D., Osgood, W. and Marshall, I.H. (1995) 'Criminal careers in the short-term: intra-individual variability in crime and its relation to local life circumstances', *American Sociological Review*, 60 (5), 655–73.

Hussong, Andrea M., Curran, Patrick J., Moffitt, Terrie E., Caspi, Avshalom and Carrig, Madeleine M. (2004) 'Substance abuse hinders desistance in young adults' antisocial behavior', *Development and Psychopathology*, 16 (4): 1029–46.

Janson, Carl-Gunnar (1975) *Project Metropolitan – A Presentation*. Project Metropolitan Report No. 1. Stockholm: Stockholm University.

Janson, Carl-Gunnar (1982) *Delinquency Among Metropolitan Boys*. Project Metropolitan Report No. 17. Stockholm: Stockholm University.

Kazemian, Lila and Farrington, David P. (2005) 'Comparing the validity of prospective, retrospective, and official onset for different offending trajectories', *Journal of Quantitative Criminology*, 21 (2): 127–47.

Kazemian, Lila and Maruna, Shadd (2009) 'Desistance from crime', in M.D. Krohn, A.J. Lizotte and P.G. Hall (eds), *Handbook on Crime and Deviance*. New York: Springer. pp. 277–96.

Kemshall, Hazel, Marsland, Louise and Boeck, Thilo (2006) 'Young people, pathways, and crime: beyond risk factors', *Australian and New Zealand Journal of Criminology*, 39 (3): 354–70.

Killias, Martin, Redondo, Santiago and Sarnecki, Jerzy (2012) 'European perspectives', in Rolf Loeber and David P. Farrington (eds), *From Juvenile Delinquency to Adult Crime. Criminal Careers, Justice Policy, and Prevention*. Oxford: Oxford University Press. pp. 278–314.

King, Sam (2014) *Desistance Transitions and the Impact of Probation*. London: Routledge.

Krohn, Marvin D., Gibson, Chris L. and Thornberry, Terence P. (2013) 'Under the protective bud the bloom awaits: a review of theory and research on adult-onset and late-blooming offenders', in Chris L. Gibson and Marvin D. Krohn (eds), *Handbook of Life-Course Criminology*. New York: Springer. pp. 183–200.

Kyvsgaard, Britta (1998) *Den Kriminelle Karriere*. Copenhagen: Jurist- og Ekonomforbundets Forlag.

Lab, Steven P. (2014) *Crime Prevention: Approaches, Practices, and Evaluations*. London: Anderson Publishing.

# REFERENCES

Laub, John H. (2002) 'Introduction: the life and work of Travis Hirschi', in John Laub (ed.), *The Craft of Criminology: Travis Hirschi, Selected Papers.* New Brunswick, NJ: Transaction. pp. xi–xlix.

Laub, John H. and Sampson, Robert J. (2003) *Shared Beginnings, Divergent Lives. Delinquent Boys to Age 70.* Cambridge, MA: Harvard University Press.

Laub, John H., Nagin, Daniel S. and Sampson, Robert J. (1998) 'Trajectories of change in criminal offending: good marriages and the desistance process', *American Sociological Review*, 63 (2): 225–38.

Lebel, Thomas P., Burnett, Ros, Maruna, Shadd and Bushway, Shawn (2008) 'The "chicken and egg" of subjective and social factors in desistance from crime', *European Journal of Criminology*, 5 (2): 131–59.

LeBlanc, Matt (1997) 'A generic control theory of the criminal phenomenon, the structural and dynamic statements of an integrated multilayered control theory', in Terence P. Thornberry (ed.), *Developmental Theories of Crime and Delinquency.* London: Transaction Publishers. pp. 215–85.

LeBlanc, Matt and Fréchette, Marcel (1989) *Male Criminal Activity From Childhood Through Youth: Multilevel and Developmental Perspectives.* New York: Springer.

Lemert, Edwin (1951) *Social Pathology: A Systematic Approach to the Theory of Sociopathic Behavior.* New York: McGraw-Hill.

Lemert, Edwin (1967) *Human Deviance, Social Problems, and Social Control.* Englewood Cliffs, NJ: Prentice Hall.

Lilly, J. Robert, Cullen, Francis T. and Ball, Richard A. (2011) *Criminological Theory: Context and Consequences* (4th edn). London: SAGE.

Lipsey, Mark W. and Derzon, James H. (1998) 'Predictors of violent or serious delinquency in adolescence and early adulthood: a synthesis of longitudinal research', in Rolf Loeber and David P. Farrington (eds), *Serious and Violent Juvenile Offenders: Risk Factors and Successful Interventions.* Thousand Oaks, CA: SAGE. pp. 86–105.

Loeber, Rolf (2012) 'Does the study of the age/crime curve have a future?', in Rolf Loeber and Brandon C. Welsh (eds), *The Future of Criminology.* Oxford: Oxford University Press. pp. 11–19.

Loeber, Rolf and Farrington, David P. (eds) (2012) *From Juvenile Delinquency to Adult Crime.* Oxford: Oxford University Press.

Loeber, Rolf, Burke, Jeffrey D. and Pardini, Dustin A. (2009) 'Development and etiology of disruptive and delinquent behavior', *Annual Review of Clinical Psychology*, 5: 291–310.

Loeber, Rolf, Farrington, David P., Stouthamer-Loeber, Magda, Moffitt, Terrie E. and Caspi, Avshalom (1998) 'The development of male offending: key findings from the first decade of The Pittsburgh Youth Study', *Studies on Crime and Crime Prevention*, 7 (2): 141–71.

Losel, Friedrich and Farrington, David P. (2012) 'Direct protective and buffering protective factors in the development of youth violence', *American Journal of Preventive Medicine*, 43 (2, Supp. 1) : S8–S23.

# REFERENCES

Lowenkamp, Christopher, Latessa, Edward J. and Holsinger, Alexander (2006) 'The risk principle in action: what have we learned from 13,676 offenders and 97 correctional programs?', *Crime and Delinquency*, 52 (1): 77–93.

McCord, Joan (2007) 'A thirty-year follow up of treatment effects', in Geoffrey Sayre-McCord (ed.), *Crime and the Family: Selected Essays of Joan McCord*. Philadelphia, PA: Temple University Press. pp. 13–21.

McGee, Tara and Farrington, David P. (2010) 'Are there any true adult-onset offenders?', *British Journal of Criminology*, 50 (3): 530–49.

McGloin, Jean (2009) 'Delinquency balance: revisiting peer influence', *Criminology*, 47 (2): 439–77.

McGloin, Jean M., Sullivan, Christopher, Piquero, Alex R. and Pratt, Travis C. (2007) 'Local life circumstances and offending specialization/versatility: Comparing opportunity and propensity models', *Journal of Research on Crime and Delinquency*, 44 (3): 321–46.

MacLeod, John F., Grove, Peter G. and Farrington, David P. (2012) *Explaining Criminal Careers: Implications For Justice Policy*. Oxford: Oxford University Press.

Maruna, Shadd (2001) *Making Good. How Ex-Convicts Reform and Rebuild Their Lives*. Washington, DC: American Psychological Association.

Maruna, Shadd (2010) 'Mixed method research in criminology: why not go both ways?', in Alex R. Piquero and David Weisburd (eds), *Handbook of Quantitative Criminology*. New York: Springer. pp. 123–40.

Matsueda, Ross (2006) 'Criminological implications of the thought of George Herbert Mead', in Mathieu Deflem (ed.), *Sociological Theory and Criminological Research: Views From Europe and The United States*. Oxford: Elsevier. pp. 77–108.

Matza, David (1964) *Delinquency and Drift*. New Brunswick, NJ: Transaction Publishers.

Matza, David (1969) *Becoming Deviant*. New Brunswick, NJ: Transaction Publishers.

Mednick, Sarnoff A. (1977) 'A biosocial theory of the learning of law-abiding behavior', in Sarnoff A. Mednick and Karl O. Christiansen (eds), *Biosocial Bases of Criminal Behavior*. New York: Gardner Press. pp.1–8.

Meisenhelder, Thomas (1977) 'An exploratory study of exiting from criminal careers', *Criminology* 15 (2): 319–34.

Meisenhelder, Thomas (1982) 'Becoming normal: certification as a stage in exiting from crime', *Deviant Behavior*, 3 (2): 137–53.

Merton, Robert K. (1938) 'Social structure and anomie', *American Sociological Review*, 3 (5): 672–82.

Merton, Robert K. (1945) 'Sociological theory', *American Journal of Sociology*, 50 (6): 462–73.

Messerschmidt, James W. (1993) *Masculinities and Crime. Critique and Reconceptualization of Theory*. Lanham, MD: Rowman and Littlefield.

# REFERENCES

Mills, C. Wright (1959) *The Sociological Imagination*. Oxford: Oxford University Press.

Moffitt, Terrie E. (1993) 'Adolescence-limited and life-course persistent antisocial behavior: a developmental taxonomy', *Psychological Review*, 100 (4): 674–701.

Moffitt, Terrie E. (2006) 'Life-course persistent and adolescence-limited antisocial behavior: a research review', in Dante Cicchetti and Donald Cohen (eds), *Developmental Psychopathology*. New York: Wiley. pp. 570–98.

Moffitt, Terrie E. (2007) 'A review of research on the taxonomy of life-course persistent and adolescence-limited antisocial behavior', in Daniel J. Flannery, Alexander T. Vazsonyi and Irwin D. Waldman (eds), *The Cambridge Handbook of Violent Behavior and Aggression*. New York: Cambridge University Press. pp. 49–74.

Moffitt, Terrie E., Caspi, Avshalom, Rutter, Michael and Silva, Phil A. (2001) *Sex Differences in Antisocial Behaviour*. Cambridge: Cambridge University Press.

Molero Samuelson, Yasmina (2011) *Antisocial Behaviour over the Life Course Among Females and Males Treated for Substance Misuse*. Stockholm: Karolinska institutet.

Monsbakken, Christian, Lyngstad, Torkild and Skardhamar, Torbjörn (2013) 'Crime and the transition to parenthood: the role of sex and relationship context', *British Journal of Criminology*, 53 (1): 129–48.

Nagin, Daniel S. (2005) *Group-Based Modelling of Development*. Cambridge, MA: Harvard University Press.

Nagin, Daniel S. and Land, Kenneth C. (1993) 'Age, criminal careers, and population heterogeneity: specification and estimation of a nonparametric, mixed poisson model', *Criminology*, 31 (3): 327–62.

Nagin, Daniel S. and Paternoster, Raymond (1991) 'On the relationship of past to future participation in delinquency', *Criminology*, 29 (2): 163–89.

Nagin, Daniel S. and Paternoster, Raymond (2000) 'Population heterogeneity and state dependence: state of the evidence and directions for future research', *Journal of Quantitative Criminology*, 16 (2): 117–45.

Neter, John and Waksberg, Joseph (1964) 'A study of response errors in expenditures data from household interviews', *Journal of the American Statistical Association*, 59 (305): 18–55.

Nilsson, Anders, Bäckman, Olof and Estrada, Felipe (2013) 'Involvement in crime, individual resources, and structural constraints: processes of cumulative (dis)advantage in a Stockholm birth cohort', *British Journal of Criminology*, 53 (2): 297–318.

Nilsson, A., Bäckman, O. and Estrada, F. (2014) 'Offending, drug abuse and life chances: a longitudinal study of a Stockholm birth cohort', *Journal of Scandinavian Studies in Criminology and Crime Prevention* (Advance Access).

Odgers, Candice and Morretti, Marlene M. (2002) 'Aggressive and antisocial girls: research update and challenges', *International Journal of Forensic Mental Health*, 1 (2): 103–19.

# REFERENCES

Olofsson, Birgitta (1971) *Vad var det vi sa! Om kriminellt och konformt beteende bland skolpojkar*. Stockholm: Utbildningsförlaget.

Opsal, Tara (2012) '"Livin' on the straights": identity, desistance, and work among women post-incarceration', *Sociological Inquiry* 82 (3): 378–403.

Paternoster, Ray and Bushway, Shawn (2009) 'Desistance and the "feared self": toward an identity theory of criminal desistance', *Journal of Criminal Law & Criminology*, 99 (4): 1103–56.

Paternoster, Raymond, Brame, Robert and Farrington, David P. (2001) 'On the relationship between adolescent and adult convictions', *Journal Of Quantitative Criminology*, 17 (3): 201–25.

Piquero, Alex R. (2001) 'Testing Moffitt's neuropsychological variation hypothesis for the prediction of life-course persistent offending', *Psychology, Crime, and Law*, 7 (1–4): 193–215.

Piquero, Alex R. (2004) 'Somewhere between persistence and desistance: the intermittency of criminal careers', in Shadd Maruna and Russ Immarigeon (eds), *After Crime and Punishment: Pathways to Offender Reintegration*. Devon: Willan Publishing. pp. 102–27.

Piquero, Alex R. (2009) 'Methodological issues in the study of persistence in offending', in Joanne Savage (ed.), *The Development of Persistent Criminality*. Oxford: Oxford University Press. pp. 271–87.

Piquero, Alex R., Brame, Robert, Mazerolle, Paul and Haapanen, Rudy (2002) 'Crime in emerging adulthood', *Criminology*, 40 (1): 137–70.

Piquero, Alex R., Farrington, David P. and Blumstein, Alfred (2007) *Key Issues in Criminal Career Research*. Cambridge: Cambridge University Press.

Piquero, Alex R., Paternoster, Raymond, Mazerolle, Paul, Brame, Robert and Dean, Charles W. (1999) 'Onset age and offense specialization', *Journal of Research in Crime and Delinquency*, 36 (3): 275–99.

Quetelet, Adolphe (1831) *A Treatise on Man and the Development of His Faculties*. Edinburgh: William and Robert Chambers.

Raine, Adrian (2013) *The Anatomy of Violence. The Biological Roots of Crime*. New York: Vintage Books.

Raskin, Bernard S. (1987) 'The measurement of time intervals between arrests', in Marvin E. Wolfgang, Terence P. Thornberry, and Robert M. Figlio (eds), *From Boy to Man, From Delinquency to Crime*. Chicago, IL: University of Chicago Press. pp. 59–67.

Reiss, Albert (1951) 'Delinquency as the failure of personal and social controls', *American Sociological Review*, 16 (2): 196–207.

Robins, Lee (1966) *Deviant Children Grown Up: A Sociological and Psychiatric Study of Sociopathic Personality*. Baltimore, MD: Williams and Wilkins.

Rosenfeld, Richard and Messner, Steven F. (2011) 'The intellectual origins of institutional anomie-theory', in Francis T. Cullen, Cheryl Lero Johnson, Andrew J. Myer, and Freda Adler (eds), *The Origins of American Criminology*. Brunswick, NJ: Transaction Publishers. pp. 121–35.

# REFERENCES

Rowe, David C., Flannery, Alexander T. and Flannery, Daniel J. (1995) 'Sex differences in crime: do means and within-sex variation have similar causes?', *Journal of Research in Crime and Delinquency*, 32 (1): 84–100.

Rutter, Michael (1994) 'Continuities, transitions, and turning points in development', in Michael Rutter and D.F. Hay (eds), *Development Through Life: A Handbook for Clinicians*. Oxford: Blackwell. pp. 1–25.

Rutter, Michael, Giller, Henri and Hagell, Ann (1998) *Antisocial Behavior by Young People*. Cambridge: Cambridge University Press.

Rutter, Michael, Maughan, Barbara, Mortimore, Peter and Ouston, Janet (1979) *Fifteen Thousand Hours: Secondary Schools and Their Effects on Children*. Cambridge, MA: Harvard University Press.

Sampson, Robert J. (2013) 'The place of context: a theory and strategy for criminology's hard problems', *Criminology*, 51 (1): 1–31.

Sampson, Robert J. and Laub, John H. (1993) *Crime in The Making: Pathways and Turning Points Through Life*. Boston, MA: Harvard University Press.

Sampson, Robert J., and Laub, John H. (1997) 'A life-course theory of cumulative disadvantage and the stability of delinquency', in Terence P. Thornberry (ed.), *Developmental Theories of Crime and Delinquency*. London: Transaction Publishers. pp. 133–61.

Sampson, Robert. J. and Laub, John H. (2005) 'A general age-graded theory of crime: lessons learned and the future of life-course criminology', in David P. Farrington (ed.), *Integrated Developmental and Life-Course Theories of Offending: Advances in Criminological Theory, Vol. 14*. London: Transaction Publishers. pp. 165–82.

Sandahl, Julia (2014) *Skolan som skyddsfaktor [The School as Protective Factor]*. Stockholm: City of Stockholm.

Sarnecki, Jerzy (1985) *Predicting Social Maladjustment. Stockholm Boys Grown Up I*. Stockholm: Esselte Tryck.

Sarnecki, Jerzy (1990) *Social anpassning och samhällssyn. Uppföljning av 1956 års klientelundersökning*. [Social Adjustment and Societal Views. Follow-Up of the Clientele Study of 1956.] Report 1990: 4. Stockholm: National Council of Crime Prevention.

Sarnecki, Jerzy (1996) 'Problem profiles for adolescents enrolled in special youth homes in Stockholm 1990–1994', in B-Å Armelius, Sara Bengtzon, P-A Rydelius, Jerzy Sarnecki and Kerstin Söderholm Carpelan (eds), *Treating Youths with Social Problems: An Overview of Research*. Stockholm: Liber Utbildning/SiS [in Swedish].

Sarnecki, Jerzy (2005) *Delinquent Networks. Youth Co-Offending in Stockholm*. Cambridge: Cambridge University Press.

Sarnecki, Jerzy (2006) *Är Rättvisan Rättvis? [How Just is Justice?]* SOU 2006:30. Stockholm: Fritzes.

Savage, Joanne (2009) 'Understanding persistent offending: linking developmental psychology with research on the criminal career', in Joanne Savage (ed.), *The Development of Persistent Criminality*. Oxford: Oxford University Press. pp.3–27.

# REFERENCES

Savolainen, Jukka (2009) 'Work, family and criminal desistance: adult social bonds in a Nordic welfare state', *British Journal of Criminology*, 49 (3): 285–304.

Schroeder, Ryan D., Giordano, Peggy C. and Cernkovich, Stephen A. (2007) 'Drug use and desistance processes', *Criminology*, 45 (1): 191–222.

Shanahan, Michael J. and Macmillan, Ross (2008) *Biography and the Sociological Imagination*. New York: Norton.

Shapland, Joanna and Bottoms, Anthony (2011) 'Reflections on social values, offending, and desistance among young adult recidivists', *Punishment and Society*, 13 (3): 256–82.

Shaw, Clifford R. (1930) *The Jack-Roller. A Delinquent Boy's Own Story*. Chicago, IL: University of Chicago Press.

Shaw, Clifford R. and McKay, Henry D. (1942) *Juvenile Delinquency and Urban Areas*. Chicago, IL: University of Chicago Press.

Sherman, Lawrence W. and Harris, Heather M. (2014) 'Increased death rates of domestic violence victims from arresting vs. warning suspects in the Milwaukee Domestic Violence Experiment (MilDVE)', *Journal of Quantitative Criminology*, 11 (1): 1–20.

Sherman, Lawrence W., Gottfredson, Denise C., MacKenzie, Doris L., Eck, John, Reuter, Peter and Bushway, Shawn D. (1998) 'Preventing crime: what works, what doesn't, what's promising', *National Institute of Justice*, July 1998: 1–19.

Shover, Neal (1996) *Great Pretenders. Pursuits and Careers of Persistent Thieves*. Boulder, CO: Westview Press.

Sivertsson, Fredrik and Carlsson, Christoffer (2015) 'Continuity, change, and contradictions: risk and agency in criminal careers to age 59', *Criminal Justice and Behavior*, 42 (4): 382–411.

Skardhamar, Torbjörn (2009) 'Reconsidering the theory on adolescence-limited and life-course persistent anti-social behaviour', *British Journal of Criminology*, 49 (6): 863–78.

Skardhamar, Torbjörn (2010) *Criminal Careers and Crime at Different Stages of Life. Theoretical and Methodological Perspectives, Childhood Risk Factors, and Desistance*. Oslo: Department of Sociology and Human Geography, Oslo University.

Skardhamar, Torbjörn and Lyngstad, Torkild H. (2011) 'Nordic register data and their untapped potential for criminological knowledge', in Michael Tonry and Tapio Lappi-Seppälä (eds), *Crime and Justice in Scandinavia. Crime and Justice: A Review of Research, Vol 40*. Chicago, IL: University of Chicago Press. pp. 613–45.

Smith, Carolyn and Thornberry, Terence P. (1995) 'The relationship between childhood maltreatment and adolescent involvement in delinquency', *Criminology*, 33 (4): 451–81.

Soothill, Keith, Ackerley, Elizabeth and Francis, Brian (2003) 'The persistent offenders debate: a focus on temporal changes', *Criminology and Criminal Justice*, 3 (4): 389–412.

Soothill, Keith, Fitzpatrick, Claire and Francis, Brian (2009) *Understanding Criminal Careers*. Devon: Willan Publishing.

## REFERENCES

SOU (1969:1) *Faktisk Brottslighet Bland Skolbarn. 1956 års klientelundersökning rörande ungdomsbrottslingar.* Stockholm: Esselte Tryck.

SOU (1971:49) *Unga Lagöverträdare I. Undersökningsmetodik. Brottsdebut och återfall. 1956 års klientelundersökning rörande ungdomsbrottslingar.* [Juvenile Delinquents I. Research method. Onset of crime and recidivism. The Clientele Study of 1956.] Stockholm: Esselte Tryck [in Swedish].

SOU (1972:76) *Unga lagöverträdare II. Familj, skola och samhälle i belysning av officiella data.* Stockholm: Justitiedepartementet.

SOU (1973:25) *Unga lagöverträdare III. Hem, uppfostran, skola och kamratmiljö i belysning av intervju och uppföljningsdata.* Stockholm: Justitiedepartementet.

SOU (1973:49) *Unga lagöverträdare IV. Kroppslig-psykisk utveckling och status i belysning av föräldraintervju och uppföljningsdata.* Stockholm: Justitiedepartementet.

SOU (1974:31) *Unga lagöverträdare V. Personlighet och relationer i belysning av projektiva metoder.* Stockholm: Justitiedepartementet.

Spanjaard, Han, J.M., Van der Knap, Leontien M., van der Put, Claudia E. and Stams, Geert Jan J.M. (2012) 'Risk assessment and the impact of risk and protective factors', in Rolf Loeber, Machteld Hoeve, N. Wim Slot and Peter H. van der Laan (eds), *Persisters and Desisters in Crime From Adolescence Into Adulthood. Explanation, Prevention, and Punishment.* London: Ashgate. pp. 127–58.

Stattin, Håkan and Magnusson, David (1991) 'Stability and change in criminal behavior up to age 30', *British Journal of Criminology*, 31 (4): 327–46.

Stattin, Håkan and Magnusson, David (1995) 'Onset of official delinquency: its co-occurrence in time with educational, behavioral, and interpersonal problems', *British Journal of Criminology*, 35 (3): 417–49.

Stattin, Håkan, Romelsjö, Anders and Stenbacka, Marlene (1997) 'Personal resources as modifiers of the risk for future criminality: an analysis of protective factors in relation to 18-year-old boys', *British Journal of Criminology*, 37 (2): 198–223.

Steffensmeier, Darrell and Allan, Emilie (1996) 'Gender and crime: toward a gendered theory of female offending', *Annual Review of Sociology*, 22: 459–87.

Steffensmeier, Darrell J. and Ulmer, Jeffery T. (2005a) *Confessions of a Dying Thief: Understanding Criminal Careers and Illegal Enterprise.* New Brunswick, NJ: Transaction.

Steffensmeier, Darrell, Schwartz, Jennifer, Zhong, Hua and Ackerman, Jeff (2005b) 'An assessment of recent trends in girls violence by using diverse longitudinal sources: is the gender gap closing?', *Criminology*, 43 (2): 355–406.

Stenberg, Sten-Åke (2013) *Född 1953. Folkhemsbarn i Forskarfokus.* Umeå: Boréa.

Sutherland, Edwin H. (1937) *The Professional Thief.* Philadelphia, PA: Lippincott.

Sutherland, Edwin H. (1947) *Principles of Criminology.* Philadelphia, PA: Lippincott.

Sveri, Knut (1960) *Kriminalitet og Alder.* Stockholm: Almqvist & Wiksell.

Swedberg, Richard (2012) 'Theorizing in sociology and social science: turning to the context of discovery', *Theory and Society*, 41 (1): 1–40.

# REFERENCES

Sweeten, Gary, Piquero, Alex R. and Steinberg, Laurence (2013) 'Age and the explanation of crime, revisited', *Journal of Youth and Adolescence*, 42 (6): 921–38.

Tannenbaum, Frank (1938) *Crime and the Community*. Boston, MA: Ginn.

Theobald, Delphine and Farrington, David P. (2014) 'Onset of offending', in Gerben Bruinsma and David Weisburd (eds), *Encyclopedia of Criminology and Criminal Justice*. New York: Springer. pp. 3332–42.

Thoits, P.A. (2003) 'Personal agency and multiple role-identities', in P.J. Burke, T.J. Owens, R.T. Serpe and P.A. Thoits (eds), *Advances in Identity Theory and Research*. New York: Kluwer. pp. 179–94.

Thomas, W.I. and Znaniecki, Florian (1974) *The Polish Peasant in Europe and America*. Chicago, IL: University of Illinois Press.

Thornberry, Terence P. (1987) 'Toward an interactional theory of delinquency', *Criminology*, 25 (4): 863–91.

Thornberry, Terence P. and Krohn, Marvin D. (2000) 'The self-report method for measuring delinquency and crime', in David Duffee (ed.), *Measurement and Analysis of Crime and Justice*. Washington: National Institute of Justice. pp. 33–84.

Thornberry, Terence P., Giordano, Peggy C., Uggen, Christopher, Matsuda, Mauri, Masten, Ann S., Bulten, Erik and Donker, Andrea G. (2012) 'Explanations for offending', in Rolf Loeber and David P. Farrington (eds), *From Juvenile Delinquency to Adult Crime. Criminal Careers, Justice Policy, and Prevention*. Oxford: Oxford University Press. pp. 47–85.

Tibbetts, Stephen G. and Alex R. Piquero (1999) 'The influence of gender, low birth weight, and disadvantaged environment in predicting early onset of offending: a test of Moffitt's interactional hypothesis', *Criminology*, 37 (4): 843–78.

Tremblay, Gilles, Tremblay, Richard E. and Saucier, Jean-Francois (2004) 'The development of parent-child relationship perceptions in boys from childhood to adolescence: a comparison between disruptive and non-disruptive boys', *Child and Adolescent Social Work Journal*, 21 (4): 407–26.

Tumminello, Michele, Edling, Christofer, Liljeros, Fredrik, Mantegna, Rosario N. and Sarnecki, Jerzy (2013) 'The phenomenology of specialization in criminal suspects', *PLoS ONE*, 8: e64703.

Uggen, Christopher (2000) 'Work as a turning point in the life course of criminals: a duration model of age, employment, and recidivism', *American Sociological Review*, 65 (Aug.): 529–46.

Ulmer, Jeffery T. and Spencer, William J. (1999) 'The contributions of an interactionist approach to research and theory on criminal careers', *Theoretical Criminology* 3 (1): 95–124.

von Hofer, Hanns (2008) *Brott och Straff i Sverige. Historisk Kriminalstiatisk 1750–(2005) Diagram, Tabeller Och Kommentarer*. Stockholms Universitet: Kriminologiska institutionen.

Walsh, Anthony (2009) *Biology and Criminology. The Biosocial Synthesis*. London: Routledge.

# REFERENCES

Warr, Mark (2002) *Companions in Crime*. Cambridge: Cambridge University Press.

Weber, Max (1978) *Economy and Society. Outline of an Interpretive Sociology*. Berkeley, CA: Berkeley University Press.

Weisburd, David and Waring, Elin (2001) *White-Collar Crime and Criminal Careers*. Cambridge: Cambridge University Press.

West, Donald (1982) *Delinquency: Its Roots, Careers and Prospects*. London: Heinemann.

White, Jennifer L., Moffitt, Terrie E., Earls, Felton, Robins, Lee and Silva, Phil A. (1990) 'How early can we tell? Predictors of childhood conduct disorder and adolescent delinquency', *Criminology*, 28 (4): 507–35.

Widom, Catherine S. (1989) 'The cycle of violence', *Science*, 244 (4901): 160–6.

Wiesner, Margit and Windle, Michael (2004) 'Assessing covariates of adolescent delinquency trajectories: a latent growth mixture modeling approach', *Journal of Youth and Adolescence*, 33 (5): 431–42.

Wikström, Per-Olof H. (2005) 'The social origins of pathways in crime: towards a developmental ecological action theory of crime involvement and its changes', in David P. Farrington (ed.), *Integrated Developmental and Life-Course Theories of Offending*. New Brunswick, NJ: Transaction Publishers. pp. 211–46.

Wikström, Per-Olof H. and Loeber, Rolf (2000) 'Do disadvantaged neighborhoods cause well-adjusted children to become adolescent delinquents? A study of male juvenile serious offending, individual risk and protective factors, and neighborhood context', *Criminology*, 38 (4): 1109–42.

Wilson, James Q. and Herrnstein, Richard J. (1985) *Crime and Human Nature*. New York: Simon and Schuster.

Wolfgang, Marvin. E., Figlio, Robert M. and Sellin, Torsten (1972) *Delinquency in a Birth Cohort*. Chicago, IL: University of Chicago Press.

Wolfgang, Marvin E., Thornberry, Terence P. and Figlio, Robert M. (1987) *From Boy to Man, from Delinquency to Crime*. Chicago, IL: University of Chicago Press.

Yamaguchi, Kazuo and Kandel, Denise B. (1985) 'On the resolution of role incompatibility: a life event history analysis of family roles and marihuana use', *American Journal of Sociology*, 90 (6): 1284–325.

Zamble, Edward and Quinsey, Vernon L. (1997) *The Criminal Recidivism Process*. Cambridge: Cambridge University Press.

Zara, George and Farrington, David P. (2009) 'Childhood and adolescent predictors of late onset criminal careers', *Journal of Youth and Adolescence*, 38 (3): 287–300.

# INDEX